Indigenous Participation in Australian Economies

Historical and anthropological perspectives

Indigenous Participation in Australian Economies

Historical and anthropological perspectives

Edited by Ian Keen

THE AUSTRALIAN NATIONAL UNIVERSITY

E PRESS

ANU
E PRESS

Published by ANU E Press
The Australian National University
Canberra ACT 0200, Australia
Email: anuepress@anu.edu.au
This title is also available online at: http://epress.anu.edu.au/ip_citation.html

---

National Library of Australia
Cataloguing-in-Publication entry

Title: Indigenous participation in Australian economies : historical and
                anthropological perspectives / edited by Ian Keen.

ISBN: 9781921666865 (pbk.) 9781921666872 (ebook)

Notes: Includes bibliographical references.

Subjects: Aboriginal Australians--Economic conditions.
                Business enterprises, Aboriginal Australian.
                Aboriginal Australians--Employment.
                Economic anthropology--Australia.
                Hunting and gathering societies--Australia.
                Australia--Economic conditions.

Other Authors/Contributors:
                Keen, Ian.

Dewey Number: 306.30994

Cover design and layout by ANU E Press

Cover image: Camel ride at Karunjie Station ca. 1950, with Jack Campbell in hat. Courtesy State
Library of Western Australia image number 007846D.

Contents

Acknowledgements

This volume arose out of a panel on Indigenous participation in the Australian economy at the joint annual conference of the Australian Anthropological Society, the Association of Social Anthropologists (UK), and the Association of Social Anthropologists of Aotearoa (New Zealand) in Auckland 2008. I would like to thank the organisers of the conference, especially Professor Veronica Strang and Dr Mark Busse, and participants in the panel, especially Professor Jon Altman who was the discussant. The panel arose out of a research project funded by an ARC Linkage grant (LP0775392), based at the Australian National University and with the National Museum of Australia as the industry partner. The researchers on the project: Professor Christopher Lloyd, Dr Anthony Redmond, Dr Fiona Skyring, Mr John White, and myself, contributed both to the panel and to this volume. I thank in particular Dr Michael Pickering of the National Museum of Australia, and staff of the School of Archaeology and Anthropology at the Australian National University for their support. I am grateful to two anonymous referees for their helpful comments, Jan Borrie who edited the manuscript, and Karen Westmacott and Duncan Beard of the ANU E-press for shepherding the manuscript through the publication process.

List of figures

Contributors

Jeremy Beckett, Emeritus Associate Professor, University of Sydney

Lorraine Gibson, Vice-Chancellor Innovation Research Fellow, Macquarie University

Chris Haynes, Honorary Research Fellow, Discipline of Anthropology and Sociology, The University of Western Australia

Sarah Holcombe, Research Fellow, National Centre for Indigenous Studies, The Australian National University

Ian Keen, Visiting Fellow, School of Archaeology and Anthropology, College of Arts and Sciences, The Australian National University

Christopher Lloyd, Professor of Economic History, University of New England

Anthony Redmond, consultant anthropologist and Visiting Fellow, Centre for Aboriginal Economic Policy Research, The Australian National University

Fiona Skyring, consultant historian

John M. White, PhD scholar, School of Archaeology and Anthropology, College of Arts and Sciences, The Australian National University

Diana Young, Director, Anthropology Museum, University of Queensland

1. Introduction

IAN KEEN

This volume arises out of a panel on Indigenous participation in Australian 'frontier' economies at the annual conference of the Australian Anthropological Society, held jointly with the British and New Zealand anthropological associations in Auckland in December 2008. The panel arose in turn out of an Australian Research Council (ARC) Linkage Grant project on Indigenous participation in Australian colonial economies involving the National Museum of Australia as the partner organisation and the School of Archaeology and Anthropology at The Australian National University. The researchers engaged in this project (2007–10) were Ian Keen (The Australian National University), Christopher Lloyd (University of New England), Anthony Redmond (Centre for Aboriginal Economic Policy Research, The Australian National University), Michael Pickering (National Museum of Australia), John White (The Australian National University) and Fiona Skyring (consultant historian). These researchers were among the contributors to the panel and most are represented in this volume. The organisers of the panel invited other scholars to contribute papers on the general theme, several of whom have contributed to this volume. The resulting chapters bring new theoretical analyses and empirical data to bear on a continuing discussion about the variety of ways in which Indigenous people in Australia have participated in the colonial and post-colonial economy.

Invisibility in economic histories

Indigenous Australians have been more or less invisible in many economic histories of Australia (for example, Abbott 1969; Fitzpatrick 1941; Griffin 1967; Shaw 1965). Where they are mentioned, topics include frontier violence, sheep and cattle stealing and differences in concepts of property (for example, Bain 1975; Shann 1948; Shaw and Nicholson 1966; Sinclair 1983; Wells 1989). Butlin (1993) outlined a pre-colonial, colonial and national economic history of Australia, but neglected the degree of variation in both Indigenous economy and Indigenous participation in the colonial and national economy. He regarded Aborigines as having been largely excluded from the market economy, apart from in the pastoral industry. An early exception to this trend was the work of Geoffrey Bolton (1969), who proposed a model of the 'feudal' position of Aborigines in the pastoral industry and who discussed Aboriginal labour in various other sectors including independent wolfram mining by Aboriginal people.

C. D. Rowley's work (1970a, 1970b) arising out of the Aborigines Project of the Social Sciences Research Council of Australia brought about a sea change in the recognition of Indigenous involvement in the colonial economy. Rowley records Aboriginal participation in several sectors including the provision of labour on small farms, the pastoral industry and other rural work; and labour in exchange for rations from government agencies, in the cedar industry and in land clearing. Rowley documents attempts to create self-sufficient Aboriginal settlements and to teach farming skills and he outlines policy and legislative contexts including master–servant legislation in Western Australia. He theorises internal Aboriginal economic relations in terms of 'reciprocity', which shaped Indigenous expectations in relations with settlers in his view. Reynolds' *With the White People* (1990) covers a similarly broad scope of relations between Aborigines and settlers including relations with explorers, work as trackers and domestic servants, farm work and the pearling industry.

This volume, and the research project from which it arises, seeks to contribute to the body of anthropological and historical studies of Indigenous participation in the Australian economy. In spite of the relative invisibility of Aboriginal people and Torres Strait Islanders in economic histories, there has been a wealth of studies of Indigenous participation in various sectors of the economy. It will be useful to outline this body of research before turning to theoretical approaches to Indigenous participation in the economy, and the contributions to this volume.

Previous research on specific sectors

Unlike the effects of relations between Aboriginal people and Macassan visitors (for example, MacKnight 1976; Thomson 1949; Warner 1937), there has been little systematic research on transformations of Indigenous economic relations and exchange systems brought about by British colonisation. Anthropologists have recorded the entry of introduced goods into Indigenous exchange networks (for example, Berndt and Berndt 1945; Falkenberg 1962), while researchers such as Thomson (1949) sought to reconstruct pre-colonial systems. Redmond and Skyring (this volume) examine transformations in the *Wurnan* exchange network in the Kimberley.

Turning to Indigenous involvement in marine industries, several studies have focused on the appropriation of Aboriginal women by white sealers (Begg 1979; Butlin 1993:197; Gibbs 2000; Murray-Smith 1973; Rowley 1970a; Ryan 1996), and on whaling (Lawrence and Staniforth 1998). There is also a substantial amount of published research on the pearling industry, in which Aborigines were employed (Bain 1982; De La Rue 1979; Ganter 1994; Mullins 2001; see also Rowley 1970a; Searcy 1905). Beckett's (1987) work covered pearling in the Torres Strait.

A variety of sources and studies has documented and analysed relations in early settlements including Port Jackson (for example, Clendinnen 2003) and King George Sound (for example, Barker 1992). Among early farming settlements, Attwood (1986) has written about Aboriginal itinerant workers in Gippsland working 'off the missions'. As for early missions themselves, New Norcia is perhaps the most fully researched (for example, Hetherington 2002). A number of studies examine the position of Indigenous female domestic servants (for example, Haskins 2004; Huggins 1995; Walden 1995). In other examples, Hunt (1983) has made a study of women's labour and sexual relations in north-western Australia from 1860 to 1900, while Watson (1998) has carried out research on the sexual economy in south-western Queensland.

Studies of Aboriginal people in the pastoral industry abound, including employment as shepherds in some districts, but most commonly in the cattle industry (for example, Doohan 1992; Jebb 2002; Kelly 1966; McGrath 1987; Makin 1972; May 1994). Early anthropological studies include Berndt and Berndt (1986). The buffalo industry in the Alligator Rivers region and Coburg Peninsula provides a good example of a 'hybrid economy' (Levitus 1982; Robinson 2006), as does Anderson's (1983) research on relations between Aboriginal people and early tin miners on Cape York Peninsula—important for its modelling of the adaptation of Indigenous social and economic relations to the wider market (see also Kirkman 1978 on goldmining on the Palmer River).

As Anderson (1988:157) points out, following early anthropological studies a second phase of research on Aboriginal involvement in the market economy focused on Aboriginal 'labour' and poverty (for example, Rowley 1970b; Sharp and Tatz 1966; Stevens 1974). Recent research has focused on Aboriginal labour history (Castle and Hagan 1998; Curthoys 1995; McGrath et al. 1995; Robinson 2003), the Indigenous labour market and regional industry (Taylor 2005) and exclusion from the labour market (Hunter 2005).

What have been the dominant theoretical approaches to Indigenous participation in the Australian economy? I shall outline these under two headings: those concerned with 'internal' relations within Indigenous domains, and those concerned with the articulation of Indigenous and 'external' domains or sectors, including the market and the state.

Characteristics of the internal Indigenous economy

An 'economy' includes the production, distribution, exchange and consumption of the material means of life, the ways in which they articulate with other valued items, particularly through exchange, and the organisation of these processes. On the assumption that 'internal' properties of Indigenous economies or sectors of the wider economy can be distinguished from 'external' ones (see Rowse 2005), their properties have been analysed in a number of ways. The economic goals, processes and values within the Aboriginal domain in 'settled' Australia have been distinctive (Keen 1988). Writers such as Calley (1956:207) and Bell (1965) described a category of people who pursued target employment and remained in short-term employment for limited economic goals and for whom accumulation was not a value. This category has been distinguished from those who adopted European values of property accumulation, thrift and regular employment and tended to be accused by others of lacking generosity and cutting themselves off from their kin (Keen 1988:15).

Aboriginal economic relations have been depicted as shaped by obligations to kin, as taking the form of reciprocity and as demand sharing. According to the first of these approaches, kinship obligations, social relationships and each category of relationship had its own particular obligations. As Berndt and Berndt (1977:122) express the first view: 'there is in every community an arrangement of obligations which every growing child has to learn. In this network of duties and debts, rights and credits, all adults have commitments of one kind or another. Mostly, not invariably, these are based on kin relationships.' The social theory behind this model is the juralistic one of rights and duties entailed by social statuses.

Obligations have a particular shape according to the second approach, in which gifts or services require a return. Berndt and Berndt (1977:122) continue: 'All gifts and services are viewed as reciprocal. This is basic to [Aboriginal] economy—and not only to theirs, although they are more direct and explicit about it. Everything must be repaid, in kind or equivalent, within a certain period.' The concept of 'reciprocity' owes much to Marcel Mauss's theory of the gift, which involves the obligation to repay. Along with redistribution and householding, reciprocity appears in Karl Polanyi's (1944) threefold classification of kinds of economic relations, linked to three types of social organisation. Sahlins (1972:193–5) developed Polanyi's concept of reciprocity, relating each form of reciprocity to a general pattern of social relations.

What Peterson (1993) calls 'inertial generosity' is the tendency to respond to demands rather than make unsolicited gifts. In a small community, the accumulation of mutual obligations would make it difficult for a person with a surplus to decide with whom to share it and on what grounds; should he or she rank debts, meet the largest or oldest debts or recompense only close kin?

An alternative to this bookkeeping approach is simply to respond to demands as they are made. This has at least four advantages: difficult decisions are avoided; the onus is placed on others; discrepancies in the evaluation of relationships are not laid bare; and an excellent excuse is provided for not meeting some obligations within the context of behaving generously. Further, it fully recognises the inherent difficulty in delayed reciprocity: time alters the value of objects and the perception of relationships, compounding the difficulties of calculating the correct return (Peterson 1993:864). A person could evade a request by hiding items that were the likely targets of requests, by lying or by vesting ownership of an item in a close relative.

Sansom (1980:132–5) applies the concept of 'service economy' to the internal economy of a Darwin fringe camp, where life is centred on the consumption of alcohol. The owner of a ceremony, of 'trouble' or a problem owned a 'slice of actions' and offered service. Each category of ownership had a capacity to generate and regenerate debt in the exchange economy. Sansom (1988) describes orders of service within which he calls a 'grammar' of services. The premises on which the economy of the fringe camp were grounded were not those of capitalist economics; rather, a voluntaristic philosophy of action counter-posed the Western philosophy of money. A person with a surplus was subject to continued demands for 'help'. One who helped others thereby made a long-term investment, with a generalised potential to collect a return rather than a specific one, and without going rates. The amount in a reclaimed debt is a function of the liquidity of the debtor, which depends on circumstances, balanced against the creditor's powers of extraction, which depends in turn on the relationship. People can resist the claims of others by 'vectoring' cash allocated to some morally unchallengeable purpose.

The concept of moral economy has been used in a variety of ways, but generally to focus on beliefs and values underlying economic behaviour and relations. Scott (1976:vii, cited in Peterson and Taylor 2003:105) used the expression to refer to the moral content of the subsistence ethic: 'The problem of exploitation and rebellion is…not just a problem of calories and income but is a question of peasant conceptions of social justice, of rights and obligations, of reciprocity.'

In Thompson's (1971) use of the concept, the moral economy involves a set of beliefs and understandings that assign economic roles to classes and that endorse aspects of customary relations and practices across these class relationships. Others have used it to point to the allocation of resources for the reproduction of social relationships, but at the cost of the maximisation of profit and obvious immediate personal benefit (Cheal 1989).

Peterson picks out two aspects of the moral economy model in the context of encapsulated fourth-world peoples (Peterson 2002; Peterson and Taylor 2003). The first relates to the allocation of resources in the reproduction of social relations internal to the Indigenous social order. The second relates to ideas about relations with the encapsulating society. At least initially, relations typical of the domestic moral economy are likely to be the basis for relationships with outsiders. Peterson takes four elements to be important to the place of kinship and sharing in the domestic moral economy

- an ethic of generosity informed by a social pragmatics of demand sharing
- a universal system of kin relations that requires a flow of goods and services to reproduce them
- the constitution of personhood through relatedness, but valuing egalitarian relations and personal autonomy
- an emphasis on politeness and indirectness in interaction, making overt refusal difficult.

For Austin-Broos (2009), a parallel Arrernte concept has been 'a kin-based and emplaced life that rendered the subject first and foremost as a relative'. The marginalisation of Western Arrernte 'has left them struggling with different and conflicting regimes of value' (Austin Broos 2009:268). In an earlier work, Austin-Broos (2003) addresses Western Arrernte attempts to articulate their kinship networks with the welfare economy and the state, and the transitions involved as kin relations are 'objectified' in terms of commodities and cash and less in terms of detailed knowledge and experience of country. The contrast Noel Pearson (2000) draws between the 'artificial' economy of Aboriginal communities on welfare and the 'real' Indigenous and market economies bears some relation to the moral economy concept. In his remarks on 'passive welfare as an economy', Pearson writes:

> Our traditional economy was a real economy and demanded responsibility (you don't work, you starve). The white fella market economy is real (you don't work, you don't get paid).

> After we became citizens with equal rights and equal pay, we lost our place in the real economy. What is the exception among white fellas— almost complete dependence on cash handouts from the government—is

the rule for us. There is no responsibility and reciprocity built into our present artificial economy...Passive welfare has undermined Aboriginal Law—our traditional values and relationships. (Pearson 2000:Foreword, cited in Austin-Broos 2009:251)

A second body of theory covers the articulation of Indigenous economies and the wider society.

Approaches to the articulation of Indigenous economies with colonial and post-colonial economies

Among the more influential approaches to the articulation of Indigenous and market economies are internal colonialism, welfare colonialism and the concept of hybrid economy. Rowley's work foreshadowed the concept of internal colonialism. In this model, Indigenous modes of production were partly conserved in their 'articulation' with the capitalist mode; the subsistence sector met part of the costs of reproduction of the labour force. Several scholars applied the theory to the pastoral industry in Australia (Hartwig 1978; May 1983) and to marine industries in the Torres Strait (Beckett 1987; see also Buckley and Wheelwright 1988).

In welfare colonialism (Paine 1977; Beckett 1987), the flow of resources from colony to colonising country is reversed, with the net flow of funds going to the colony. Integration of the Indigenous population within the broader economy radically undermines their previous livelihoods and they are placed on transfer payments such as unemployment benefits. Welfare colonialism defines welfare as a vehicle for stable governance through the exercise of a non-demonstrative and dependency-generating form of neo-colonial social control that pre-empts local autonomy. It creates paralysing dependencies on the 'centre' on the part of a 'peripheral' population, preventing political mobilisation and autonomy (Paine 1977; Reinert 2006). Citizenship and welfare 'colonialise indigenousness' with the state's distinctive norms, rather than actualising Indigenous culture and identity (Bernardi 1997). Beckett (1987:17) sums up:

Welfare colonialism...is the state's attempt to manage the political problem posed by the presence of a depressed and disenfranchised indigenous population in an affluent, liberal democratic society. At the practical level it meets the problem by economic expenditure well in excess of what the minority produces. At the ideological level the 'native', who once stood in opposition to the 'settler' and outside the pale of society, undergoes an apotheosis to emerge as its original citizen.

Bernardi, following Morris (1989), takes welfare colonialism to be a Foucauldian 'disciplinary technology'.

Austin-Broos (2009:185) has traced the effects of welfare colonialism at the level of Western Arrernte outstation communities:

> [O]utstations had begun to proliferate as civil rights increased. In this context, Morony's reports had a further significance: they marked the emergence of a shadow economy in Arrernte life where welfare became the major source of income for outstation residents. This downside of outstations—caused by their remoteness—was initially masked by other dimensions of the land rights process.

Austin Broos (2009:133) also examines how the market sector impinges on the kinship domain and the dilemmas involved in the transition to a cash economy (p. 101).

The concept of welfare colonialism focuses on 'top-down' processes whereas the concept of a hybrid economy models the intersection of sectors, each treated equally analytically. It has been deployed by a number of scholars in several distinct contexts. Muldavin (1997) and Kime (1998), for example, describe the complex amalgam of capitalism and central planning in China as a 'hybrid economy', as does Fahey (1997) in relation to Vietnam. Yang (2000) uses the expression to refer to a local economy in rural China that combined indigenous, state-socialist and market components, and in which ritual consumption subverts the logic of capitalism. In the Australian context, hybrid-economy models have been proposed as alternative perspectives to models of economic exclusion, development and marginalisation (Altman 2004). Altman (2001, 2004, 2005) defines the hybrid economy as comprising the intersection of customary, market and state sectors, and applies the concept to the economies of contemporary remote Aboriginal communities. His model of hybrid economy is readily adaptable to capture the variety of local economies that emerged on the frontier (see Lloyd, this volume). One might add a central 'intercultural' field (Merlan 1998) at the intersection of the customary sector with the state and/or the market sectors (cf. Altman 2004:515, who applies 'intercultural' to regional structures), and include a dynamic dimension in the model to accommodate transformations in each sector and in relations between them—as does Altman in his longitudinal research.

The present volume

The chapters in this volume add to the array of studies of specific sectors or industries and address, directly or indirectly, the theoretical stances outlined above.

Following this introduction, the chapters begin with a broad overview of the relationship of Indigenous people to the settler-colonial economy in Australia by Christopher Lloyd. Australian settler capitalism, Lloyd argues, emerged under the tutelage of the British state in the early nineteenth century. The landmass of Australia was 'cleared' of impediments to pastoral and other extractive forms of capitalism and the Aboriginal inhabitants were marginalised and decimated. The greatest barrier to unfettered capitalist accumulation within the settler mode of production was that of labour. Lloyd also addresses the concept of hybrid economy. Recent research, he argues, has rediscovered the hybrid local economic forms that emerged in many places, in which Aboriginal people supplied labour and developed varying economic relations with settlers in Australia. His chapter examines some of this recent research and writing and develops an argument about how these hybrid local economic formations were able to emerge and survive within the expanding world market of the nineteenth century. Economic hybridity, Lloyd argues, became a possibility and in some cases a necessity in the process of incorporating colonies into larger social and geopolitical structures. In Australia, hybrid economies required initial transformations of Indigenous economies, but hybridity also involved Aborigines maintaining essential elements of their traditional ways of life.

Remaining in the nineteenth and early twentieth centuries, Ian Keen's chapter examines the concepts of property that observers and commentators brought to bear on Aboriginal concepts and institutions of possession—both of land and of 'moveable property'—and how these understandings contrast with Aboriginal concepts and institutions of possession. The usual terms in which this kind of question has been posed have been the doctrine of *terra nullius* and Lockean justifications of dispossession. The chapter moves away from these particular perspectives to examine the property concepts and assumptions brought to bear by individuals in their day-to-day encounters on the frontier and in their reflections on the nature of Aboriginal society. Discussions about changes in property concepts and property law through the early modern period in England are enlightening as to the background of such interpretations. Against this background, the chapter traces the construal of Aboriginal concepts and institutions of possession—from those of early nineteenth-century observers and commentators, through the amateur anthropologists later in the century to the beginnings of professional anthropology in the twentieth. The somewhat surprising result is that commentators not only interpreted Aboriginal concepts and institutions of 'owning' in terms of the all-encompassing concept of 'property' that emerged in early modern England, but also projected English social structure onto Aboriginal social relations.

Following on from his analyses of internal colonialism and welfare colonialism in the Torres Strait Islands, Jeremy Beckett draws on his long-term research and extensive knowledge of Torres Strait Islander society to provide a succinct overview of Islanders in the labour force. From the mid-nineteenth century, Islanders worked in the commercial marine industry in the strait, but with the collapse of the markets an exodus began after World War II from the strait to the towns and cities of north Queensland and beyond. Currently seven times as many people of Islander descent live on the mainland as in the strait. Developing infrastructure in Queensland provided the 'pull'—the majority of Islanders worked for the state railway as fettlers, and others as cane cutters. Meanwhile, the strait economy recovered, with a revival of fishing, pearling and bêche-de-mer markets. From the late 1970s, social service benefits increased, and later the Community Development Employment Projects (CDEP) scheme was introduced in the Torres Strait Islands. Employment conditions in north Queensland have transformed once again with the mechanisation of cane cutting and fettling, so that Islander employment on the mainland has now diversified.

The particular ways in which Indigenous economic relations have been adapted to new conditions and the cultural significance attached to these adaptations have been important to internal colonial relations in Australia. The chapters by Anthony Redmond and Fiona Skyring, and by Diana Young, consider relationships from the early 1920s and 1930s in the Kimberley and the Western Desert, with a focus on the pastoral and sandalwood economies and dogging. Redmond and Skyring examine the adaptation of the *Wurnan* trading network of the Kimberley to the influx of Western commodities and challenges arising from employment of Aboriginal people in large numbers in the pastoral industry from the 1920s. In particular, they consider relations with 'Afghan' cameleers at Moonlight Valley on the Salmond River and with white pastoralists. Relations were mediated through the relationship of Aboriginal women to pastoralists; violence was another pervasive dimension. Aboriginal populations became more sedentary and dependent on rations in return for labour, supplemented by hunting and fishing. Tobacco, tea and sugar—available only from the settlers— were highly prized. The senior men who were most involved in *Wurnan* exchange had some of the most intimate relations with white and Afghan bosses, but there was an imbalance in the meaning of the relationship. The engagement provided some advantages to Aboriginal people, such as the ability to travel and sustain the *Wurnan* trading network and ceremonies, so sustaining a 'parallel economy'.

With the passing of the *Wild Dogs Act* in South Australia in 1912, the dingo was reframed as a commodity, creating specific conditions for encounters between Aboriginal people in the far north-west of South Australia and the 'doggers', who pursued the bounty. Diana Young attributes the establishment of the Presbyterian mission at Ernabella to the Act—at least indirectly: 'Through the medium of the dingo skin, it is possible to discern specific distributions of power', she writes. Her chapter traces the involvement of Anangu in the seasonal dogging camps and their relations with doggers. In a similar way to labour in the Kimberley, Anangu were paid for skins with rations and clothing; nevertheless, Young shows that Anangu were greatly attracted to the camps and the mission had to compete with the doggers in providing attractions. Young shows, then, that dog skins were 'wealth' to Anangu, allowing them access to country and to valued goods. Clothing in turn had its own particular value, becoming essential as both part of the person and an item of trade in ritual. In this way, an 'economy of surfaces' developed, linking skins with clothes.

Neither the welfare colonialism nor the internal colonialism model applies strongly to the next case, in which Aboriginal people formed the mainstay of farming on the NSW South Coast, as in Gippsland, Victoria, and the subsistence sector was small. John White's chapter offers a critique of the concept of 'dependence' in earlier analyses of the role of Indigenous workers in the horticultural sector on the South Coast in the mid-twentieth century. These earlier researchers argued that seasonal engagement in bean and pea picking put Aboriginal people in a position of structural dependence, whereas the decline of the industry, increasing political engagement and broadening employment opportunities brought about a transition to greater independence. White argues that this research took little account of non-marketised resources such as fish. Moreover, the notion of dependency as unsuccessful assimilation obfuscates the innovative and socially meaningful ways in which Aboriginal people interacted with the economy. The chapter traces the history of colonisation on the NSW South Coast and Indigenous engagement with the settler economy. Reciprocal relations of exchange for labour for cash or kind began early and, with dispossession, people engaged in seasonal employment on farms—relegated to low-paid work in an increasingly competitive market. With the rise of bean and pea production after World War II, Aboriginal labour was the mainstay of the industry. Fishing also provided an avenue for some degree of autonomy. These activities are best seen as 'seasonal responses to changing economic circumstances' rather than indicative of dependency. The relation between farms of the Tuross Valley and Aboriginal pickers was one of 'interdependence'.

Remaining in New South Wales, in an exploration of Aboriginal attitudes to work and employment in Wilcannia, Lorraine Gibson begins with the basis of identity in terms of interpersonal relations rather than in terms of job or profession. People ask 'Who you is?' rather than 'What do you do?' In Wilcannia, non-Aboriginal people hold most of the better-paid jobs and Aboriginal people ask why their own people do not get them. Yet those who do succeed in getting (and keeping) good jobs tend to be seen as 'coconuts' (black on the outside, white on the inside). The threat of social ostracism is ever present for those who do not participate in the sharing economy. An increasing number of Aboriginal people choose this position, however, and there are increasing social divisions in relation to employment and the possession of material goods. Nevertheless, Aboriginal subjectivity in Wilcannia is connected to kinship and its associated social obligations rather than mainstream employment. The importance of family tends to override commitment to employment, and paid work imposes less of a moral obligation than for non-Aboriginal people. For many Aboriginal people, hunting, fishing and spending the day with kin and friends are 'a form of production' in its fullest sense, Gibson argues. The sense of self is determined not by engagement in the capitalist division of labour, but by birth into a family. Gibson's chapter thus resonates with the concept of domestic moral economy and its values of demand sharing and kinship obligation, and shows how these impinge on relations with the market economy and its values.

The hybrid-economy model would require some elaboration to cover the subject matter of the final two chapters, which discuss mining and national parks in remote regions in more recent decades (see also Trigger 2005). Both are concerned with the intersection of Indigenous, market and state sectors.

Sarah Holcombe's chapter examines implications for structures established by the state to govern relations between Indigenous people and corporations. The chapter describes the activities of Gumala Aboriginal Corporation, which was set up to manage the *Yandicoogina Land Use Agreement* in the context of iron-ore mining in the Pilbara. She examines the regional economy following the agreement and its implications for Gumala. For example, some 50 per cent of the income of Gumala members derives from Centrelink payments, and only one-third from wages. Holcombe discusses the utility of the sustainable livelihoods approach for wider policy—an approach used internationally, but little in remote Australia. Gumala is potentially well placed to address gaps in research and practice in community and regional development, she suggests. The sustainable livelihoods approach focuses on existing capabilities of individuals, families and households, and examines various forms of 'capital': human, social, natural, physical and financial. While not directly applicable to Australian conditions, the value of the methodology lies in its flexibility and 'bottom-up' approach, and it could assist Gumala to extend community planning and incorporate those who are not employed. Planning for more mine closures—especially landscape rehabilitation, the support of homelands centres and heritage clearances—is a potential area for the application of the approach.

Indigenous, market and state sectors intersect in a different way in the Alligator Rivers region of the Northern Territory. In a critical assessment of the connection between tourism and the Indigenous economy, Chris Haynes considers the impact of the tourism industry in the context of Kakadu National Park. Aboriginal people have had a long-term engagement with mining and Kakadu National Park in the Alligator Rivers region. The park was declared as the result of the report of the Ranger Uranium Environmental Inquiry, which also heard an Aboriginal land claim over the region under the *Aboriginal Land Rights (Northern Territory) Act* (1976) as a result of which a considerable proportion of the park was granted to a Land Trust on behalf of traditional Aboriginal owners. Agreements between traditional owners, the national park and the mining company govern relations in the park. Haynes examines the effects of tourism engendered by the opening of the park, which he sees as significantly disadvantageous to traditional owners. He points to a mismatch between expectations of an experience of traditional Aboriginal culture on the part of tourists and the degree of willingness of Aboriginal people to comply. A relatively small proportion of tourism revenues accrues to Aboriginal people, Haynes argues, which could explain why traditional owners are unwilling to embrace tourism. Haynes also addresses the commodification of traditional culture; objectified forms promulgated by the tourist operators and the park alike have little to do with the lived culture or 'webs of significance' of Aboriginal people and tend to challenge their authenticity. Tourism needs to be more fully controlled by Aboriginal people themselves (see also Levitus 2005 on local economies in Kakadu National Park).

The chapters in this volume thus add to the body of research on the engagement of Aboriginal and Torres Strait Islander people in the economy of the colonial era and through the twentieth and early twenty-first centuries, with contributions on Torres Strait Islanders in the mainland economy, the pastoral industry in the Kimberley, doggers in the Western Desert, bean and pea picking on the South Coast of New South Wales, attitudes to employment in general in western New South Wales, relations of Aboriginal people to mining in the Pilbara and relations with the uranium mine and Kakadu National Park in the Top End. They also contribute to discussions about theoretical and analytical frameworks relevant to these kinds of contexts and bring critical perspectives to bear on current issues of development. It is to be hoped that research and writing of a kind represented here will foster a dialogue between the perspective of economic history and anthropological and historical perspectives on Indigenous participation in Australian economies.

Bibliography

Abbott, G. J. (ed.) 1969, *Economic Growth of Australia 1788–1821*, Melbourne University Press, Carlton.

Altman, J. C. 2001, *Sustainable development options on Aboriginal land: the hybrid economy in the twenty-first century*, Centre for Aboriginal Economic Policy Research Discussion Paper No. 226/2001, Centre for Aboriginal Economic Policy Research, The Australian National University, Canberra.

Altman, J. C. 2004, 'Economic development and Indigenous Australia: contestations over property, institutions and ideology', *The Australian Journal of Agricultural and Resource Economics*, vol. 48, no. 3, pp. 513–34.

Altman, J. C. 2005, 'Economic futures on Aboriginal land in remote and very remote Australia: hybrid economies and joint ventures', in D. Austin-Broos and G. Macdonald (eds), *Culture, Economy and Governance in Aboriginal Australia*, University of Sydney, NSW, pp. 121–34.

Anderson, J. C. 1983, 'Aborigines and tin mining in north Queensland: a case study in the anthropology of contact history', *Mankind*, vol. 13, no. 6, pp. 473–98.

Anderson, J. C. 1988, 'Economy', in R. M. Berndt and R. Tonkinson (eds), *Social Anthropology and Aboriginal Studies*, Aboriginal Studies Press, Canberra, pp. 127–88.

Attwood, B. 1986, 'Off the mission stations: Aborigines in Gippsland 1860–1890', *Aboriginal History*, vol. 10, no. 2, pp. 131–51.

Austin Broos, D. 2003, 'Places, practices, and things: the articulation of Arrernte kinship with welfare and work', *American Ethnologist*, vol. 30, no. 1, pp. 118–35.

Austin Broos, D. 2009, *Arrernte Present, Arrernte Past: Invasion, violence and imagination in Indigenous Central Australia*, University of Chicago Press, Ill.

Austin Broos, D. and Macdonald, G. (eds) 2005, *Culture, Economy and Governance in Aboriginal Australia*, University of Sydney, NSW.

Bain, M. 1975, *Ancient Landmarks: A social and economic history of the Victoria district of Western Australia 1839–1894*, University of Western Australia Press, Nedlands.

Bain, M. 1982, *Full Fathom Five*, Artlook, Perth.

Barker, C. 1992, *Commandant of Solitude: The journals of Captain Collet Barker*, Melbourne University Press at the Miegunyah Press, Carlton.

Beckett, J. 1987, *Torres Strait Islanders: Custom and colonialism*, Cambridge University Press, UK.

Begg, A. C. 1979, *The World of John Boultbee, Including an Account of Sealing in Australia and New Zealand*, Whitcoulls, Christchurch.

Bell, J. H. 1965, 'The part-aborigines of New South Wales: three contemporary social situations', in R. M. Berndt and C. H. Berndt (eds), *Aboriginal Man in Australia*, Angus and Robertson, Sydney.

Bernardi G. 1997, 'The CDEP scheme: a case of welfare colonialism', *Australian Aboriginal Studies*, vol. 1997, no. 2, pp. 36–46.

Berndt, R. M. and Berndt, C. H. 1945, *A Preliminary Report on Fieldwork in the Ooldea Region, Western South-Australia*, Australian Medical Publishing Service, Sydney.

Berndt, R. M. and Berndt, C. H. 1977, *The World of the First Australians: An introduction to the traditional life of the Australian Aborigines*, Ure Smith, Sydney.

Berndt, R. M. and Berndt, C. H. 1986, *End of an Era: Aboriginal labour in the Northern Territory*, Australian Institute of Aboriginal Studies, Canberra.

Bolton, G. 1969, 'The development of the north', in R. Preston (ed.), *Contemporary Australia: Studies in history, politics, and economics*, Duke University Press, Durham, NC, pp. 120–50.

Buckley, K. and Wheelwright, T. 1988, *No Paradise for Workers: Capitalism and the common people in Australia 1788–1914*, Oxford University Press, Melbourne.

Butlin, N. 1993, *Economics and the Dreamtime: A hypothetical history*, Cambridge University Press, UK.

Calley, M. 1956, 'Race relations `on the north coast of New South Wales', *Oceania*, vol. 27, no. 3, pp. 190–209.

Castle, R. and Hagan, J. 1998, 'Settlers and the state: the creation of an Aboriginal work force in Australia', *Aboriginal History*, vol. 22, pp. 24–35.

Cheal, D. 1989, 'Strategies of resource management in household economies: moral economy or political economy?', in R. Wilk (ed.), *The Household Economy: Reconsidering the domestic mode of production*, Westview Press, Boulder, Colo., pp. 11–22.

Clendinnen, I. 2003, *Dancing with Strangers*, Text Publishing, Melbourne.

Curthoys, A. 1995, 'Working for the white people: an historiographic essay on Aboriginal and Torres Strait Islander labour', in A. McGrath, K. Saunders and J. Huggins (eds), *Aboriginal Workers*, Australian Society for the Study of Labour History, Sydney, pp. 1–29.

De La Rue, K. 1979, *Pearl Shell and Pastures: The story of Cossack and Roebourne, and their place in the history of the north west, from the earliest explorations to 1910*, Cossack Project Committee, Roeburne, WA.

Doohan, F. 1992, *One Family, Different Country: The development and persistence of an Aboriginal community at Finke, Northern Territory*, University of Sydney, NSW.

Fahey, S. 1997, 'Vietnam and the "third way": the nature of socio-economic transition', *Tijdschrift voor economische en sociale geografie*, vol. 88, no. 5, pp. 469–80.

Falkenberg, J. 1962, *Kin and Totem: Group relations of Australian Aborigines in the Port Keats district*, Humanities Press, New York.

Fitzpatrick, B. 1941, *The British Empire in Australia: An economic history, 1834–1939*, Melbourne University Press with Oxford University Press, Carlton.

Ganter, R. 1994, *The Pearl-Shellers of Torres Strait: Resource use, development and decline 1860s–1960s*, Melbourne University Press, Carlton.

Gibbs, M. 2000, 'Conflict and commerce: American whalers and the Western Australian colonies, 1826–1888', *The Great Circle: Journal of the Australian Association for Maritime History*, vol. 22, no. 2, pp. 3–23.

Griffin, J. (ed.) 1967, *Essays in Economic History of Australia, 1788–1939*, Jacaranda Press, Brisbane.

Hartwig, M. C. 1978, 'Capitalism and Aborigines: the theory of internal colonialism and its rivals', in T. Wheelwright and K. Buckley (eds), *Essays in the Political Economy of Australian Capitalism*, Australia and New Zealand Book Company, Sydney, pp. 119–41.

Haskins, V. 2004, '"A better chance"?: sexual abuse and the apprenticeship of Aboriginal girls under the NSW Aborigines Protection Board', *Aboriginal History*, vol. 28, pp. 33–58.

Hetherington, P. 2002, *Settlers, Servants & Slaves: Aboriginal and European children in nineteenth-century Western Australia*, University of Western Australia Press, Crawley.

Huggins, J. 1995, 'White aprons, black hands: Aboriginal women domestic servants in Queensland', in A. McGrath, K. Saunders and J. Huggins (eds), *Aboriginal Workers*, Australian Society for the Study of Labour History, Sydney, pp. 188–95.

Hunt, S.-J. 1983, Women in the north: a study of women's lives in northern Western Australia, 1860–1900, Unpublished MA thesis, University of Western Australia, Perth.

Hunter, B. 2005, 'The role of discrimination and the exclusion of Indigenous people from the labour market', in D. Austin-Broos and G. Macdonald (eds), *Culture, Economy and Governance in Aboriginal Australia*, University of Sydney, NSW, pp. 78–94.

Jebb, M. 2002, *Blood, Sweat and Welfare: A history of white bosses and Aboriginal pastoral workers*, University of Western Australia Press, Perth.

Keen, I. 1988, 'Introduction', in I. Keen (ed.), *Being Black: Aboriginal cultures in 'settled' Australia*, Australian Institute of Aboriginal Studies, Canberra.

Kelly, J. H. 1966, *Struggle for the North*, Australasian Book Society, Sydney.

Kime, K. M. 1998, 'Seigniorage, domestic debt and financial reform in China', *Contemporary Economic Policy*, vol. 16, no. 1, pp. 12–21.

Kirkman, N. 1978, 'A Snider is a splendid civilizer: European attitudes to Aborigines on the Palmer River goldfield, 1873–1883', in H. Reynolds (ed.), *Race Relations in North Queensland*, Department of History, James Cook University, Townsville.

Lawrence, S. and Staniforth, M. (eds) 1998, *The Archaeology of Whaling in Southern Australia*, Brolga Press for the Australasian Society for Historical Archaeology and the Australian Institute for Maritime Archaeology, Gundaroo, NSW.

Levitus, R. 1982, 'Everybody bin all day work': a report to the Australian Parks and Wildlife Service on the social history of the Alligator Rivers region of the Northern Territory 1869–1973, Unpublished manuscript.

Levitus, R. 2005, 'Land rights and local economies: the Gagudju Association and the mirage of collective self-determination', in D. Austin-Broos and G. Macdonald (eds), *Culture, Economy and Governance in Aboriginal Australia*, University of Sydney, NSW, pp. 29–40.

McGrath, A. 1987, *Born in the Cattle: Aborigines in cattle country*, Allen & Unwin, Sydney.

McGrath, A., Saunders, K. and Huggins, J. (eds) 1995, *Aboriginal Workers*, Australian Society for the Study of Labour History, Sydney.

MacKnight, C. C. 1976, *The Voyage to Marege': Macassan trepangers in northern Australia*, Melbourne University Press, Carlton.

Makin, J. 1972, *The Big Run: The story of Victoria River Downs Station*, Rigby Seal Books, Adelaide.

May, D. 1983, 'The articulation of the Aboriginal and capitalist modes on the north Queensland pastoral frontier', *Journal of Australian Studies*, vol. 12, pp. 34–44.

May, D. 1994, *Aboriginal Labour and the Cattle Industry: Queensland from white settlement to the present*, Cambridge University Press, Melbourne.

Merlan, F. 1998, *Caging the Rainbow: Places, politics, and Aborigines in a north Australian town*, University of Hawai'i, Honolulu.

Morris, B. 1989, *Domesticating Resistance: The Dhan-gadi Aborigines and the Australian state*, Berg, Oxford.

Muldavin, J. S. S. 1997, 'Environmental degradation in Heilongjiang: policy reform and agrarian dynamics in China's new hybrid economy', *Annals of the Association of American Geographers*, vol. 87, no. 4, pp. 579–613.

Mullins, S. 2001, 'Australian pearl-shellers in the Moluccas: confrontation and compromise on a maritime frontier', *Great Circle*, vol. 23, no. 2, pp. 3–23.

Murray-Smith, S. 1973, 'Beyond the pale: the islander community of Bass Strait in the nineteenth century', *Tasmanian Historical Research Association, Papers and Proceedings*, vol. 20, no. 4, pp. 167–200.

Paine, R. 1977, 'The path to welfare colonialism', in R. Paine (ed.), *The White Arctic: Anthropological essays on tutelage and ethnicity*, Memorial University of Newfoundland, St John, pp. 3–28.

Pearson, N. 2000, *Our Right to Take Responsibility*, Pearson and Associates, Cairns, Qld.

Peterson, N. 1993, 'Demand sharing: sociobiology and the pressure for generosity among foragers', *American Anthropologist*, vol. 95, no. 4, pp. 860–74.

Peterson, N. 2002, From mode of production to moral economy: kinship and sharing in fourth world social orders, Paper delivered at the Ninth International Conference on Hunting and Gathering Societies, 9–13 September 2002, Edinburgh.

Peterson, N. and Taylor, J. 2003, 'The modernising of the Indigenous moral economy', *The Australia and Pacific Journal of Anthropology*, vol. 4, no. 1, pp. 105–22.

Polanyi, K. 1944, *The Great Transformation*, Rinehart, New York.

Reinert, E. S. 2006, *Development and social goals: balancing aid and development to prevent 'welfare colonialism'*, Working Papers 14, Department of Economics and Social Affairs, United Nations, New York.

Reynolds, H. 1990, *With the White People*, Penguin, Ringwood, Vic.

Robinson, C. J. 2006, 'Buffalo hunting and the feral frontier of Australia's Northern Territory', *Social and Cultural Geography*, vol. 6, no. 6, pp. 885–901.

Robinson, S. 2003, '"We do not want one who is too old": Aboriginal child domestic servants in late 19th and 20th century Queensland', *Aboriginal History*, vol. 27, pp. 162–82.

Rowley, C. D. 1970a, *The Destruction of Aboriginal Society*, Penguin Books, Ringwood, Vic.

Rowley, C. D. 1970b, *Outcasts in White Australia*, Penguin Books, Ringwood, Vic.

Rowse, T. 2005, 'The Indigenous sector', in D. Austin-Broos and G. Macdonald (eds), *Culture, Economy and Governance in Aboriginal Australia*, University of Sydney, NSW, pp. 213–30.

Ryan, L. 1996, *The Aboriginal Tasmanians*, Allen & Unwin, St Leonards, NSW.

Sahlins, M. 1972, *Stone Age Economics*, Aldine-Atherton, Chicago.

Sansom, B. 1980, *The Camp at Wallaby Cross: Aboriginal fringe dwellers in Darwin*, Australian Institute of Aboriginal Studies, Canberra.

Sansom, B. 1988, 'A grammar of exchange', in I. Keen (ed.), *Being Black: Aboriginal cultures in 'settled' Australia*, Australian Institute of Aboriginal Studies, Canberra, pp. 159–78.

Scott, J. 1976, *The Moral Economy of the Peasant: Rebellion and subsistence in Southeast Asia*, Yale University Press, New Haven, Conn.

Searcy, A. 1905, *In Northern Seas*, W. K. Thomas, Adelaide.

Shann, E. O. G. 1948, *An Economic History of Australia*, Cambridge University Press, UK.

Sharp, I. G. and Tatz, C. (eds) 1966, *Aborigines in the Economy: Employment, wages and training*, Jacaranda Press, Melbourne.

Shaw, A. G. L. 1965, *The Economic Development of Australia*, Longmans, Croydon, Vic.

Shaw, A. G. L. and Nicholson, H. D. 1966, *Growth and Development in Australia: An introduction to Australian history*, Angus and Robertson, Sydney.

Sinclair, W. A. 1983, *The Process of Economic Development in Australia*, Longman Cheshire, Melbourne.

Stevens, F. 1974, *Aborigines in the Northern Territory Cattle Industry*, The Australian National University Press, Canberra.

Taylor, J. 2005, 'The Indigenous labour market and regional industry', in D. Austin-Broos and G. Macdonald (eds), *Culture, Economy and Governance in Aboriginal Australia*, University of Sydney, NSW, pp. 109–20.

Thompson, E. P. 1971, 'The moral economy of the English crowd in the eighteenth century', *Past and Present*, vol. 50, pp. 76–136.

Thomson, D. F. 1949, *Economic Structure and the Ceremonial Exchange Cycle in Arnhem Land*, Macmillan, Melbourne.

Trigger, D. 2005, 'Mining projects in remote Australia: sites for the articulation and contesting of economic and cultural futures', in D. Austin-Broos and G. Macdonald (eds,), *Culture, Economy and Governance in Aboriginal Australia*, University of Sydney, NSW, pp. 41–62.

Walden, S. 1995, '"That was slavery days": Aboriginal domestic servants in New South Wales in the twentieth century', in A. McGrath, K. Saunders and J. Huggins (eds), *Aboriginal Workers*, Australian Society for the Study of Labour History, Sydney, pp. 196–207.

Warner, W. L. 1937, *A Black Civilization: A social study of an Australian tribe*, Harper, New York.

Watson, P. L. 1998, *Frontier Lands and Pioneer Legends: How pastoralists gained Karuwali land*, Allen & Unwin, St Leonards, NSW.

Wells, A. 1989, *Constructing Capitalism: An economic history of eastern Australia 1788–1901*, Allen & Unwin, Sydney.

Yang, Mayfair Mei-hui 2000, 'Putting global capitalism in its place', *Current Anthropology*, vol. 41, no. 4, pp. 477–509.

2. The emergence of Australian settler capitalism in the nineteenth century and the disintegration/ integration of Aboriginal societies: hybridisation and local evolution within the world market

CHRISTOPHER LLOYD

Introduction

Australian settler capitalism emerged under the tutelage of the British state, which permitted the blending of public interest and private property, within an imperial geopolitical and capitalist dynamic, in the early nineteenth century. The landmass of Australia was more or less 'cleared' over time of impediments to extractive, land-extensive, capitalist pastoralism and agriculture and the Aboriginal inhabitants were marginalised and decimated. The greatest barrier, however, to unfettered capitalist accumulation within the settler mode of production—in Australia as elsewhere—was that of labour, as Wakefield (1929) and Marx (1996) understood. Labour was soon scarce, especially when convictism ended, and far from homogenous and those searching for suitable low-cost and preferably servile supplies roamed across the world. Meanwhile, Aboriginal Australians managed to remain as a living presence in the frontier districts, despite the ravages of disease and violence, but with negligible incorporation into capitalist relations until the late nineteenth century and then in very limited contexts. Suitable supplies of proletarianised wage labour came as immigrants.

The settler economic form—typically characterised by land-extensive resource extraction, free immigrant labour and capitalistically intense development—did not arrive with the colonists in any of what became the neo-European settler societies of the temperate zones. This formation emerged over time out of the material conditions the settlers found, their institutional and socioeconomic baggage, their encounters with indigenous peoples and the later intermeshing with the world economy in the nineteenth century through resource extraction and large-scale labour and capital importation. Recent research and understanding about settler economies in several places are rediscovering the older hybrid socioeconomic forms that emerged in these places—often in the interstices of the formal colonial world and in an uneasy oppositional alliance with some local European settlers. As in North America and southern South America—the two main earlier regions of incipient settler development—in Australia, Indigenous people developed economic relations with settlers in some places and supplied some labour, while at the same time being marginalised and impoverished due to land seizures, but culturally and socially viable within their own, shrinking milieux. This chapter examines some of this recent research and writing and develops an argument about how these hybrid local economic formations were able to emerge and survive within the expanding world market of the nineteenth century. This account has important resonances for contemporary debates about the nature of nineteenth and twentieth-century settler capitalism in Australia and the place of Aboriginal people in Australia today.

Settlement, land and Indigenous people

The European settlement of New South Wales that began in 1788 with a penal colony at Sydney was designed initially to provide a service function for the British Empire—as a depository for the criminal and later political prisoner population of the British Isles and wider Empire.[1] There was limited thinking about economic and strategic possibilities, but no serious planning or provisioning for such a colony. The solving of a serious social problem— the burgeoning of the rootless lumpen class of urban and rural fringe dwellers that swarmed from the countryside to the cities in the world's first industrial revolution, a problem that has reappeared in every country around the world in successive socioeconomic transformations ever since—greatly exercised the minds of the ruling British classes, who feared the collapse of social stability. The British practice of exiling convicts had existed since the early eighteenth century (Meredith and Oxley 2007)—well before the discovery of the hospitable

---

1 'Settlement' is preferred to 'invasion' for, in the initial period, Europeans arrived relatively unopposed and began the process of building a neo-European settler society with imported and then transformed organisms, institutions, social relations and economic systems. As European numbers increased and the settlement spread, conflict with the Indigenous people intensified and became more widespread and the concept of invasion can be applied to the process—at least in some districts. What happened subsequently is the main topic for this chapter.

eastern coast of Australia by Cook in 1770—and was followed also by French, Dutch, Portuguese and Russian governments. The loss of the American colonies forced the search for new places of exile.

The British authorities had a view of Australia as an empty land. The recent debate about the meaning and use of the concept of *terra nullius* as applied to Australia in the late eighteenth century (Attwood 2004; Broome 2002; Buchan 2007) has highlighted—whatever the exact meaning and use of the expression— that the Aboriginal Australians were not considered as landowners in any Western sense and were not considered as examples of *homo economicus* or, indeed, as civilised beings. The land was supposedly 'available' to Europeans for the taking for it was apparently not possessed by anyone. No legal question was involved. The whole territory was taken as crown land. The Aborigines were in the landscape as natural beings but not as lawful owners or occupiers, according to British precepts. Just how, in the late eighteenth century, they fitted into the pantheon of humanity was a subject of interest and uncertainty for some scholars and colonists at the time (see Keen, this volume). The later concepts and certainties of the nineteenth century under the influence of eugenics and social Darwinism were not readily to hand (Turnbull 2007). Nevertheless, the first Governor, Arthur Phillip, was enjoined to treat Aboriginal people with respect and lawfully, although the legal status of Aborigines under British law was uncertain. Initial relations between colonists and Aborigines were friendly (Clendinnen 2003), but soon deteriorated as the colonists moved further inland. Resistance began as it must have become very clear to the Aborigines that not only did the invaders intend to stay, they were competing for the same natural resources of game, water and agricultural land. Lopsided low-intensity guerrilla warfare soon broke out with rifles against spears. Indeed, Governor Phillip himself was severely wounded in one skirmish. Even more devastating to the Aboriginal population was disease, especially smallpox and measles.

Aboriginal economy

Australian Aborigines were foragers or hunter/gatherers before European colonisation. Neither agriculture in the sense of settled communities of cultivators nor pastoralism in the sense of settled or nomadic groups with domestic animals existed in Australia. There were areas of partially sedentary material culture where food sources were abundant, such as some river valleys and coastlines. There were, however, no permanent dwellings, no real villages and very few possessions. Nomadic foraging was by far the dominant socioeconomic system. As with foragers elsewhere, however, here there was a wide variety of activity, dependent to a large degree on the environment in which people lived. Aboriginal people did a great deal to mould the landscape to their needs by, for example, firestick farming to improve grasslands for grazing animals, building fish traps in shallow riverbeds and coastal zones or building canoes for hunting marine mammals and fish. There was much local specialisation in food production depending on natural conditions, and the manufacture of tools was a matter of local specialisation—again, depending on resources. Trade of tools and special materials with neighbouring peoples and over long distances across many language boundaries has been well studied (see Butlin 1993; Keen 2004). It seems clear that there was a continent-wide system of cultural diffusion and trading networks.

The origins and character of Australian settler capitalism

While the British colonisation of New South Wales (including Van Diemen's Land) was motivated primarily as providing a service for the release of social and political pressure at home, and soon for the release of political pressure in Ireland and elsewhere in the Empire, the colony was required to become materially self-sufficient from the beginning. This proved to be very difficult in the early years, although state-directed but largely privatised economic activity became the central economic-regulatory regime from the beginning (Butlin 1993; Lloyd 2003). By the early nineteenth century and especially after the end of the Napoleonic wars, when British socioeconomic conditions worsened and the flow of convict exiles rapidly increased, much private economic activity emerged in the colony. Free immigration increased rapidly and the convict and emancipist population provided a rapidly growing labour supply for the emergence of capitalist economic activity.

Settler capitalism as a distinctive form of capitalist regime began to emerge, then, from the second decade of the nineteenth century. In this development, the Australian experience began to replicate certain features of similar settler-colonial zones in other parts of the world—especially in North America and southern South America (Denoon 1983; Lloyd and Metzer 2011; Rock 1987). This form of capitalism had certain key features that became central through the nineteenth century. By this time, the importance of the world market—created largely through the economic activities of European empires and by the beginnings of European industrialisation—was crucial. Worldwide flows of strategic raw materials, manufactures, capital and labour were already well under way and were to expand enormously in the nineteenth century. One of the key materials consequent on the emerging industrialisation of Western Europe was lubricant oil from animal sources, which was the principal export from the very beginning of the Australian colony, since Australian coastal waters had a large resource of seals and whales.

The initial conditions and the world market context set the pattern of subsequent economic development of Australia: capital-intensive and land-extensive extractive industries; exports of raw materials for Britain's industrialisation; imports of capital, labour and manufactured goods. Crucial to the settler-capitalist pattern that emerged was the natural environment: extensive grasslands and the temperate climate of the south-east of the continent, which made the importation of European agricultural processes possible but on a much vaster scale. Later, vast mineral resources were unlocked by capital after a brief era of small-scale, artisanal mining activity. Despite the availability of a large servile convict labour supply, plantation agriculture did not emerge on the Caribbean model because of the environment, with the partial exception of sugar plantations for a brief period on the Queensland tropical coast. Besides, convicts had rights and could not be enslaved. The environment lent itself to sheep and cattle grazing and, through selective breeding, the Australian wool supply soon dominated British imports in quantity, quality and price. European crops, European animals and European techniques were all easily adaptable to Australian conditions. In addition, minerals—especially copper and later gold and many base metals—were discovered in vast quantities and the story of Australian economic development became hitched firmly to the wealth and industrialising effects of raw-material exports.

The land/labour regulation regime of Australia's early settler capitalism was one of a mixture of semi-coercion and market relations, but the convict component was soon eclipsed by free labour and a purely capitalist model of wage labour was dominant by the 1830s. Conflicts over land and labour control in the 1840s resulted largely in the victory of urban commercial and liberal interests against atavistic quasi-feudal landed interests. The remnants of convictism soon disappeared (Lloyd 2004; McMichael 1984). In any case, convictism could be considered an undeveloped form of wage labour and differed significantly from more servile forms of labour. Attempts to create a yeoman class of small-scale agricultural tenants or proprietors by the Wakefieldian reformers in the 1830s failed in the face of geographical conditions and the disastrous economic conditions of the 1840s. Land reform in the interests of commercial 'family farmers' was partially successful from the 1860s.

As the settler socioeconomic pattern spread out from Sydney and Hobart (from 1803) and later from Brisbane (1825) and Melbourne (1835), the impact on Aboriginal societies was immense. There was a population crash due mainly to disease and malnutrition as the Aborigines were dispossessed of their customary lands and herded into government and church settlements. And, as Rowley pointed out, even where the Aborigines were treated with humanity it was always within the framework of British law, such as on Alexander Berry's estate in the Shoalhaven Valley:

> But even such a rare adjustment, in the absence of any provision for a settlement relating to property rights and anchored in the European Law, became, in the long run, just another road to unconditional surrender. The descendants of those who were charmed by Berry or other entrepreneurs may have been more numerous; but there is no evidence that they were in the long run any better off than those of groups which had stubbornly resisted to the last. (Rowley 1970:29)

Aboriginal nomadism and sheep pastoralism were in direct competition once the early attempts to confine settlement were breached. The martial law declaration in the Bathurst district in 1824—a declared form of de facto civil war—was the official consequence of the type of unofficial guerrilla grassland conflict prevalent in New South Wales and Van Diemen's Land at that time. Once the early skirmishes and massacres had occurred, disease and alcohol were even more destructive than official and unofficial violence (Rowley 1970:33–43). The total absence of legal recognition of Aboriginal 'property' was at the heart of the issue. It is worth asking, however, what difference such recognition would have made. Comparisons with indigenous/settler relations in other settler societies—including North America, southern South America and New Zealand, in all of which there were forms of recognition of indigenous land rights to some extent through treaties—serves to show that it was only through highly organised armed indigenous resistance that any remnants of traditional lands were held on to. The conquest of eastern North America and later of the prairies of central North America after the civil war were very lopsided affairs, despite various treaties. The Sioux and Lakota failed in their attempts to buy artillery pieces but had they done so their eventual destruction could have been even more catastrophic. In the cases of Argentina and Chile, the use of cavalry and limited access to modern weaponry, including even artillery, did forestall some settler conquests. In Argentina, however, the pampas wars of the nineteenth century were explicitly designed by the Argentinian state, under the *estanciero* class, to conquer the land resource and even exterminate the 'troublesome' native people who posed a severe military threat to settlements, even though the rights to land were partly recognised in law in some states and the people were settled agriculturalists and/or nomadic pastoralists. In Chile, the strength of the Mapuche nation was sufficient—with Western arms and military organisation—to hold off the Chilean state until the late nineteenth century and even retain very limited devolved quasi-sovereignty until today, but in a much constrained form. In New Zealand, North Island Maori resistance was strong enough to force the British to fight their biggest military engagement between the Crimean and Boer Wars, but even that was insufficient to prevent social and economic defeat. As these examples show, the great land grabs of the nineteenth-century temperate zone went on as fundamental consequences of the development of settler-capitalist possibilities within a world market. The wealth to be had from commodity production and exports drove the rapacious alliances of the settler states and capitalist landed, mining and financial classes in all the settler zones.

Socioeconomic hybridity

The European–Aboriginal encounter in the early decades of Australian settlement was one of mutual dislike, distrust and open hostility. While hostility and depredation by settlers continued in many areas even into the early twentieth century, in other areas, however, economic accommodation soon emerged. It can be argued that necessity was the mother of accommodation and cooperation. Moreover, the emergence of settler-based markets provided the context for European–Aboriginal socioeconomic hybridisation.

The concepts of socioeconomic hybridity and the hybridisation process refer to the emergence of a socioeconomic formation with elements from the very contrasting systems of Indigenous and settler societies. 'Hybrid' is a term referring to a synthetic or accommodative socioeconomic formation in which there are elements of traditional as well as settler/market relations, technologies and economic power. Settler hybridity, then, while always the consequence of colonialism in certain contexts, has many forms with varying degrees of coercion. In its most benign form, there is retention of a significant degree of human agency by the Indigenous people. Economic hybridity became a possibility or necessity as part of the process of incorporation of colonised regions into larger social and geopolitical contexts. This was the case wherever settler societies were formed in the world socioeconomic and demographic system dominated by European imperialism from the sixteenth century onwards, and indeed during earlier processes of colonisation involving large-scale settlement of colonists in already occupied lands in medieval and ancient times, such as in the Mediterranean and South and East Asia. In many places during early modern times where there were large indigenous populations, such as in Mexico and the Andean region, forms of hybrid and then mestizo societies and economies developed. In all these cases, there was a high degree of initial violence, degradation and coercion by colonists and colonial states.

It has been argued that in northern and central Australia today, where Aboriginal societies and cultures are most 'intact' in the sense of being closer to their original forms and ways of life and less impacted by European colonisation and degradation, a form of hybrid economy has emerged. As John Altman has argued, in parts of Arnhem Land in the Northern Territory:

> The non-market or subsistence sector based on harvesting of wildlife was the dominant component of the economy. This late 20th century economy was not 'traditional', pristine, or precontact, even though colonization had come relatively late to Arnhem Land. This economy is…distinctly indigenous. This economy is not a single sector, it also has market and state sectors, and it does not exist in isolation. While this hybrid economy has its own values, especially in the customary sector, it is also based on a series of conjunctures or articulations between all sectors. (Altman 2006:1)

Altman (2005, 2006) represents this economy as three overlapping circles of the market, the state and the customary, with four segments of articulation or overlap (Figure 2.1).

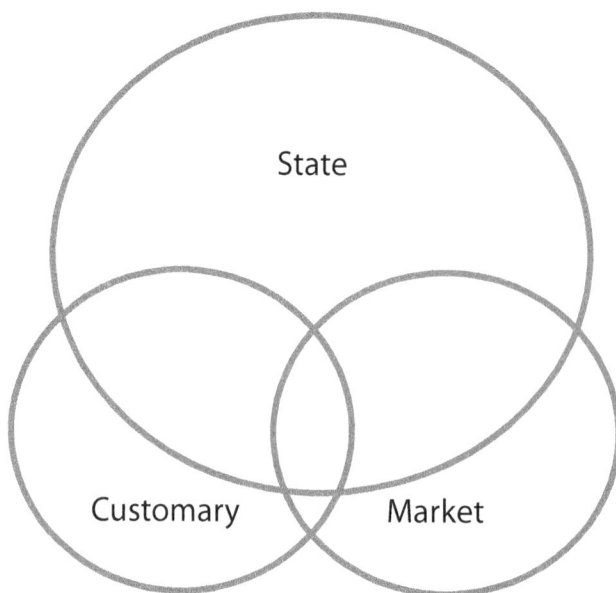

Figure 2.1 Overlapping sectors of the hybrid economy

A key idea here is that conjunctures and articulations make this kind of accommodation possible. In order for there to be this kind of partially merged way of life, the capacity of each system to incorporate elements from the other had to be there first. In the case of Indigenous societies, this could become so only after significant impact and transformation through colonialism. Traditional foraging could not easily be incorporated into the capitalist market economy of settlers, if at all. Only by incorporating and somehow synthesising elements of traditional and capitalist structures could the Indigenous people become open to this new hybrid form of production and organisation. In other words, Indigenous societies were 'made ready' as it were for the possibility of hybridisation. That process was one of partial destruction of their traditional ways of life through the ravages of disease, violence, land seizure and miscegenation, and their forced adaptation to European settler socioeconomic systems in order to survive. Their traditional lands had been penetrated and they were now in a partially dependent relationship. On the other hand, the emerging settler-capitalist forms on the frontier also had to adapt, and that meant sometimes using Indigenous people as labourers, trading with Indigenous people for food supplies and using traditional knowledge. Hybridity also implies that significant elements of traditional ways of life and economic activity are the basis of both settler and Indigenous survival in these contexts.

Hybridity can come about and be understood from either the Aboriginal or the settler-colonial side of the economic exchange relationship. It is also possible for hybridity to be a development on both sides in the sense that settlers can accommodate to some extent at the same time as Aborigines become partially incorporated into some new form of economic relationship with the capitalist economy. Something like this seems to have been the case in the early colonisation of areas of Van Diemen's Land, according to Boyce (2008), where a mutual accommodation between settlers and Aborigines emerged. Similar developments have been studied in North America (for example, the fur trade of the Great Lakes region and the buckskin and beaver fur trades in Appalachia before the nineteenth century), in southern South America (for example, the development of a feral-cattle hunting economy on the pampas of Argentina until the late-nineteenth century) and in New Zealand (for example, Maori whaling in the mid-nineteenth century).

The possibilities that were open to hybridisation in early nineteenth-century Australia depended on several factors being present. Aborigines could become articulated with the local economy in only two ways: by providing resources, especially food and animal skins, and by providing labour. While there was limited hybridisation in the very first few years of the Sydney settlement through Aborigines supplying fish and game meat (Atkinson 1997:163)—unlike in North America, where animal skins and furs were an important commodity, and in Argentina, where cattle hides and later dried meat were important—the only animal products Aborigines could 'sell' in significant quantities were ones in which they had no prior interest and which became significant only through European technology and demand: seal and whale oil. Certainly, significant numbers of Aborigines became involved in the fishery but only as workers (often semi-enslaved) within the capitalist world market or as female concubines and wives of sealers. This was not hybridisation. Insofar as hybridisation occurred in coastal areas it was through the supply of marine food sources. Here, there is some reason to think that hybridisation did occur and that it continued in limited coastal areas. Aboriginal people had knowledge and effective traditional fishing techniques such that they could trade with local settlers.

The possibility of a hybridised labour supply depended on local Aborigines being able to supply labour while at the same time maintaining a strong place for their traditional way of life. Most Australian capitalist agricultural industries had no place for such an articulation. Shepherding, which gave way to fenced sheep stations in the second half of the nineteenth century, could permit such a form of labour in the early years of the pastoral industry and there were few examples of Aboriginal shepherds. The pastoral industry soon needed a full-time working class of shepherds, shearers, fencers and other workers. Aboriginal people became, in Rowley's (1970:34) words, 'a useful last resort for any kind of labour' on sheep stations but there was little need of them. Arable cropping also required full-time workers. Sharefarming of wheat or dairy cattle, although not significant, was a full-time occupation—likewise mining, with one exception, as discussed in the next section.

One significant area where some form of hybridisation was possible was on cattle stations. Here, the need for labour was intermittent and the kind of labour supplied was one in which local workers could live on the land, especially in the very land-extensive form of cattle station development that took place in northern and semi-arid zones where these landholdings could be as large as 1 million hectares. The work was partly nomadic and took place across the traditional lands of local Aboriginal people, who could at least in some places become partially incorporated into the production process—first by supplying food, and later by supplying labour as horsemen (stockmen or ringers in Australian terminology). This work was seasonal, poorly paid (often only via rations), but highly valued by the station lessees, some of whom were absentee capitalist corporations based in some cases outside the country.[2] The Australian meat and livestock industry became globalised and highly profitable from the 1860s via canning and more so from the late 1880s with the advent of refrigeration. Securing labour supply in those northern, sparsely inhabited areas was always a major problem, which relations with the Aboriginal people were crucial in overcoming.

Such articulations did not necessarily imply the emergence of a hybrid form of Indigenous economy of the sort defined by Altman. For articulation to be the basis

---

2   Most agricultural land in Australia, especially in the northern half of the continent, was crown (that is, state-owned) land tenanted on leases up to 99 years.

of hybridity, it had to be possible for Aborigines to maintain essential elements of their traditional ways of life. If they were simply corralled into the capitalist economy as 'wage slaves' then of course they were simply proletarianised or worse. From the settler-capitalist side, for hybridity to emerge or be sustained, Aborigines had to articulate with but not be incorporated into the capitalist economy. There was an incentive for capitalists in some places, especially in the cattle industry, to keep Aborigines as a separate, semi-subsistence and subservient supply of seasonal labour. That they became remarkably skilled horsemen with greater capacity for work than European workers but much cheaper was a model that the capitalists were keen to maintain. Only with the advent of consciousness of the abuse of their rights from the 1960s did any form of revolt occur, such as at Wattie Creek by the Gurindji people.

More examples of hybridity

An earlier striking example of hybridity in colonial Australia emerged in Van Diemen's Land (later named Tasmania) in the early decades of colonisation, before 1824. James Boyce (2008) has argued powerfully that in rural areas in the centre and east of the island what was in effect a hybrid subsistence rural society of convicts, emancipists and Aborigines emerged on the basis of the rich food resources to be found there. The natural environment was significantly different from the surrounds of Sydney and the landscape supported this remarkable development. It was only with a change of socio-political regime in 1824, once the British landowning establishment and the colonial administration of the convict transportation system wished to seize these valuable lands and eliminate the hybrid society that had emerged, that this 'garden of Eden' was incorporated into the settler-capitalist system of sheep stations. The associated war on the Aborigines succeeded in eliminating or exiling many of them.

A second example of hybridity concerns, as already mentioned, the cattle industry in northern Australia from the mid to late nineteenth century. Originally, the white settlers depended on Indigenous labour—often drawn from the traditional landowners who had been dispossessed and then induced to cooperate with the cattle farmers. By the late nineteenth century, a pattern of mutuality had emerged in several areas in which each side came to depend on the other. Of course, the mutuality varied and in some places there was outright 'enserfment' (Anthony 2004). In others there was a stable hybrid situation in which the Aborigines were able to maintain close contact with and even a sort of stewardship over parts of their ancestral domains (Harrison 2004; McGrath 1987). By the late twentieth century, the situation had evolved in such a way that the hybrid pastoral form had developed a much more Indigenous agency in some places in the sense that many pastoral leases had become the property again of traditional owners under the *Northern Territory Land Rights Act* or the Mabo process (Davis 2005). Nevertheless, pastoralism of this kind is still a hybrid form in that there is a blending of traditional ways of life on ancestral lands with production for a market.

A third example is the tin-mining area of Cape York between 1885 and 1940, as researched in detail by Christopher Anderson (1983). In this case, the first significant contact between local Aboriginal people and Europeans in the Annan River valley of south-eastern Cape York occurred in 1885 when tin fossickers moved into the area. As tin mining developed, it significantly damaged the ecological foundation of Aboriginal life because of its effects on the beds and banks of creeks and rivers and through the introduction of alien animals such as cattle, horses and pigs. The availability of tea, tobacco, alcohol and opium as trade or payment goods, flour and beef as food supplies and axes and pieces of glass as technologies all induced the Aboriginal people to remain in close contact with the incoming settlers (Anderson 1983:484–5). In order to obtain and increase access to these commodities, Aboriginal people entered into extensive labouring and service arrangements—both through formal wage contracts registered with the police in Cooktown and through self-employment within the mining sector, usually supplying game-food sources. There were also a few cases of Aboriginal men becoming tin miners (Anderson 1983:485–6).

This Cape York case is striking because of the rapid and thorough development of a hybrid Aboriginal/settler economy so soon after the arrival of Europeans. The Aboriginal people evolved a working arrangement in some places between the maintenance of important aspects of their traditional way of life, including living in camps that had aspects of subsistence hunting and gathering, while articulating with the settler economy through wage work and trade. Once the tin declined in value and quantity from the late 1920s, the social structure of the hybrid arrangements began to break down and many local Aboriginal people moved away or were removed by government agents to southern settlements (Anderson 1983:495–6).

A fourth example involves the development of the Aboriginal acrylic-painting movement in the second half of the twentieth century. Here, traditionally oriented Aboriginal people of remote parts of desert regions of the Northern Territory and Western Australia began to use new materials to permanently record their age-old abstract representations of creation and mythical legends. Hitherto these abstractions were used as body adornments for ceremonies and as ephemeral sand drawings. Beginning at Papunya Tula settlement in 1971, where many Aborigines had 'come in' from remote areas, this artistic movement spread to many areas and became one of the most important new forms of artistic expression in the world by the late twentieth century. The initial artistic development and diffusion owed much to the facilitation of the white supporters of traditional artists, and then to the global art market networks. Along the way there was much exploitation and also much assistance. The origin and continuation of the movement were, nevertheless, crucially dependent on the maintenance of traditional ways of life and cultural knowledge, without which the richness and power of the meanings and expression of the artists could not continue in full form (Bardon 2006). This is an example of the kind of intersection of state, customary and market relations and forces that Altman identified and that Myers (2005) has called 'blurred genres'.

The evolution of Australian settler capitalism in the nineteenth century and the disintegration/integration of Aboriginal societies

These examples of hybridity were, when all is said and done, rare exceptions in the story of the disintegration of Aboriginal society. Hybridity is of course already a transformed state from earlier traditional modes of existence but one in which there is agency on both sides of the encounter. That encounter, given its provenance and its socio-ideological era, could not be other than destructive of Aboriginal cultures and people. Colonial Europeanised Australia was embedded in the world economy from the very beginning. The conjuncture of imperial service function, state direction of economic activity and rapid development of resource-extraction industries meant that the colonial economy, once it developed after the early stuttering years of commissariat dependence, was premised completely on exports of primary products, the inflow of investment and consumption goods and the inflow of labour supply. Labour was key for the settler production system. The other factors of production—land and capital— were abundant but fixed in location in the case of land and abundant and highly mobile in the case of capital through a range of new institutions established at an early stage to facilitate its deployment. Labour of the right kind (that is, open to pecuniary incentives, malleable and disciplined) had, however, to be created through a process of transport, manipulation, 'training' and force, as Edward Wakefield half understood. Mere robust bodies were not enough, as the settlers soon discovered with the Aborigines. Proletarianisation in Europe had gone on for centuries and was continuing in the nineteenth century (for example, the Scottish Highland clearances and English enclosures) and many settlers hoped that the Aborigines might be available in situ. This proved impossible, however, with rare exceptions. The proletarianisation of English and Scottish peasants was premised on the language, culture, religion, social relations, customs, and so on that workers and capitalists shared. None of these was shared between settlers and Aborigines. Thus, the 'choice' for Aborigines in the nineteenth century was stark, as Rowley explains:

> [I]n Aboriginal morality reciprocal generosity was the basis of economics. The whites shocked those whose lands they were taking by their failure to recognise their reciprocal obligations. Soon the hard niggardliness, as it must have appeared to the Aborigines, backed by shooting in defence of personal property, had brought retaliation; and the monotonous story of the Australian frontiers had begun. (Rowley 1970:27–8)

Once the frontier of settlement in the south-eastern and eastern third and the south-western corner of the continent had reached the limits of pasturage, by the 1850s to 1860s, it seems clear that no traditional Aboriginal societies survived.

The Australian economy experienced several phases or regimes of organisation and regulation through the nineteenth and twentieth centuries—each a transformation of an earlier structure (Lloyd 2002, 2004, 2008). Throughout all this history the Aboriginal people were marginalised and left to eke out an existence on the periphery of non-Aboriginal society, with a few places where they managed to retain, develop or defend a hybrid way of life. In most cases, particularly in the southern half of the continent where the large majority of settler Australians lived and where the bulk of the Aboriginal people lived (most of whom today are of mixed descent), they became partially absorbed in a sense into the mainstream society within urban areas but still on the fringes of that society. Within northern Australia, the Aborigines have retained some of their traditional ways of life, their languages or remnants of them and their cultures. They have not become fully integrated into the regime of global capitalism (notwithstanding attempts by governments and mining companies in the twenty-first century) but remain in complex and varying hybrid relationships with mainstream capitalism and/or impoverished welfare recipients on reserves.

With the fundamentally important recognition of native title in 1992 and the subsequent development of a new regime of Aboriginal reconciliation (Ritter 2007; Veracini 2006), culminating in the national apology of March 2008 by Prime Minister Kevin Rudd, a new era of Aboriginal–settler relations began— but one that has much distance to travel. It seems clear that hybrid economic developments offer viable possibilities still in certain locales where resources of labour, land and traditional knowledge can be their foundation.

References

Altman, J. 2005, 'Development options on Aboriginal land: sustainable Indigenous hybrid economies in the twenty-first century', in L. Taylor, G. Ward, G. Henderson, R. Davis and L. Wallis (eds), *The Power of Knowledge: The resonance of tradition*, Aboriginal Studies Press, Canberra.

Altman, J. 2006, *The Indigenous hybrid economy: a realistic sustainable option for remote communities?*, Topical Issue 2 [electronic publication], Centre for Aboriginal Economic Policy Research, The Australian National University, Canberra.

Anderson, J. C. 1983, 'Aborigines and tin mining in north Queensland: a case study in the anthropology of contact history', *Mankind*, vol. 13, no. 6, pp. 473–98.

Anthony, T. 2004, 'Labour relations on northern cattle stations: feudal exploitation and accommodation', *The Drawing Board: An Australian Review of Public Affairs*, vol. 4, no. 3, pp. 117–36.

Atkinson, A. 1997, *The Europeans in Australia: A history. Volume One*, Oxford University Press, Melbourne.

Attwood, B. 2004, 'The law of the land or the law of the land?: history, law and narrative in a settler society', *History Compass*, vol. 2, pp. 1–30.

Bardon, G. 2006, *Papunya: A place made after the story: the beginnings of the Western Desert painting movement*, Burlington, Aldershot, UK.

Boyce, J. 2008, *Van Diemens Land*, Black Inc., Melbourne.

Broome, R. 2002, *Aboriginal Australians: Black responses to white dominance 1788–2001*, (Third edition), Allen & Unwin, Sydney.

Buchan, B. 2007, 'Traffick of empire: trade, treaty and terra nullius in Australia and North America, 1750–1800', *History Compass*, vol. 5, no. 2, pp. 386–405.

Butlin, N. G. 1993, *Economics and the Dreamtime*, Cambridge University Press, UK.

Clendinnen, I. 2003, *Dancing with Strangers*, Text Publishing, Melbourne.

Davis, R. 2005, 'Identity and economy in Aboriginal pastoralism', in L. Taylor et al. (eds), *The Power of Knowledge: The resonance of tradition*, Aboriginal Studies Press, Canberra.

Denoon, D. 1983, *Settler Capitalism: The dynamics of dependent development in the southern hemisphere*, Oxford University Press, UK.

Harrison, R. 2004, 'Contact archaeology and the landscapes of pastoralism in the north-west of Australia', in T. Murray (ed.), *The Archaeology of Contact in Settler Societies*, Cambridge University Press, UK, pp. 109–43.

Keen, I. 2004, *Aboriginal Economy and Society: Australia at the threshold of colonisation*, Oxford University Press, Melbourne.

Lloyd, C. 2002, 'Regime change in Australian capitalism: towards a historical political economy of regulation', *Australian Economic History Review*, vol. 42, no. 3, pp. 238–66.

Lloyd, C. 2003, 'Economic policy and Australian state-building: from labourist-protectionism to globalisation', in A. Teichova and H. Matis (eds), *Nation State and the Economy in History*, Cambridge University Press, UK, pp. 404–23.

Lloyd, C. 2004, *The 1840s depression and the origins of Australian capitalism*, Working Paper, School of Business, Economics and Public Policy, University of New England, Armidale, NSW, <http://www.une.edu.au/bepp/working-papers/econ-history/index.php>

Lloyd, C. 2008, 'Australian capitalism since 1992: a new regime of accumulation?', *Journal of Australian Political Economy*, vol. 61, pp. 31–56.

Lloyd, C. and Metzer, J. 2011, 'Settler colonization and societies in world history: patterns and concepts', in C. Lloyd, J. Metzer and R. Sutch (eds), *Settler Economies in World History*, Brill Publishers, Leiden.

McGrath, A. 1987, *Born in the Cattle*, Allen & Unwin, Sydney.

McMichael, P. 1984, *Settlers and the Agrarian Question*, Cambridge University Press, UK.

Marx, K. 1996 [1867], 'Capital. Volume One', in Karl Marx and Frederick Engels, *Collected Works. Volume 35*, International Publishers, New York, Ch. 33.

Meredith, D. and Oxley, D. 2007, 'Condemned to the colonies: penal transportation as the solution to Britain's law and order problem', *Leidschrift*, vol. 22, no. 1, pp. 19–39.

Myers, F. 2005, 'Unsettled business: acrylic painting, tradition, and Indigenous being', in L. Taylor, G. Ward, G. Henderson, R. Davis and L. Wallis (eds), *The Power of Knowledge: The resonance of tradition*, Aboriginal Studies Press, Canberra.

Ritter, D. 2007, 'Myths, truths and arguments: some recent writings on Aboriginal history', *Australian Journal of Politics and History*, vol. 53, no. 1, pp. 138–48.

Rock, D. 1987, *Argentina: 1856–1918: From Spanish Colonization to Alphonsin* (Updated Edition), University of California Press, Berkeley.

Rowley, C. D. 1970, *The Destruction of Aboriginal Society*, The Australian National University Press, Canberra.

Turnbull, P. 2007, 'British anatomists, phrenologists and the construction of the Aboriginal race, c 1790–1830', *History Compass*, vol. 5, no. 1, pp. 26–50.

Veracini, L. 2006, 'A prehistory of Australia's history wars: the evolution of Aboriginal history during the 1970s and 1980s', *Australian Journal of Politics and History*, vol. 52, no. 3, pp. 439–54.

Wakefield, E. G. 1929 [1829], *A Letter from Sydney and Other Writings*, Dent, London.

3. The interpretation of Aboriginal 'property' on the Australian colonial frontier

IAN KEEN

Prologue

Captain Collet Barker took command of Fort Wellington garrison outpost at Raffles Bay in the Northern Territory in August 1828 and, after it was abandoned a year later, he commanded the garrison at King George Sound in the south-west of Western Australia, where he remained until the end of March 1831. He has been described as one of the more enlightened of the British officers in his dealings with Aboriginal people (Mulvaney and Green 1992:42). Relations between personnel of these outposts and local Aboriginal people have been described as amicable, and that is the impression one gets from Barker's journals. These record a variety of kinds of interaction—from tentative approaches at the beginning of relations to the acceptance of the presence of Aborigines on the garrisons, and with several Aboriginal people taking up regular residence in both garrison camps, with regular visits by others. The amicable relations between Aboriginal people and the personnel of these garrisons had everything to do with the short-term nature of these settlements, and at Raffles Bay the acquaintance of Aboriginal people with previous visits from Macassan trepangers. Particular circumstances explain the friendly relations at King George Sound: earlier attacks by sealers and enmity between Minong people and more northerly groups against which the presence of the garrison offered some protection.

Relations at Raffles Bay were marked by the constant exchange of gifts, some of which had the character of barter: a man gave a stone hatchet, basket and grasstree cord, demanding a steel hatchet in return (Mulvaney and Green 1992:113). There were exchanges of performances: local people sang and danced for the soldiers, and in turn witnessed a parade. Soldiers demonstrated shooting at a target; Aboriginal men demonstrated throwing spears. What Peterson (1993) has called 'demand sharing' was well in evidence. Barker describes how a man they called 'Waterloo' 'begged the pencil case from me, which I gave him' (Mulvaney and Green 1992:87). The demand side of demand sharing sometimes appeared excessive to Barker: a man called 'Wellington' by the British, Barker writes, 'bye and bye asks for everything he sees' (Mulvaney and Green 1992:90).

Conflict between the garrison and local men, as Barker describes it, centred not on land but on moveable property, and concerned 'theft'—a recurrent theme on the early frontier. A man named Luga, for example, made off with a garrison canoe at Raffles Bay and Barker had him whipped for it (Mulvaney and Green 1992:181). Those with whom relationships were established, however, recognised garrison property; a man called Mago, for example, borrowed a frying pan and pot from one Mrs Mills and on returning them 'would give them to nobody but her' (Mulvaney and Green 1992:113).

While he took pains to understand local Aboriginal people, and recorded names, vocabulary and customs, Barker does not reflect on Aboriginal concepts of property. Rather, he sees attitudes to the possessions of others as a matter of personal 'character' and 'trust'. Isaac Scott Nind, the surgeon under Barker's command at King George Sound in the south-west of Western Australia, does include remarks about property in his ethnographic sketch, published in the *Journal of the Royal Geographical Society*. Land is divided into districts, he remarks, and 'is the property of families or individuals' (Nind 1831:44). He has nothing to say, however, about personal possessions.

These remarks lead me to ask, what concepts of property did British colonisers bring to bear in their interpretations of Aboriginal actions and apparent attitudes and how did these understandings contrast with Aboriginal concepts and institutions of possession? The now familiar story is that according to colonial ideologies hunters and gatherers had no concepts of property, as they did not till the soil (Buchan 2001). Jurists such as Vattel provided legal justification for acquiring colonies by 'discovery' and 'settlement'; and the doctrine of *terra nullius* was applied to Australia—deemed to be a settled colony. A key legal case was the Gove case (*Milirrpum* 1971), in which Blackburn J. found both that communal native title was not recognised in the common law and that the relation between a Yolngu clan and its land was not a proprietary one, for it lacked diagnostic features, especially exclusive possession and the ability to alienate the land. The Blackburn judgment contrasts with that of Marshall in the United States (1823), which recognised Native American rights of occupation, and that of Chapman in New Zealand (1847). This ground has been well covered by writers such as Henry Reynolds (1987) and Nancy Williams (1986), although Reynolds (1987:136) found that there was a greater awareness and acceptance of 'native title' than previous accounts had suggested.

I shall move away from these particular perspectives and examine, rather, the property concepts and assumptions brought to bear by individuals in their day-to-day encounters on the frontier and in their reflections on the nature of Aboriginal society. These are rather hard to get at, but discussions about changes in property concepts and property law through the early modern period in England are enlightening as to the background of such interpretations.

Property concepts in late eighteenth-century England

What seems to have taken place through the early modern period is the coming together of land and personal possessions under the rubric of 'property', with the commodification of land, the extension of the law of contract and widening of the scope of contract relations (Lieberman 1995:150, 155). In Blackstone's view, the then new 'commercial mode of property' set new legal requirements to 'facilitate exchange and alienation', so that although many aristocratic families held land in entail, land was becoming more readily alienable (Atkinson 1998; Lieberman 1995:148–9). Common rights in land continued and shared use rights such as the right to glean were widespread, but the enclosures movement reduced the importance of common rights in land (Atkinson 1998). The overarching category of 'property' had come to include all forms of commodities, of which the main subcategories were 'real' and 'moveable' property. The contrast between land and money as forms of property, seen also as a moral and psychological distinction, were entrenched in the early modern period (Klein 1995:222–3).

By the early twentieth century, property was no longer regarded in legal theory as 'absolute dominion', as in Blackstone's ideal, or as *sui generis*, but as a disaggregated 'bundle of rights'. The rights afforded by property were no longer absolutely distinguishable from those offered by other legal categories and no longer carried a clearly definable set of incidents (Davies and Naffine 2001:36). The modern understanding of property as 'disaggregated' is traced to the writings of Hohfeld in the early twentieth century (Hohfeld 1913, 1917; see also Gordon 1995:96), although scholars attribute the expression 'bundle of rights' to Maine (Hann 1998).

Given the fundamental distinctions between personal and real property, and between commerce and landed interests, how was Aboriginal 'property' understood through the nineteenth and early twentieth centuries?[1]

---

1 Atkinson (1998) points out the variety of forms of landownership in early colonial Australia. These included grants of 'common lands' by Governor King to various communities and Governor Macquarie's

The interpretation of Aboriginal 'property'

The 'no-property' view

One opinion expressed in the late eighteenth and early nineteenth centuries was that Aborigines had no concept of property at all—in relation to either land or personal possessions. Governor Phillip's initial dispatches wrote of the Indigenous peoples as living in a 'state of nature', desiring 'little ornaments' but 'having no conception of ownership' (*HRA*:vol. 1, p. 145). 'Fidelis' in the *Sydney Gazette* of 1824 argued that the colony was not the 'property of its original inhabitants', who had 'no notion of property as applicable to territorial possessions', for people wandered 'wherever inclination prompted' (Reynolds 1987:167). The country was to be regarded as 'an unappropriated remnant of common property' (Reynolds 1987:168). The main justification was Lockean: it was 'the right and duty of civilization to occupy and subdue the soil' (*North Australian* 1861, cited in Reynolds 1987:171).[2] Eyre quotes a letter in the *South Australian Register* of 1 August 1840:

> It would be difficult to define what conceivable proprietary rights were ever enjoyed by the miserable savages of South Australia, who never cultivated an inch of soil, and whose idea of the value of its direct produce never extended beyond obtaining a sufficience of pieces of white chalk and red ochre wherewith to bedawb their bodies for their filthy corroborees. (Eyre 1845:vol. 2, pp. 296–7)

The familiar link is made here between the origin of property and agriculture. Eyre (1845:vol. 2, p. 296), however, argued strongly against the no-property view: 'It has generally been imagined, but with great injustice, as well as incorrectness, that the natives have no idea of property in land, or proprietary rights connected with it. Nothing can be further from the truth than this assumption.' The same unjust assumption is made in 'the public journals of the colonies' (Eyre 1845:vol. 2, p. 296).

The no-property view seems to have been a minority one, however, if Taplin's (1879) survey is a reliable indication. Three of Taplin's respondents replied to his question of whether the Aborigines had no property; one respondent was the principal of an institution, one a crown land ranger and one a police trooper.

---

grant of freehold land to Aboriginal people (Atkinson 1998:13). Property in land had a confused status, especially in the case of squatting, which burgeoned from the 1830s. Thus, land was not straightforwardly private property.

2   Reynolds (1987) notes the contradiction: that a very small proportion of Australia was brought under the plough.

Eleven others described inheritance or in some cases destruction of personal possessions; most were police troopers, one was Gason the ethnographer of the Dieri, and one a telegraph station master.

In a contrary vein, a number of late eighteenth and early nineteenth-century commentators—both in Van Diemen's Land (Tasmania) and on the mainland—commented on the strength of Aboriginal assertions of ownership of land. Collins (1798:598–9) thought that Aboriginal conceptions of property related not simply to objects of use, but 'strange as it may appear' to their 'real estates' held as a kind of 'hereditary property, which they retained undisturbed' (see also Buchan 2001:145). Bishop Broughton reported to a House of Commons Select Committee that the Aborigines had a 'conception of our having excluded them from what was their original property' (Reynolds 1987:139). G. F. Moore, a West Australian settler, described the delight of an Aboriginal man in his own country, as did the Tasmanian historian West (Reynolds 1987:139), who described a place on Flinders Island as 'a station of his [the Aboriginal man's] people'.

Barrington (1810) and Paterson (1811) draw on very similar material for their views on Aboriginal property, though Paterson's is the fuller account. Paterson comments, '[t]heir spears and shields, their clubs and lines, &c., are their own property; they are manufactured by themselves, and are the whole of their personal estate' and echoes Collins' remark about possessing 'real estates' (Reynolds 1987:126–7). He reports Bennelong's assertion that Goat Island (Me-mel, in Sydney Harbour) was 'his own property'—it had been his father's and he would give it to By-gone, 'his particular friend and companion'—and his attachment to the place. Bennelong also spoke of others 'who possessed this kind of hereditary property, which they retained undisturbed' (by other Aboriginal groups presumably) (p. 127). Paterson thought women, however, to be 'the slaves of men' (Reynolds 1987:118). Drawing on Collins, Barrington (1810:24) adds canoes, hatchets and fish-gigs to the list of 'property', and notes that Bennelong took great pleasure in being on Goat Island with his wife.

Isaac Scott Nind writes (1831:44) of Minong people at King George Sound in the south-west of Western Australia that '[t]hey are very jealous as to encroachments on their property, and the land is divided into districts, [each of] which is the property of families or individuals'. Except during seasons when people move away from their own country,

> those natives who live together have the exclusive right of fishing or hunting upon the neighbouring grounds, which are in fact divided into individual properties; the quantity of land owned by each individual being considerable. Yet it is not so exclusively his, but others of his family have certain rights over it; so that it may be considered as partly

belonging to the tribe. Thus all of them have a right to break down grass trees, kill bandicoots, lizards, and other animals, and dig up roots; but the presence of the owner of the ground is considered necessary when they fire the ground for game. (Nind 1831:28)

Thus for Nind, 'property' is equated with land. He applies a tribe/family/individual model of relations to land, understands 'districts' to be owned by family groups or individuals and uses the language of 'rights' to grapple with the subtleties of use and control. Indeed, the 'tribe/district' model was common in early writings about Aboriginal property in land.

Tribe, family and individual as property holders

The most common interpretation of Aboriginal relations to land through the first half of the nineteenth century was cast in terms of tribe, family and individual. Some accorded 'property in land' to the tribe and some interpreted ownership as exclusive possession that was defended, although what was referred to as the 'district' or 'locality' of the tribe was frequently described as a place of residence rather than ownership. Phillip referred to tribes 'residing' in their particular districts rather than owning them, while John Hunter (1793:62) wrote of each 'tribe' having a locality or place 'where the tribe resides'.

Eyre (1845:vol. 2, p. 297) generalises that Aboriginal 'districts' were about 10 to 20 miles (16–32 km) in radius, 'being the property and hunting grounds of the tribes who frequent them', and 'parcelled out' among individual members, such that '[e]very male has some portion of land, of which he can always point out the exact boundaries' (this passage is ambiguous; does it mean that men of a group had individual connections to particular portions of land or that males had joint rights?). A 'tribe' could enter another tribe's district only with the permission or invitation of that tribe (Eyre 1845:vol. 2, 297). Eyre thought that a father subdivided his property during his lifetime and that properties 'descend in almost hereditary succession', although females, he thought, did not inherit (Eyre 1845:vol. 2, p. 297). Eyre does not describe personal property; the issue was property as land, seen as belonging to the individual and the tribe, the boundaries defended, and as entailing rights in animals on the land, and indirectly the grass.

Eyre cites Grey (1841), who thought that 'landed property' belonged to individual males, each of whom accurately knew the 'limits of his property' and that 'various objects' marked the boundary (Eyre 1845:298, citing Grey 1841:232). The Grey extract cites a letter from Lang to one Dr Hodgkin, affirming that Aborigines had an idea of 'property in land'. Every 'tribe' has its own 'district', with boundaries well known 'to the natives generally'. Within a district all wild animals 'are considered as much the property of the tribe inhabiting, or rather ranging on, its whole extent, as the flocks of sheep and herds of cattle…are held by European law and usage the property of their respective owners' (Eyre 1845:298). People of a particular tribe 'regard the intrusion of any other tribe of Aborigines upon that district, for the purposes of kangaroo hunting, &c, as an intrusion, to be resisted and punished by force of arms' (Eyre 1845:299).

Lang thought that within tribal territories, 'particular sections or portions of these districts are universally recognised by the natives as the property of individual members of these tribes' (Eyre 1845:299), and he describes how an owner might invite tribes from other districts as well as his own to participate in burning off the country. The Reverend W. Yates testified to a House of Commons Select Committee (which reported in 1836 and 1837) as to the relation of a 'tribe' to a 'district' as 'their own property'.

Salvado (1977) gives a picture of each 'family' owning a 'district' such that each individual member had a distinct foraging territory (he is referring to the New Norcia district in the south-west of Western Australia). The heading to Salvado's Chapter 17 includes 'Proprietary rights over terrain'. The entry is brief, but he describes exclusive possession:

> Every individual has his own territory for hunting, gathering gum and picking up yams, and the rights he has here are respected as sacred. I have often heard them say in dispute—even to their friends: 'Nichia n-agna cala, nunda cala Canturbi; iei nunda uoto' ('This is my district, yours is Canturbi [the name of a place near New Norcia]; get out of here straightaway!'). Consequently, each family regards one particular district as belonging exclusively to itself, though the use of it is freely shared by nearby friendly families. But if an enemy or a stranger is caught there, he is put to death by the owner. (Salvado 1977:181)

Several early sources use the language of 'rights' to describe Aboriginal relations to land. Salvado's use of the expression 'proprietary rights' has already been noted. Governor Gawler of South Australia and Charles Sturt, then Land Commissioner, argued that Aborigines had 'natural indefeasible rights invested in them as their birthright'. Before settlement, they 'possessed well understood and distinct proprietary rights over the whole of the available lands in the Province' (Reynolds 1987:147). In a similar vein, L. E. Threlkeld wrote of Aborigines' 'rights of birth' (Reynolds 1987:150). Nind (1831), the assistant surgeon at King George Sound, described varieties of 'rights', including the exclusive rights of a residence group to use 'neighbouring grounds'.

Early commentators categorise personal possessions as property. Governor Phillip 'seemed willing to protect those articles of use and possession such as spears and "fiz-gigs" [harpoons] that the settlers invariably stole whenever they found them unattended' (Buchan 2001:145). Most of Taplin's correspondents in Victoria who responded to the question about property a little later in the century described the inheritance of personal items by close relatives. Early accounts also describe exchange, under the headings of 'trade' and 'barter' (Taplin 1879). Captain Barker had made observations of gift giving at King George Sound (Mulvaney and Green 1992). Ethel Hassell (1936) and Daisy Bates (1985) describe exchange in the south-west of Western Australia; items included spear shafts from the mulga country, stone flakes, throwing sticks and various foods.

The terms in which Aboriginal 'property' is described

What, then, are the terms in which Aboriginal owning is described by such commentators? To sum up, we find the following:

* concepts of 'owner' and 'property', 'landed property' and 'property in land'
* property described in terms of the possession of rights: proprietary rights, exclusive rights, 'natural indefeasible rights' and birthright
* conceptions of tribes and families as occupiers of land or holders of property
* territories and 'sections' or 'portions' of territories associated with such groups and with individuals, described as places of residence or use, or as property or 'real estates', and in one case, 'station'
* both land and personal possessions, where recognised, are seen as inherited or passed down by 'descent' or 'hereditary succession'
* exchange is described in terms of 'trade' and 'barter'.

Amateur anthropologists' accounts of Aboriginal property

Among interested amateur anthropologists of the latter part of the nineteenth century, Taplin (1879) was a missionary of the Ngarrindjerri of the River Murray mouth in South Australia and Howitt (1880, 1904) was a magistrate, Protector of Aborigines and farmer who employed Kŭrnai people on his hop farm in Gippsland, eastern Victoria. Both circulated questionnaires to property owners, police, protectors, and so on. Others such as Ethel Hassell (1936) (the wife of a property owner in the south-west) and Dawson (1881) (a property owner in western Victoria), as well as Howitt, wrote ethnographic notes on particular peoples with whom they had economic relations. (Others included Gideon S. Lang [1865]; Curr [1886–87]; Spencer and Gillen [1938]; and Horne and Aiston [1924].)

Lang (1865:5) writes that:

> Every tribe occupies its own territory, which is as distinctly defined as any estate in England, and is on no account encroached upon by any stranger, unless upon pain of death…This tribal right to exclusive occupation is, however, modified in certain cases for the benefit of the tribes generally.

He reports access by others for particular kinds of food and raw materials: 'these are general laws giving all the tribes authority to resort to the place without offence either to the tribe permanently located there, or to those through whose country it is necessary to pass in order to reach it' (Lang 1865:5–6).

Tribal land also 'belongs to different members of families of the tribe; it is always jealously watched, and transmitted from generation to generation' (Lang 1865:13). Lang also describes 'personal right of property' in trees and resources found in trees, citing the same sources as Smyth (Lang 1865:13; Smyth 1878).

Curr (1886–87:vol. I, p. 42) thought that for Aboriginal people, '[a]t present, the accumulation of property, or even the care of it, seems to him not worth the trouble it costs'. Curr compares the freedom of the individual in English and Aboriginal societies:

> Thus, civilization aims at restricting governmental interference to *property*, and as far as possible leaving the *person* untouched. In savage life in Australia, on the contrary, there is no interference with property; with the net, shield, and spear a man has made, and the food he has obtained, he may do as he chooses, but no individual, male or female, passes through life without many interferences with his or her person. (Curr 1886–87:vol. I, p. 51; emphasis in original)

Curr had in mind here bodily mutilation associated with initiation, mourning, and so on. He thought Taplin wrong in saying that among the Ngarrindjerri ('Narrinyeri') property such as weapons, implements and ornaments belonged to the tribe in common; rather, 'such things are personal property' (Curr 1886–87:vol. I, p. 66): 'the rights of personal property are as much regarded within the tribes as amongst ourselves.'

Concerning land, Curr (1886–87:61) writes that tribes 'occupy practically in common, and to the exclusion of all others, a tract of country which they claim as their own'. Tribes within 'associations' of tribes 'are always distinct; their lands are not held in common' (Curr 1886–87:63), but each tribe's land is divided into portions with known though imprecise boundaries, not artificially marked, and 'each of which is the personal property of a single male'. People had 'a very elaborate nomenclature for their lands' (Curr 1886–87:64). Curr (p. 64) thought that a father would divide his lands among his sons before he died, letting the tribe know what he had done, although the sons did not inherit the land until after his death, but females did not inherit, he thought. In the absence of sons, the land would go to the nearest male relative. He writes that 'prior to the coming of the Whites each tribe held its territory, when necessary, *vi et armis*, against all intruders' (p. 69). Curr thought that 'the wife is the property of the husband', but he allowed her 'undisputed possession of the bags, ornaments, &c., which she may make or acquire; so that I have often seen a woman give such things away, and have heard husbands ask permission of their wives to take something out of their bags' (p. 66).

Foelsche (1895) also subscribed to the tribe model: 'Each tribe has a recognised land boundary', he writes,

> which is always sacredly respected, and each family or clan in the tribe have their particular portion of land within this boundary. I have never heard of any quarrelling or disputes over boundaries. All families or clans camp promiscuously together anywhere they choose within the tribal boundary. (Foelsche 1895:195)

Like Howitt (1880, 1904), Taplin (1879) thought that tribes (defined by common language and common customs) were divided into exogamous 'clans', each with its own name and symbol and with an ideology of common descent. He depicts the clan as highly corporate; even a man's property rights in his implements and weapons were 'subject to the superior rights of his clan' (Taplin 1879:11).

Writing about Aboriginal people of the Western District of Victoria, Dawson (1881) uses a stronger language of property, including terms such as 'rights', 'inheritance', 'owner', 'landed property' and 'estate'. Property for Dawson was just 'land'; he does not include personal possessions. He writes of the 'territory belonging to a tribe' being 'divided among its members':

> Each family has the exclusive right by inheritance to a part of the tribal lands, which is named after its owner; and his family and every child born on it must be named after something on the property.

> When the father of a family dies, his landed property is divided equally among his widow and his children of both sexes. Should a child of another family have been born on the estate, it is looked upon as one of the family, and it has an equal right with them to a share of the land, if it has attained the age of six months at the death of the proprietor. (Dawson 1881:7)

Moving to the early twentieth century, A. W. Howitt (1904) rarely uses the term 'property' and it does not appear in the index of his comparative study of Aboriginal peoples of south-eastern Australia. Rather, he writes of 'tribal organisation' and 'local organisation' contrasted with 'social organisation'. A 'tribe' is associated with a 'locality'; divisions of the tribe are 'local' and are 'geographical divisions' (Howitt 1904:42–4, 71). He writes of a tribe as 'occupying' country or being of 'their country' and of Wiradjuri 'boundaries' (central New South Wales) or country 'inhabited' by a tribe (Howitt 1904:49, 54–7). In the case of the Kŭrnai 'tribe' (eastern Victoria), clans were divided and subdivided, 'each subdivision having its own tract of hunting and food ground' (Howitt 1904:73). He names 'divisions' according to a place or locality, briefly defined (pp. 76–7), and writes of 'the country of the Brabralung' clan (p. 73). The Bunjil-baul division claimed Raymond Island in the Gippsland Lakes and the swans' eggs laid on it 'as their exclusive property' (Howitt 1904:73).

Spencer and Gillen (1968:590) mention property only once; they report that among the Arrernte (Arunta) of Central Australia, the pebbles for a type of hatchet were obtained from particular localities 'which were the property of local groups of men without the permission of whom the stone could not be removed', and note that A. W. Howitt (1880:232) reports similar ownership of quarries in Victoria.

'Of property, as such,' write Horne and Aiston (1924:33) of the Wangkangurru ('Wongkonguru') people of the Simpson Desert, 'there is but little definite trace'. A person's personal possessions 'are respected absolutely', however, for it 'is not considered right or proper to use anything that has belonged to another man' (Horne and Aiston 1924:33). A weapon or implement may lie in the fork of a tree or on the ground and not be touched —neither would a store of seeds (Horne and Aiston 1924:33). They describe trade and barter for locally made implements (p. 34). What they refer to as 'tribal possession' among Blinman people, who were a 'subdivision' of the Kuyani ('Kooyiannie') people (Lake Torrens, South Australia), included ochre deposits. Others would send a message stick to obtain permission to mine the ochre: 'Until the whites came the tribal boundaries were religiously kept, and it is sufficient for them that these are their lands and have been for generations' (Horne and Aiston 1924:35). Horne and Aiston (1924:35) recount traditions that Wangkangurru formerly lived where Ngamini ('Ngameni') people now dwell (Simpson Desert), however, they were pushed south by them, displacing the Diyari ('Dieri'), who moved further south. Aiston was a policeman and chief protector in the region.

Thus, the 'tribe/district' model of relations to land persists in these authors' works, although Taplin and Howitt recognise another layer of relations of people to country: the clan, and (in Howitt's case) its subdivisions. To sum up the property concepts deployed in these writings:

- concepts of property, 'exclusive property' and 'rights' persist: the 'right to exclusive occupation' of a territory on the part of a tribe, the exclusive right of a family to a part of the tribal land (Dawson), land and swan eggs as the 'exclusive property' of a particular division of a 'clan' (Howitt) and quarries controlled as the property of a local group (Howitt, Spencer and Gillen)

- conceptions of tribes and families also persist, augmented by 'clan' and divisions and subdivisions of the clan in Howitt's model, and in Spencer and Gillen, 'local groups of men' who own quarries

- the land of a tribe and clan is described in terms of territories, estates (Lang, Dawson) and 'country' (Lang), and as 'portions' (Curr) or 'parts' (Dawson) of tribal land, and the 'locality' of a tribe or division (Howitt)

- once again, land is seen as inherited or 'transmitted' from generation to generation (Lang)

- Lang and Smyth add individual rights to trees or resources within trees

- Curr was alone in thinking that a woman was the property of her husband

- Taplin thought members of a clan had 'common rights' in weapons and implements, though others depicted such items as personal property.

Early professional anthropologists' accounts

Turning to trained anthropologists of the early twentieth century, Radcliffe-Brown built on the tribe/clan/family model. In his 1913 and 1918 articles, he uses the term 'local group' rather than clan, and in his 1918 notes on Australian tribes, he writes of 'the territory and its products' as 'belonging to' each local group. He introduces the term 'horde' to denote a group of people who lived together, complementing 'clan' as a descent group. A person required the permission of other groups to hunt (and presumably gather) on their country, unless following game. 'Acts of trespass', he thought, were punishable by death (Radcliffe-Brown 1913:146). A local group is, however, clan-like in this model, for he writes that each child belongs to the local group of its father (Radcliffe-Brown 1913:145, 146). His account of the relationship between clan and horde varies; the Yaralde 'clan-horde' (River Murray mouth) consisted of 'persons who regarded themselves as being closely related in the male line' (Radcliffe-Brown 1918:228) and the group included wives and unmarried children (p. 231). In his later overview, he writes of the horde (rather than the clan) as possessing proprietary rights over the land and its products (Radcliffe-Brown 1931).

W. Lloyd Warner (1937) was the first to carry out long-term fieldwork with an Aboriginal community (this was in the late 1920s): Yolngu or 'Murngin' of north-east Arnhem Land in the Northern Territory. He was also perhaps the first of the major ethnographers to question the 'property' analysis of Aboriginal land, and he extends the concept of property to include 'incorporeal property' such as ritual. He distinguishes three 'types' of property: items of technology, land and incorporeal property such as names and totemic designs.

It is the Yolngu ('Murngin') 'clan' rather than the residence group that owns land and other property in his account. Land is divided among the clans, he writes, 'and definite areas and their natural objects such as trees, water holes, and the like are considered as belonging to these exogamic units' (Warner 1937:146). The moieties are also supposed to have an 'owning' relationship to these areas of land, by derivation (Warner 1937:140). The ownership of land includes the use of it, but members of other clans are not excluded from its use, but in the case of two friendly groups, encouraged (Warner 1937:147). Items of technology are 'personally owned', although a number of fathers, sons and brothers who have cooperated in an enterprise such as building a boat 'have a feeling of collective ownership' (Warner 1937:147).

Among elements of incorporeal property, the concept of which he saw as 'not very highly developed' (Warner 1937:147; cf. Keen 1994), were a man's name, 'which is his own', although others may share it, and totemic designs associated with clans and moieties: 'it would be impossible for members of the other clans or moiety to use these designs or emblems unless given permission under special circumstances.' Totemic designs, like totems themselves and rituals, 'are not so much properties in an economic sense as integral parts of the structure of the clan'; moreover, '[t]o a great extent this is also true of the land' (Warner 1937:147). They belong to 'an economic category' only in a secondary and derivative sense, 'yet the effect of their being part of the clan and moiety configuration has many of the attributes of our concept of property' (Warner 1937:147). No songs or painted designs are considered the property of any one individual or group, Warner thought (incorrectly) (p. 147; cf. Keen 1994; Morphy 1991). The ritual belonging to a healer ('medicine man', *marrngitj*) is not so much owned as acquired through inherent ability in combination with a mystical experience (Warner 1937:148).

Warner (1937:147–8) thought the Yolngu sense of property to be 'undeveloped', as the result of their 'lack of interest in developing their technological equipment', ultimately as a result of the need for mobility and hence portability. He qualifies the use of the expression 'property'. Land, the natural features on it and 'incorporeal property' including ritual and totemic designs, he writes, were less the 'property' of the clan and more an integral 'part' of it (Warner 1937:146–9). This reflects Yolngu distinctions rather more closely than does the property model.

Donald Thomson (1972), who carried out fieldwork in eastern Cape York Peninsula in the late 1920s, describes subtleties of property relations among particular categories of relative. Young men could use the possessions of those with whom relations were unconstrained without asking permission; these included his close father's father, mother's father and mother's older brother. Among Umpila speakers, a *poladu* (SS) could borrow his *pola*'s (FF's) spears and other possessions without asking him: 'He looks [sees] but he doesn't talk [say anything]' (Thomson 1972:11); and similarly 'a person may use the spear or canoe of his *ngatjimo* [MF/FMB] without having to ask permission' (p. 11). Such freedom was also customary between a man's younger sister's child and his mother's older brother, but not his mother's younger brother, with whom relations were reserved (Thomson 1972:12). It is implicit in Thomson's account that one should ask other relatives' permission before using their possessions.

To sum up the views of these professional anthropologists:

- concepts of property and 'proprietary' rights again persist, with a local group, horde or clan having proprietary rights over its territory and products, together with attendant concepts of trespass and permission (Radcliffe-Brown)

- there are qualifications from Warner: land 'belongs to' the clan, but is a part of it rather than being its property, as are songs and totemic designs (Warner)

- ideas about personal property persist, although more subtly described by Thomson.

The grid of English categories of property

The overall picture seems to be, then, that commentators interpreted Aboriginal possessions not only in terms of the all-encompassing concept of 'property', including personal possessions, land, wives (in one view) and 'incorporeal' things, but also projecting English social structure onto Aboriginal social relations. The tribe is the equivalent of the nation, with its common language, territory (which the tribe defends) and body of custom. It is divided into family groups, each with an 'estate'. In several accounts, individuals inherit property in land from the father post mortem and pass it down to sons or to other close relatives in the absence of sons. The 'family' is thus constituted as a succession of individual landholders—reminiscent of aristocratic families holding land in entail. Radcliffe-Brown's 'horde' with its property in land is in effect an expanded family. Certain class elements are read into Aboriginal social relations in interpretations of prominent individuals as 'chiefs' (for example, Dawson 1881). (The later 'clan' model introduces an element with a Scottish but not an English equivalent.)

While both personal and real property are said to be held exclusively—especially land at the level of tribe—they are not described in terms of commodities. The language of commodities creeps in, however, when it comes to the exchange of moveable items, described as 'trade' or 'barter'. After all, 'trade' was a synonym for 'commerce' in eighteenth-century England and contrasted with the landed interest.

Thus, Aboriginal society—at least in its dimension of 'property'—is depicted through the nineteenth and early twentieth centuries as a primitive form of English society. Terms such as 'tribe' (from Latin *tribus*) and (later) 'clan' (adopted into Gaelic from Latin *planta*) give the structure its exotic, primitive character—'tribe' used initially to label elements of Hebrew society and clan to denote Scottish kin groups. It is only when we come to Warner (1937) that 'property' begins to be qualified and the possessions of 'clans' are given a special status, more closely reflecting the kinds of distinctions made by Aboriginal people themselves.

Kinds of Aboriginal 'property'

How does present anthropological understanding of things 'owned' in Aboriginal societies of the kinds encountered in the early nineteenth century accord with these early colonial views? To generalise, in contrast with the all-encompassing meta-category of 'property', things owned are divided into two broad domains.

First, the holding of land and waters ('country') and related sacred things including songs, designs, rituals and sacred objects is conceptualised in terms of connections to totemic ancestors who left traces in land and waters, and of kin relations to ancestors and among owners. Anthropologists have described such connections as implying intrinsic connections (Myers 1991:55), as inalienable or 'inclusive' (Hann 1998; Keen 2004:352–3) or in terms of 'consubstantial' connections (Bagshaw 1998). Kin relations permit degrees of connection to places—described in the anthropological literature in terms of kinds and degrees of 'rights' (for example, Williams 1986). Myers (1991:55) writes of a dialectic between autonomy residing in the right to be asked and relatedness in the tendency to include and share with others.

Second, ownership of moveable and consumable items is not thought of as inalienable, but is subject to demand sharing (Peterson 1993) (see also Chapter 5 this volume on trade and exchange), although people recognise the personal ownership of equipment. Ownership of larger items such as canoes (Thomson 1934) or more recently motor vehicles is strongly asserted, although regarded as belonging to a kin group more than an individual. With some exceptions, material culture items are excluded from the ancestral domain. Contract relations apply very widely to marriage in Aboriginal societies, which also links to the exchange nexus (Keen 2004:204–5). (This explains, perhaps, why some Europeans saw wives as chattels, for the relationship was read as a commodity relation.) In at least some Aboriginal societies, people are able to link personal possessions to the ancestral domain—reserving an item to personal or kin group use by, for example, painting a totemic design on the object (Keen 2004:301; Thomson 1939a). Items from the ancestral domain enter the nexus of gift exchange, including gifts in exchange for wives.[3]

Thus, in strong contrast with the assimilation of all kinds of things 'owned' to 'property' in British and similar cultures, 'country', associated rituals, and so on are treated very differently from personal possessions (and marriage) in Aboriginal ones. Are there equivalents, however, to 'owner' and 'property' in Aboriginal languages? The closest to 'owner', perhaps, are suffixes such as -waltja in Western Desert languages (Myers 1986:55) and -watangu in Yolngu dialects (Keen 1994), but the second of these at least has a more restricted range of application than 'owner' and connotes what linguists call inalienable possession (part-whole and kin relations). There is no equivalent to the overarching concept of property.

Concluding remarks

The results of this brief exercise have been somewhat surprising. Commentators drawing on their experience on the colonial frontier (as well as the experiences of others) interpreted Aboriginal 'property' relations as simulacra of English property relations, albeit gradually modified with systematic research. One might have expected a more exotic, 'savage' society to be constructed, consonant with the depiction of 'superstitions' and 'magic'.

Can it be said that the interpretation of Aboriginal ownership shaped relations on the frontier? Much more important factors seem to have included economic and political interests and particular circumstances. The interpretation of Aboriginal 'property' relations has, however, been significant at the wider legal and political levels, as in the Gove Case, the *Aboriginal Land Rights (Northern Territory) Act* and native title. It is here that their main impact lies.

In the Gove case (*Milirrpum* 1971), Justice Blackburn rejected the property model, for it appeared inconsistent with the Yolngu evidence (Williams 1986). Clans did not seem to hold land to the exclusion of others and it was not alienable. It is significant that in recognising the existence of native title at

---

3   There is a parallel on the north-west coast of North America. Among Gitksan people, for example (Cove 1982), the holding of land and waters is conceived of in terms of a group's sharing a spirit essence with the land and its creatures—extended to the group's crest, stories and songs.

common law in *Mabo II*, the High Court avoided the term 'property', preferring to treat native title as a *sui generis* form of title, and wrote rather of 'connection' to land (Bartlett 1993), avoiding the difficulties faced in the Gove case, although 'title' embeds the concept of property. Six of the seven judges declared that the content and nature of common-law native title are determined according to the traditional laws and customs of the Indigenous people who, according to these laws and customs, have a 'connexion with the land' (Howe 1995:5). Justices Dean and Gaudron suggested that it is preferable 'to recognise the inappropriateness of forcing the native title to conform to traditional common law concepts and to accept it as sui generis or unique' (Howe 1995:6). In order for native title rights to be enforced at common law, the High Court found it necessary to equate them to some degree to common-law concepts of property rights, although the court could not reach a consensus on whether these rights were proprietary or personal (Howe 1995:6). In spite of the view that native title has a *sui generis* character, there has been a consistent push in native title litigation to treat Aboriginal ownership of land and waters in terms of divisible 'incidents' of title.

What are the implications of the ideas about the character of Aboriginal property reviewed in this chapter for ideas about Aboriginal economy as a whole? Apart from subsistence techniques and technology, and to an extent exchange, property was the main aspect of economy that early commentators addressed; Aboriginal people were not thought of as having 'economies', perhaps because economy was defined mainly through the flow of money. Anthropologists of the mid-twentieth century began to model Aboriginal ecologies (for example, Thomson 1939b), but only later in the century were Indigenous economies discussed, together with the place of Aboriginal people in the Australian economy (for example, Young 1981).

Anthropologists like to think that they are rather less ethnocentric than their nineteenth-century forebears in their depictions of cultures different from their own. When it comes to the study of 'property' cross-culturally, however, by far the most common framework for doing so is in terms of 'rights', 'obligations' and 'duties', in spite of the very particular role of these terms in British and related legal systems (for example, Hann 1998; von Benda-Beckmann and von Benda-Beckmann 1999). Strathern (1984) has been one of the very few to question the application of the concept of 'property'—in relation specifically to the Highlands of Papua New Guinea. If an anthropologist writes that Yolngu recognise a 'right to do x', how is it expressed? Is 'right' an apt translation? Anthropologists need to record and interpret more of the Indigenous discourse about 'owning' things.

Bibliography

Atkinson, A. 1998, 'The British legacy: land disposal and use in early colonial Australia', in R. Morton (ed.), *The Land and the People: The Wik lectures*, The History Institute, Carlton, Vic.

Bagshaw, G. 1998, 'Gapu dhulway, gapu maramba: conceptualisation and ownership of saltwater among the Burarra and Yan-nhangu peoples of northeast Arnhem Land', in N. Peterson and B. Rigsby (eds), *Customary Marine Tenure in Australia*, University of Sydney, NSW, pp. 154–77.

Barrington, G. 1810, *The History of New South Wales...*, M. Jones and Sherwood, Neely and Jones, London.

Bartlett, R. 1993, 'The Mabo decision', *Australian Property Law Journal*, vol. 1, no. 3, pp. 236–61.

Bates, D. 1985, *The Native Tribes of Western Australia*, National Library of Australia, Canberra.

Brewer, J. and Staves, S. 1995, *Early Modern Conceptions of Property*, Routledge, London and New York.

Buchan, B. 2001, 'Subjecting the natives: Aborigines, property and possession under early colonial rule', *Social Analysis*, vol. 45, no. 2, pp. 143–62.

Collins, D. 1798, *An Account of the English Colony in New South Wales, with Remarks on the Dispositions, Customs, Manners, &c. of the Native Inhabitants of that Country*[...], T. Cadell Jr and W. Davies, London.

Cove, J. J. 1982, 'The Gitksan traditional concept for land ownership', *Anthropologica*, vol. 24, no. 1, pp. 3–17.

Curr, E. M. 1886–87, *The Australian Race*, [2 vols], John Ferres, Government Printer, Melbourne.

Davies, M. and Naffine, Ng 2001, *Are Persons Property? Legal debates about property and persons*, Ashgate, Aldershot, UK.

Dawson, J. 1881, *Australian Aborigines: The languages and customs of several tribes of Aborigines in the Western District of Victoria, Australia*, George Robertson, Melbourne.

Eyre, E. J. 1845, *Journal of Expeditions of Discovery into Central Australia...*, T. and W. Boons, London.

Foelsche, P. 1895, 'On the manners, customs, religions, superstitions of natives of Port Darwin and west coast of Gulf of Carpentaria', *Journal of the Royal Anthropological Institute*, vol. 24, pp. 190–8.

Gordon, R. 1995, 'Paradoxical property', in J. Brewer and S. Staves (eds), *Early Modern Conceptions of Property*, Routledge, London and New York, pp. 95–110.

Grey, G. 1841, *Journals of Two Expeditions of Discovery in North-west and Western Australia, During the Years 1837, 38 and 39, Volume 2,* Boone, London.

Hassell, E. 1936, 'Notes on the ethnology of the Wheelman tribe of south Western Australia', *Anthropos*, vol. 31, pp. 679–711.

Hann, C. M. 1998, 'The embeddedness of property', in C. M. Hann (ed.), *Property Relations: Renewing the anthropological tradition*, Cambridge University Press, UK, pp. 1–47.

Historical Records of Australia (HRA), vol. 1, series 1, p. 14.

Hohfeld, W. N. 1913, 'Some fundamental legal conceptions as applied in judicial reasoning', *Yale Law Journal*, vol. 23, pp. 16–59.

Hohfeld, W. N. 1917, 'Fundamental legal conceptions as applied in judicial reasoning', *Yale Law Journal*, vol. 26, pp. 710–70.

Horne, G. and Aiston, G. 1924, *Savage Life in Central Australia*, Macmillan and Co., London.

Howe, A. 1995, 'A poststructuralist consideration of property as thin air— Mabo, a case study', *E Law: Murdock University Electronic Journal of Law*, vol. 2, no. 1, <http://www.murdoch.edu.au/elaw/issues/v2n1/how21.html>

Howitt, A. W. 1880, 'The Kŭrnai tribe: their customs in peace and war', in L. Fison and A. W. Howitt (eds), *Kamilaroi and Kŭrnai: Group-marriage and relationship, and marriage by elopement*, George Robertson, Melbourne, pp. 177–260.

Howitt, A. W. 1904, *The Native Tribes of South-East Australia*, Macmillan, London.

Hunter, J. 1793, *An Historical Journal of the Transactions at Port Jackson*, Printed for J. Stockdale, London.

Keen, I. 1994, *Knowledge and Secrecy in an Aboriginal Religion*, Clarendon Press, Oxford.

Keen, I. 2004, *Aboriginal Economy and Society: Australia at the threshold of colonisation*. Oxford University Press, Melbourne.

Klein, L. E. 1995, 'Property and politeness in the early eighteenth-century Whig moralists', in J. Brewer and S. Staves (eds), *Early Modern Conceptions of Property*, Routledge, London and New York, pp. 234–53.

Lang, G. S. 1865, *The Aborigines of Australia*, Wilson and Mackinnon, Melbourne.

Lieberman, D. 1995, 'Property, commerce, and the common law: attitudes to legal change in the eighteenth century', in J. Brewer and S. Staves (eds), *Early Modern Conceptions of Property*, Routledge, London and New York, pp. 141–58.

Milirrpum 1971, *[Judgment in the] Supreme Court of [the] Northern Territory [between] Milirrpum v Nabalco Pty Ltd and the Commonwealth of Australia (Gove Land Rights Case)*, Law Book Company, Sydney.

Morphy, H. 1991, *Ancestral Connections: Art and an Aboriginal system of knowledge*, University of Chicago Press, Ill.

Mulvaney, J. and Green, N. 1992, *Commandant of Solitude: The journals of Captain Collet Barker 1828–1831*, Melbourne University Press at the Miegunyah Press, Carlton.

Myers, F. 1986, *Pintupi Country, Pintupi Self*, Australian Institute of Aboriginal Studies, Canberra.

Myers, F. 1991, 'Burning the truck and holding the country: property, time and the negotiation of identity among Pintupi Aborigines', in T. Ingold, D. Riches and J. Woodburn (eds), *Hunters and Gatherers: Property, power and ideology*, Berg, Oxford, pp. 52–73.

Nind, I. Scott 1831, 'Description of the natives of King George's sound (Swan River Colony) and adjoining country', *Journal of the Royal Geographical Society of London*, vol. 1, pp. 21–51.

Paterson, G. 1811, *The History of New South Wales from its First Discovery to the Present Time...*, Mackenzie and Dent, Newcastle upon Tyne.

Peterson, N. 1993, 'Demand sharing: reciprocity and the pressure for generosity among foragers', *American Anthropologist*, vol. 95, no. 4, pp. 860–74.

Radcliffe-Brown, A. R. 1913, 'Three tribes of Western Australia', *Journal of the Royal Anthropological Institute*, vol. 43, pp. 143–94.

Radcliffe-Brown, A. R. 1918, 'Notes on the social organization of Australian tribes', *Journal of the Royal Anthropological Institute*, vol. 48, pp. 222–53.

Radcliffe-Brown, A. R. 1931, *The Social Organization of Australian Tribes (Oceania Monographs No. 1)*, University of Sydney, Sydney.

Reynolds, H. 1987, *Frontier: Aborigines, settlers and land*, Allen & Unwin, Sydney.

Salvado, R. 1977 [1853], *The Salvado Memoirs*, Edited and translated by E. J. Stormon, University of Western Australia Press, Perth.

Smyth, R. B. 1878, *The Aborigines of Victoria...*, J. Curry O'Neill, Melbourne.

Spencer, B. and Gillen, F. 1938 [1899], *Native Tribes of Central Australia*, Macmillan, London.

Strathern, M. 1984, 'Subject or object? Women and the circulation of valuables in Highlands New Guinea', in R. Hirschon (ed.), *Women and Property, Women as Property*, Croom Helm, London, pp. 158–75.

Taplin, G. (ed.) 1879, *The Folklore, Manners, Customs, and Languages of the South Australian Aborigines*, E. Spiller, Acting Government Printer, Adelaide.

Thomson, D. F. 1934, 'The dugong hunters of Cape York', *Journal of the Royal Anthropological Institute*, vol. 64, pp. 237–63.

Thomson, D. F. 1939a, 'Notes on the smoking pipes of north Queensland and the Northern Territory of Australia', *Man*, vol. 39 (June), pp. 81–91.

Thomson, D. F. 1939b, 'The seasonal factor in human culture, illustrated from the life of a contemporary nomadic group', *Proceedings of the Prehistoric Society*, vol. 5, pp. 209–21.

Thomson, D. F. 1972 [1950], *Kinship and Behaviour in North Queensland*, Australian Institute of Aboriginal Studies, Canberra.

Warner, W. L. 1937, *A Black Civilization: A social study of an Australian tribe*, Harper and Brothers, New York and London.

von Benda-Beckmann, K. and von Benda-Beckmann, V. 1999, 'Introduction', in Toon van Meijl and Franz von Benda-Beckmann (eds), *Property Rights and Economic Development: Land and natural resources in Southeast Asia and Oceania*, Kegan Paul International, London.

Williams, N. M. 1986, *The Yolngu and their Land: A system of land tenure and the fight for its recognition*, Australian Institute of Aboriginal Studies, Canberra.

Young, E. A. 1981, *Tribal Communities in Rural Areas*, [Aboriginal Component in the Australian Economy 1], The Australian National University, Canberra.

4. From island to mainland: Torres Strait Islanders in the Australian labour force

JEREMY BECKETT

Introduction

The Torres Strait Islanders are Australia's other Indigenous minority. Until the 1960s, their homelands were the small islands between Cape York and the Western Province of Papua New Guinea, which their ancestors had occupied since 'time immemorial'. Apart from Thursday Island, which Australian settlers have made an administrative and commercial centre since 1879, the Indigenous inhabitants remained in occupation of their home islands, free to cultivate gardens, fish or hunt turtle and dugong.[1] Finding themselves on the periphery of world capitalism since the middle of the nineteenth century, however, the Islanders had become suppliers of turtle shell and then divers and deckhands in the regional marine industry. This industry was always economically marginal and depended on cheap labour such as the Islanders provided, while providing opportunities for leadership (Ganter 1994:passim).[2] By the end of World War II, Islanders began to look to opportunities on the mainland, where it was rumoured they could earn 'proper wages, same as white man'. At the beginning of the 1960s, the markets on which the marine industry had depended collapsed, leaving hundreds of men without work. This began an exodus from the strait to the mainland.

The migration was economically viable because the collapse of the Torres Strait economy coincided with a surge in the mainland economy, creating a demand for the kind of work that Islanders could perform, so that more and more came south during the 1960s and 1970s. As wives and even aged parents joined their

---

1   Thursday Island, or Waiben, was originally part of the domain of the Kaurareg people. About the turn of the century, the Queensland Government sent them to live on neighbouring Hammond Island, but in 1923 relocated them to Moa Island. Kaurareg began returning to Horne Island after World War II.

2   Regina Ganter (1994) has written the definitive account of the Torres Strait pearling industry.

sons, the migration became a resettlement—soon with a generation of mainland-born Islanders. Today, while about 6000 Islanders still live in the strait, some 42 000 live on the mainland—concentrated mainly along the Queensland coast, but also in the Northern Territory and Western Australia; indeed, Torres Strait Islanders are to be found almost everywhere in Australia.

Ethno-history

The Torres Strait Islanders are mainly of Melanesian stock who at some time in the past settled the islands from mainland Papua (McNiven and Quinnel 2004).[3] The islands—more than 20 of which were permanently inhabited with yet others either seasonally occupied or visited occasionally—varied widely in the economic resources they provided. Overall, however, the region was richly endowed with marine life, including turtle and dugong, as well as abundant fish and crustaceans. A critical feature of the regional economy was the great seagoing double-outrigger canoe, traded in from Papua and differently rigged, which enabled full exploitation of these resources, and also trading between different ecological micro-environments (Haddon 1912; Lawrence 1994).

The one resource that the region lacked was stone of a kind that could be shaped for cutting. A few iron implements seem to have come into the area—probably from Indonesia—so that when British vessels began passing through the strait just before and in the early years of British colonial settlement, they were pursued by Islander canoes eager to exchange knives and axes for local produce (Haddon 1935). In due course, a regular traffic developed, with turtle shell as the commodity that the Europeans particularly valued (Allen and Corris 1977). In the next phase of Islander involvement in the global economy, it was their labour that they were to sell.

Until about the middle of the nineteenth century, European shipping was mostly in transit to and from the Australian colony. The 1850s saw the beginning of bêche-de-mer fisheries and, in 1869, pearl shell was discovered in considerable quantities (Ganter 1994:20). Soon many Islanders were working in the marine industry. Their early need for iron was presently supplemented by the perceived superiority of imported tobacco over local products, and the arrival of the London Missionary Society (LMS) in 1870 gave rise to a new set of needs, particularly clothing. Flour and rice, supplied on the luggers, became alternatives to yams and bananas. The labour needs of the industry fluctuated from year to year, however, so that the workforce was sustained and reproduced

---

3   The latter-day Islander population is racially mixed, as a result of intermarriage with Pacific Islanders, Asians and others who came to work in the Torres Strait fisheries during the second half of the nineteenth century.

by a combination of subsistence production and work for wages. Senior men, being less able-bodied, returned to their gardens and fishing, leaving their sons to work on the boats, and taking some of their wages (Beckett 1987). One might say that the Islanders were eased into wage labour, rather than being abruptly taken from their hunting expeditions and their gardens. Presently, however, their need for commodities created demands for cash that the industry could satisfy only in boom times.

The Queensland Government and the marine industry

Queensland annexed the islands between 1872 and 1879, but did not seriously intervene in the Islanders' affairs until the turn of the century, when it began to regulate the payment of 'native' workers in the marine industry (Beckett 1987). In a polyglot labour force, Islanders found themselves positioned in a racial hierarchy, with Malays, Japanese and Pacific Islanders paid more than them, but with Aborigines and Papuans paid less.[4] In 1904, Queensland placed the Islanders under the *Aboriginals Protection Act*, which meant, among other things, that their movements were now restricted to the islands, and in future the government would receive Islanders' wages on their behalf, allocating small amounts for approved purposes.[5] It also oversaw a number of Islander-run enterprises known as Company Boats, which provided an alternative to the privately owned 'Master Boats'. This arrangement persisted until the mid-1960s.

Working in the marine industry, combined with conversion to Christianity, reordered the pattern of community life, with lay-off time set aside for the missionaries' festivals, particularly weddings, and Islander festivals, with dancing and feasting the accepted way of celebrating both forms.[6] Young men were the preferred labour on the boats, while their fathers and uncles eventually retired to subsistence work. Except in the very early years, women did not work in the marine industry. Recognising the increasing dependence on commodities, however, the government allocated parents or families a share of the men's wages.

Learning to labour was an integral part of the Islanders' experience of colonialism. The first generation of boat skippers were Asians or Pacific Islanders—the latter particularly reputed for maintaining harsh discipline onboard the luggers. A

---

4 See Ganter (1994) for an account of the indentured labour in the industry and the role of Japanese divers.
5 This was the *Aboriginals Protection and Sales of Opium Act*, enacted and periodically revived between 1897 and 1934. In 1939, Queensland replaced it with a *Torres Strait Islanders Act*, which ran until 1965.
6 The LMS began evangelising the islands in 1871, giving way to the Church of England in 1915 (Beckett 1987).

later generation of skippers were often the sons of foreigners who had taken Islander wives and lived in one of the island communities. Among these there was competition for prestige as 'top skipper'—a local incentive combining with the quest for monetary gain. This spirit was passed on to their crews, whose earnings increased in a successful year, with more cash to take home to their families, parents and communities. There were, however, many bad years, due to international manipulation of the markets, so that there was no sure correlation between effort and reward. Discontent over wages was one of the causes of a strike on the government's boats in 1936 (see Beckett 1987; Sharp 1993).

Even in a good year, Islanders' wages were a fraction of what a white worker would earn. It is not clear when Islanders became aware of this difference, but when they were recruited into the military after Japan's entry into World War II, they found themselves serving alongside white soldiers, but receiving a fraction of their wages. This again led to a strike and some increase in their pay (Beckett 1987). Returning to civilian life with a sense of entitlement, they experienced a brief period of prosperity in the marine industry, before the old fluctuations and frustrations returned.

The mainly Chinese market for bêche-de-mer had collapsed with the outbreak of war with Japan in 1934 and did not resume until the 1980s. Pearling was also suspended for the period of the war, but it remained the staple of the local economy until about 1960, when the international garment industry, which had bought most of the shell for buttons, turned to plastics as a cheaper alternative. Before this, however, earnings in the industry had declined in real terms—a situation aggravated by Islanders' rising expectations of what they should be paid. Moreover, with a burgeoning population, scores and eventually hundreds of young men could no longer find places on the luggers (Beckett 1987). After a decade or so, the Torres Strait marine economy revived around other kinds of fishing, and somewhat later the demand for pearl shell recovered to a small degree, but in the meantime hundreds of Islanders were left without a source of money, beyond the social service benefits paid to families and to pensioners.[7] Faced with the prospect of unrest, Queensland and the local government councils no longer opposed Islanders moving to the mainland and, within months, hundreds had gone 'south' (Beckett 1987).

Work opportunities on the mainland

Shortly after the end of World War II, the chairman of Murray Island had requested the government's permission for some of his men to go south for the

---

7   Islander seamen were not at this time eligible for unemployment benefits.

cane-cutting season—an experiment that was repeated for a number of years. Cane cutting was, however, a seasonal occupation, and when Islanders began arriving in the 1960s, they were able to find year-round work on the railways, laying and servicing the lines. This was a period of rapid economic development in Queensland and Australia generally, when new lines were being laid into the interior, particularly to serve the new mines. Fettling, as this occupation was called, was a relatively low-paid occupation, which required men to work in the heat, often on remote sidings, which might take them away from town for the week. In a period of full employment, it was not attractive to white workers. It was, however, an opportunity for Islanders, who could cope with the heat and for whom the wages were several times what they could earn back in the strait, had there been jobs to get. Moreover, they were getting 'white man's wages' and they received the money 'in the hand' rather than through the government office (Beckett 1987).

The Islander migration also coincided with the development of new infrastructure in interior Queensland and, presently, the Northern Territory and Western Australia. This also required men who could work in tropical conditions, and Islanders were found to be good and adaptable workers, despite their lack of formal skills and their poor levels of education.[8]

A contractor who had employed Islander workers reported of them favourably in a letter to Conzinc Riotinto (CRA) in 1966: 'these people are good workers, are happy and should be considered for employment on other CRA operations.'[9] The report continued, in part: 'They do not like being rushed and do not appreciate being "bawled out"—in such events they stammer and revert quickly to speaking their native language.' 'They are regarded as being superior to European migrants in respect of understanding and learning to handle equipment.' 'Their hygiene habits are regarded as superior to the European migrants on the project and are better than a considerable number of Australians on the project.' (Compare Gibson this volume on Aboriginal concepts of 'work'.) If they disliked being 'bawled out', Islanders would not put up with physically abusive overseers, and bashed one who had pushed them too far. The victim took the contractors to court, arguing that the company was liable in that they should have known that 'Torres Strait Islanders were likely to indulge in the consumption of such liquor and thereby become argumentative and violent people and given to attacking others with whom they come in contact'.[10] The

8   As Williamson (1994) shows, Islanders had had schooling since the days of the LMS, but of a limited kind. It virtually ceased during the war with Japan, though there were qualified state teachers after 1946.
9   J. S. Davidson to F. F. Espie Esq. and S. Christia Esq., 10 March 1966.
10   *Clive Cedric Moon v Hornibrook (Pty) Limited and others*, Supreme Court of Queensland, February 1964.

judge decided in favour of the plaintiff (despite depositions from myself and the Director of Aboriginal Islander Advancement), but it does not seem that the event had any effect on the employment of Islanders.

As long as these projects lasted, Islanders were able to command good wages, with opportunities for overtime, but they began to slow about 1970. In the long run, it was the state railways that provided the majority of Islander workers in Queensland and elsewhere with their regular occupation, right up to retirement.[11] A Northern Terrritory pearl-culture enterprise was also flying in Islander workers for contract periods. The majority of Islanders remained concentrated along the coast of Queensland, with Cairns, Townsville and Brisbane as the main centres; but others followed the work to Western Australia and the Northern Territory, and beyond. Arthur (2003) notes that Islanders on the mainland live mainly in cities and small towns.

Getting a foothold

The Islanders' entry into the mainland labour market, and life on the mainland generally, was made easier because they already had kinfolk living in northern Queensland (Hodes 1998). These were people of mixed descent, so technically they were not 'under the Act', some of whom had come down before the war; others resettled during the war and failed to return to the islands afterwards. These recognised their Islander kinfolk and showed them hospitality. In the days of pearling, Torres Strait luggers working the Great Barrier Reef came down to Townsville and Cairns to unload their shell, so that these places were not totally unfamiliar when men later decided to come south.

These connections were no doubt helpful in finding jobs for the new arrivals—a role later played by Islander immigrants for their kin as they in turn became established. It also seems that in many cases the work gangs were all or predominantly Islanders, with a senior man as 'ganger'. Some of these gangers had been boat skippers back in the strait and, according to their workers, brought the same ethos of 'hard work' to the railways. In addition, there was the idea that Islanders had to establish their reputation as workers. Thus, one ganger had his boys work longer hours—though they could expect no extra pay—'for name'. If Islander workers did not like being 'rushed', as the CRA report suggested, their own gangers could get them to complete contracts ahead of schedule. Some workers in retrospect thought they were foolish to do so, but others remember those achievements with pride (cf. Beckett 1987:202; Lui-Chivizhe forthcoming).

---

11   The state railways were organised by the Railway Workers' Union, and the Islander workers came under the same agreements as white employees.

Ganger was as high as Islanders seemed to get in the railway system; some tried to rise higher, but only one succeeded. One who had applied for promotion abandoned the idea, suggesting it was 'too much headache', which I interpreted as meaning that his control of standard English had failed him.

The Islander migration

The first Islanders to go south were single or young married men who left their wives behind. As many told me, earning more money than ever before, they found themselves squandering it on alcohol. This was not the way things were supposed to be in the new life, and not a few turned to the Assembly of God and other Pentecostal churches who forbade drinking and smoking as well. By the 1970s, women, children and even aged parents were also making their way south, re-creating some of the constraints and expectations that had prevailed back home. As families, Islanders were able to rent accommodation built for them by the Department of Aboriginal and Islander Advancement and later the Queensland Department of Housing.

The revival of the Torres Strait economy

After a decade or so of economic decline, the regional economy began to revive, with crayfish (rock lobster)—flown south to mainland restaurants and north to Japan—as a major source of income. Some also harvested reef fish for the same markets. After some years, there were also revivals of the pearling and even bêche-de-mer markets. These activities were of course seasonal and they were also vulnerable to overfishing, but by switching from one resource to another, some Islander entrepreneurs were able to prosper as never before—without government interference. As in the days of pearling, now Badu entrepreneurs have proved the most successful, and have the largest population in the strait. Other island enterprises have failed or operate only intermittently.

Probably because of the involvement of Islander men in the military during World War II, Islander families and seniors have been in receipt of social service benefits since 1941. From the late 1970s, benefits, in various forms, became more substantial than previously and, after becoming eligible for the dole, many communities organised work under the Community Development Employment Projects (CDEP) scheme. Schooling has also improved in the strait over the years, with secondary students attending the high school on Thursday Island and exceptional children sent to high schools on the mainland. There is employment for a small number of high school graduates in several of the numerous government departments based in the strait.

Islanders on the mainland in the new millennium

Bill Arthur, who has been following the situation of Torres Strait Islanders for more than 20 years, produced a profile of their status as revealed in the 2001 Census (Arthur 2003).[12] The statistics suggest that the rate of employment of Islanders on the mainland is 46.8 per cent; their proportion in the labour force is 56.8 per cent. Allowing for regional variations, this places them somewhat higher than the Aboriginal population, but below that of the 'non-Indigenous' population.

As elsewhere in Australia (Gregory 2005), in the areas where Islanders are mostly living, the demand for unskilled workers has declined.[13] Fettling, like cane cutting, is now mechanised, and when Torres Strait railway employees retire they are not replaced. The rising generation has to find work where they can and it seems that there is no longer one occupation in which Islanders congregate. Some have returned to live in the strait; others go up for the crayfishing season and then return south. I heard of men signing on for mining work in Western Australia on a fly-in–fly-out basis.

Islanders' representation at the higher levels of employment is relatively modest, which can in part be attributed to education. According to Arthur's (2003) analysis of the 2001 Census, 23 per cent of Islanders have completed high school (compared with 39.5 per cent for non-Indigenous Australians); 2.1 per cent have graduate degrees, compared with 10.2 per cent for the non-Indigenous population.

Families living on the mainland no doubt find themselves pressed to meet the demands of day-to-day living, but Islanders also find themselves called on to meet financial obligations—particularly for the post-funerary rites, known to Islanders as the 'tombstone opening' (cf. Beckett 1987). This requires family and friends not only to erect a tombstone, but to provide an island-style feast at some urban venue. In some instances, the relatives return to the strait to conduct the ceremony. The expense can be considerable; one recent affair was rumoured to have cost $100 000.

Conclusion

The Islander migration to the mainland is a remarkable story. It was the result of a coincidence of several economic and social factors. The decline of the old marine

---

12   Bill Arthur has worked extensively with Islanders, though mainly those living in the strait. Most of his writings have appeared as Discussion Papers for the Centre for Aboriginal Economic Policy Research in Canberra. He conducted a similar analysis of the 1996 Census (Arthur 2000).

13   Here, I have simply selected from Arthur's tables. Readers should refer to his paper for additional detail.

industry in Torres Strait provided the push factor, combined with an awareness that better wages were to be had elsewhere, but the demand for tropical workers on the railways and developing infrastructure for a burgeoning economy provided the pull. The Islanders seized this opportunity with both hands; others might not have responded with the same tenacity, even enthusiasm. The work was hard and the conditions were often rough, particularly in the early days, but the Islanders were receiving 'proper wages', not the meagre pay they received on the luggers, and they were managing their money for themselves. Beyond that, they were justifying their claim to social and moral equality—implicitly if not explicitly denied them while they were 'under the Act'.

Island-born migrants might express nostalgia for 'home' (though there were those who were glad to have escaped for one reason or another) and some returned home after some months or years. For the majority, however, it seemed be enough to have kinfolk living nearby and a regular round of Islander festive and church gatherings. Islander 'culture'—mainly dance and singing—is provided for these gatherings and also for civic affairs in the wider community. As for the mainland-born generation, some have been to the islands only for brief visits. A few of these return to live, usually to take up some government job, but the young urbanites complain that in the islands 'every day the same'.

As previously suggested, the Torres Strait Islander migration to the mainland was a product of a particular time and particular economic conditions. These conditions no longer obtain. In recent years, Islanders have been affected by the disappearance of the occupations in which they used to work and the general falling off in demand for unskilled workers. The younger mainland-born generation is, however, better equipped to compete in the labour market; they have been through a normal school system, as their parents had not, and they can speak standard English as their parents could not. If they have not acquired some skill or educational qualification, they could have difficulty finding jobs, but with the difference that now they 'know their way around'.

Torres Strait Islanders identify as Indigenous, but such land or (now) sea rights that they may claim are in the strait, not on the mainland. Given the importance they attach to the disposal of their dead, however, the handsome tombstones now to be seen in many north Queensland cemeteries suggest anther kind of connection.

References

Allen, J. and Corris, P. (eds) 1977, *The Journal of John Sweatman: A nineteenth century surveying voyage in north Australia and Torres Strait*, University of Queensland Press, St Lucia.

Arthur, W. 2000, *Location and socio-economic status: Torres Strait Islanders, 1996*, Discussion Paper 199, Centre for Aboriginal Economic Policy Research, The Australian National University, Canberra.

Arthur, W. 2003, *Torres Strait Islanders in the 2001 Census*, Discussion Paper 255, Centre for Aboriginal Economic Policy Research, The Australian National University, Canberra.

Beckett, J. 1987, *Torres Strait Islanders: Custom and colonialism*, Cambridge University Press, UK.

Ganter, R. 1994, *The Pearl-Shellers of Torres Strait: Resource use, development and decline, 1860s–1960s*, Melbourne University Press, Carlton.

Gregory, B. 2005, 'Between a rock and a hard place: economic policy and the employment outlook for Indigenous Australians', in D. Austin-Broos and G. Macdonald (eds), *Culture and Governance in Aboriginal Australia*, University of Sydney Press, NSW.

Haddon, A. C. 1912, *Reports of the Cambridge Anthropological Expedition to Torres Strait. Volume IV: Arts and crafts*, Cambridge University Press, UK.

Haddon, A. C. 1935, *Reports of the Cambridge Anthropological Expedition to Torres Strait. Volume I: General ethnography*, Cambridge University Press, UK.

Hodes, J. 1998, Torres Strait Islander migration to Cairns before World War II, Unpublished MA dissertation, Central Queensland University, Rockhampton.

Lawrence, D. 1994, 'Customary exchange across the Torres Strait', *Memoirs of the Queensland Museum*, vol. 34, no. 20.

Lui-Chividze, L. (forthcoming), 'Making history: Torres Strait Islander railway workers and the 1968 Mt Newman track laying record', *Aboriginal History*.

McNiven, I. and Quinnel, M. (eds) 2004, 'Torres Strait archaeology and material culture', *Memoirs of the Queensland Museum Cultural Heritage Series*, vol. 3, part 1.

Sharp, N. 1993, *Stars of Tagai: The Torres Strait Islanders*, Aboriginal Studies Press, Canberra.

Williamson, A. 1994, *Schooling the Torres Strait Islanders 1873 to 1941: Context, custom and colonialism*, Aboriginal Research Institute Publications, Faculty of Aboriginal and Islander Studies, University of South Australia, Adelaide.

5. Exchange and appropriation: the *Wurnan* economy and Aboriginal land and labour at Karunjie Station, north-western Australia

ANTHONY REDMOND AND FIONA SKYRING

The traditional *Wurnan* trade network spans a number of socio-cultural regions in the Kimberley region of Western Australia and beyond, operating at both small-scale interpersonal and larger-scale inter-group levels, channelling ritual and simple economic objects of desire through predetermined but flexible trading routes (see also Blundell and Layton 1978; Redmond 2001a). This chapter examines *Wurnan* as practised by Ngarinyin people at Karunjie Station in the East Kimberley and the way in which successive generations of Ngarinyin participants have maintained and adapted the two very different systems of *Wurnan* and the pastoral station economy within their social worlds. The pastoral station owners, connected to local Ngarinyin people through geography, coercive labour relations and to a certain extent kinship ties, were largely unaware of the operation of *Wurnan* yet were influential players in this economic interdependency. Twenty years ago, Basil Sansom (1988) pointed to a high degree of 'incommensurability' between the traditional Aboriginal 'service economy' and a now thoroughly encapsulating market economy. Rather than being focused on an exchange of objects, the paradigmatic exchanges between northern Australian Aborigines were described by Sansom (1988:173) as 'gifts of service' for which objects simply provided vehicles for producing relatedness.[1] Far from being about the balanced reciprocity that Mauss (1954) and later Lévi-Strauss (1969) saw as the basis of all social contracts, Aboriginal gifts of service tend to constitute hierarchical relationships, because gifts of 'signal services' have a capacity to produce lifelong indebtedness even if the

---

1   Sansom's conceptualisation was consistent with Mauss's notion of *The Gift* (1954), in which the French word '*prestation*' denoted both objects and services.

roles between 'actor and patient' will transform over time. Where there is an equalising reciprocity involved, it is one that emerges only with the passage of time and the history of particular relationships.[2]

Gifts between trading partners in the inter-clan and inter-regional *Wurnan* in the Kimberley region move in a network that is locally perceived as being isomorphic with marriage exchange and the obligations between in-laws. These gifts engender formal expectations and obligations. *Wurnan*, though, may take place at multiple levels around the same object. As Gregory (1982) has shown, at the far end of the scale of formalised exchanges, objects have a capacity to enter and exit the commodity economy, so that its status as gift or commodity may alter in the course of its transmission between different social contexts (see also Appadurai 1986; Godelier 1999:14).

In the north-eastern Kimberley by the 1930s, a range of Western commodities had entered into the traditional *Wurnan* economy (see also Redmond 2001a, 2001b) where they became gifts or 'present', to use the Kimberley Kriol term. Some older Ngarinyin people described how Western commodities quickly became associated with the powerful aura that has long characterised objects obtained from afar in their traditional trade networks. By assimilating the perceived power of newly arrived commodities to the force of ancestral Dreamings (see also Munn 1970; Myers 1988) these people were able to offer a 'view from afar' on the effects of inducting Western goods into *Wurnan* trade and the impact this had on regional social relationships.

Some of my Ngarinyin co-workers also explicitly compared the *Wurnan* with European trading principles of demand and supply.

> Donald Campbell: Old Johnny from Dodnan he cart em from Gibb River, he used to tell me, he got big mob red material to get for naga, wool and cotton to make em hairbelt and everything, in return saltwater side mob send jaguli, shell, Port Keats and them send em milinggin bamboo.

> Whatever they gonna send gotta happen the same way…keep em clear, like when we go to ngarranggarni place [Dreaming sites] just like that… like people used to be trading on the ship, go to one island, then another place island, that mob got no anything, this mob can send spice to them to get food or whatever, it's all similar in a sense. Trade with other mob who haven't got that thing, like spice and silk, nother mob sell

---

2   The indeterminacy that Sansom saw as characterising Aboriginal social/economic life precluded dealing in the dependable expectations of recovering a return gift, which Western economism links with the concept of reciprocity.

em something else that they didn't have…same thing…If you sit down long time and look at things from the outside you see from gardiya [whitefella] to Blackfella side everything fall into place…

Gordon Smith: It's a governing system. (Redmond fieldwork notes, 2007)

In this discussion of the workings of the *Wurnan*, we can see a strong emphasis on material objects per se and the seeking out of objects which, through being locally unavailable, gain an aura of power from being traded from afar, creating new needs and ties between trading partners.

Once Ngarinyin people and their neighbours in the north-eastern Kimberley began to be inducted into the pastoral economy in large numbers from about 1920 or so, some serious challenges were raised to this 'governing system' that accompanied *Wurnan* exchanges. One of the most direct challenges was to Aborigines' control over the value of their own land, labour and mobility. A further serious challenge emerged with the disruption of the local sexual economy when Aboriginal women became the sexual partners of strangers: white stockmen 'bosses' and the 'Afghan' cameleers who provided the transport system for goods across the region's cattle stations. The importance of Aboriginal women in the appropriation of land by the strangers who travelled 'over the ranges' in the Kimberley has already been canvassed (Jebb 2002). The settlers needed, in addition to land, people to work the land to make it profitable. When the white men abducted or induced local Aboriginal women to stay with them, the women's relatives were also drawn into the colonising process so that it was from these initial relationships that the station workforce was established.

Two northern Indian cameleers, Sahanna and his brother, Sultan, moved into transport contracting in the Kimberley. They could have been among the first group of Afghans to migrate to the area after leaving Port Hedland following the cameleers' strike of 1908 (Bottrill and Sahanna 1991:1). Though Sahanna, at least, had served in the British Army in India, his civil and political rights and those of his fellow Indian and Afghan cameleers were restricted by racially discriminatory legislation. Classified under the law as an 'Asiatic' in Western Australia, he could not, for instance, legally employ Aboriginal people, who were the main labour force in Western Australia at the time. In the north-west and the Kimberley, Aboriginal workers were the only labour force. In the 1940s, Sahanna was targeted by the authorities, who were going to prosecute him for his illegal employment of Aboriginal people.[3]

Sahanna and Sultan sought to establish their own cattle station at Moonlight Valley on the Salmond River, as an adjunct to their cartage business. By 1920, this rugged and inaccessible area of the north-eastern Kimberley had been

---

3   Commissioner Bray, 26 October 1943, in Aborigines Department file, SROWA, 1943/1044.

virtually untouched by the bigger pastoral interests, such as the Durack family, who had earlier settled the better cattle country along the Ord River Valley. The Afghans' only neighbours were at Durack River Station, Karunjie, which was being established by a small group of Scots-born veterans of the AIF 10th Light Horse. These were the former comrades-in-arms, Dave Rust and Scotty Salmond, as well as Scotty Saddler (later convicted of the murder of a fellow stockman) and Scotty Meṇmuir. All of these men seem to have sought out alliances with local Aboriginal groups, underwritten by relationships with local Aboriginal women, which had to be concealed from the authorities because under the 1905 *Aborigines Act* in Western Australia, these relationships were prohibited. This law remained in force until 1963. While white men's relationships with Aboriginal women were central to the operation of the frontier economy and to the effective appropriation of land, the actions of the police and other government authorities and the men themselves ensured that there was no official acknowledgment of them. Although it was an offence for all non-Aboriginal men to have relationships with Aboriginal women, prosecution and arrest were usually reserved for 'Asiatic' men who formed such liaisons. This was illustrated in the difference between the experience of Sahanna and that of Rust and Salmond. Sahanna's wife, and the mother of his two children, was a local Aboriginal woman, and this attracted the attention of the Commissioner for Native Affairs, who threatened to charge Sahanna with breach of the *Aborigines Act*.[4] Sahanna's neighbours, Rust and Salmond, who also had Aboriginal wives, never received any such warnings. The selective policing of the offence of 'cohabiting' and having sexual intercourse with Aboriginal women—and these were the words used in the legislation—reinforced white men's access to Aboriginal women as a sexual resource.

Despite the differences in the policing of sexual relationships in the north-eastern Kimberley, their function in connecting the outsiders with local Aboriginal clans was the same. Sahanna took up with the daughter of a man from the Galiyamba clan on which Moonlight Valley was situated. His brother, Sultan, took up with her sister. Scotty Salmond, by all accounts a very violent returned soldier, took a woman from the Liyarr clan, on whose country Karunjie Station was established. Dave Rust took another woman (who also seems to have been from Liyarr clan country) after her father had been shot and killed by one of the roving Karunjie stockmen, Jack Carey. Donald Campbell was the son of another Liyarr woman, Eva Balandu, and a mixed-race Aboriginal man from Queensland, Jack Campbell, the head stockman for Russ and Salmond (see Figure 5.1).

---

4   Commissioner Bray, 1 December 1943, in ibid.

Figure 5.1 Camel ride at Karunjie Station ca. 1950, with Jack Campbell in hat

Courtesy State Library of Western Australia image number 007846D.

Thus, both the Afghans at Moonlight Valley and the Scots-born returned soldiers at Karunjie had taken up with women who were nearly all from the same two local clans—Liyarr and Galiyamba, already related as wife-giving and wife-receiving clans in the traditional marriage system. In addition to this monopolisation of the women of these clans, it appears that Sultan had 'grabbed out of the bush' a young Liyarr boy and 'grown him up' (Campbell Allanbra cited in Munro 1996:39–40). According to Allanbra (Munro 1996), Sultan later took up with this man's wife, taking her to work on his sandalwood collecting expeditions. Later, when the boy had grown into a young man, he was murdered by a white stockman, Peter Reynolds, in order to take his wife.

It is not always easy to tell how much agency was involved on the part of these Aboriginal women and their male kin in establishing the sometimes quite long-lasting relationship with whites and the people they called Afghans. Sometimes the violent abduction is explicit, as when Aboriginal people told how Dave Rust's Aboriginal partner's father had been shot and killed before she became Rust's wife. In other cases, the formation of relationships with the white male settlers was more complex and it is worth noting here that traditionally there was an already established capacity for women's sexual resources to be deployed for securing alliances and building ritual bonds. New factors introduced by white settlement included the depletion of the mature male population through violent encounters with the white settlers, high rates of removal and imprisonment of men for cattle-spearing offences and intensified inter-group conflict resulting from violent appropriations of Aboriginal women, waterholes and hunting grounds. Given that white men had demonstrated a ready capacity to inflict terror and destruction, it would not be surprising if Aboriginal men sought to gain leverage with the strangers by acquiescing to the strangers' need for local women, or if women themselves sometimes made such initiatives. Some of these women now speak with considerable affection for the autonomy and/or relative safety amid the frontier violence that they were able to achieve through being a white man's or Afghan's partner. Travelling with these men, collecting sandalwood, camp cooking, doing stockwork or collecting dingo scalps for cash availed some women of considerable opportunities amid the everyday drudgery of working for whites.

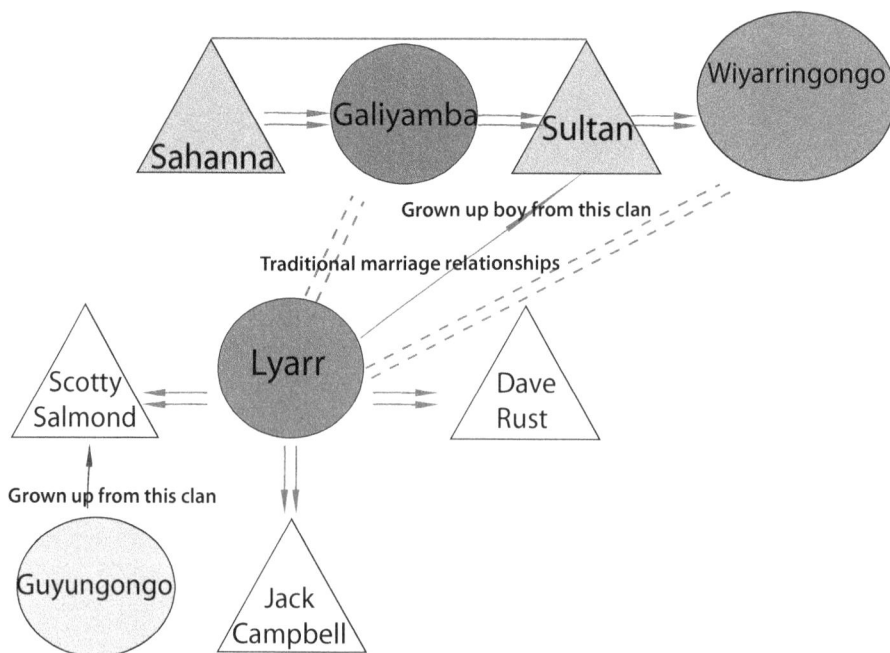

Figure 5.2 Relationships between local clans and non-local men at Karunjie

The Kimberley frontier was a violent place. Five white men were speared and killed in the first wave of invasion in the eastern Kimberley in the 1880s and Aboriginal casualties were much higher. What were called 'dispersals' were attacks on Aboriginal camps by police, in retaliation for allegations of cattle spearing (Owen 2003:105–10), but the removal of Aboriginal people from cattle-grazing country was the central motive. Police rarely recorded how many Aboriginal people they shot in 'dispersals', but in 1895 one Wyndham police sergeant described in his personal diary that the police patrol of which he was a member killed 20 men in one raid. The police patrol continued raiding camps in the area of Ivanhoe Station, eventually returning to Wyndham more than a month later with 14 prisoners who had been marched around the bush in chains. Thirteen of the prisoners were charged with 'being in the unlawful possession of beef' and sentenced to two years' hard labour plus 15 lashes of the cat-o'-nine-tails (Owen 2003:120–1).

Local station owners and white stockworkers were also participants in the killing of Aboriginal people. Evidence from police journals suggests that the Duracks, who appropriated the first and largest pastoral leases along the Ord River, had a 'gentlemen's agreement' with the Police Commissioner, whereby white men on Durack-owned stations would not be investigated or prosecuted for murdering Aboriginal people. There were several such murders and Patsy Durack told one constable that 'the police who put away a man for doing in the blacks always got the chuck out of the police' (Owen 2003:126–7). During the 1901 trial of two Aboriginal youths for the murder of another Durack, Jeremiah, young Patsy Durack agreed that they 'generally used Winchester rifles to shoot natives' (Skyring 2001:23–4).

Salmond's own recollections suggest that the threat of murderous violence was a strategy used at Karunjie as well, and that this could coexist with relatively stable relationships. Salmond recounted to a journalist in 1970 how he had formed a partnership with Dave Rust after World War I, and Salmond went into 'unknown country' to establish the station. He described the early years of Karunjie as 'lively' when 'natives constantly tried to spear the cattle and kill the whites', presumably including him. Salmond contended that the only thing 'natives' understood was 'savagery and strength', and he trained dogs to defend the homestead against 'blacks'. He recalled 'we had just come back from a war in which we were taught to kill. And when it came to a showdown we were the strongest.' Salmond seemed comfortable with his nickname, 'debbil-debbil' (Moroney 1970).

In addition to this violence perhaps one of the most profound changes of circumstances for local Aborigines was the profusion of new needs that emerged in the Aboriginal economy as populations became relatively sedentary in station out-camps dependant on rations that stimulated new appetites and capacities for work such as the rapidly addictive substances tobacco, tea and sugar. The diet for Aboriginal station workers provided by their employers until the late 1960s was usually well below the standards set by government, and people had to hunt and fish to supplement the meagre rations they received in return for their labour. It meant, however, that goods such as tobacco, tea and sugar were available only from whites or the Afghans, and quickly became highly prized items. Campbell Allanbra told Mary Anne Jebb (2002:40), 'Oh Afghans had really good tobacco too. One little bit in that bottle with a pipe used to make us work all day. Really good tobacco.' Rations were the basis of exchange between the whitefellas at the outposts of settlement and the Aboriginal people on whose labour and local knowledge of the land they relied. If pastoralists had paid the full exchange value for Aboriginal labour in a labour-scarce market, the whole pastoral economy would have collapsed. This new desire for introduced goods built on an existing social reality in which there were always degrees of interdependency to be negotiated:

> Jilgi Edwards: No money that time on sandalwood, only rations the Afghans gave us...only now we see the money...Working for the damper and meat, tobacco, everyday Tuesday we got it at Moonlight Valley, we helped Afghans find that sandalwood, two tonne on each camel...big mob of camel. I learnt how to handle them camel too...they good those camel. (Redmond fieldwork notes, 2007)

It seems from both documentary and oral history sources that Aborigines got a better deal from the camel drivers than they did from their white bosses, so preferred to work for them. Since the introduction of the 1905 *Aborigines Act*, authorities rigorously policed the prohibition on 'Asiatics' employing Aboriginal people. A circular sent out by the Chief Protector in 1907 sought responses on the issue of employment of Aboriginal people by 'Afghans'. While some local police and protectors in the north-west and the Kimberley condemned any interaction with camel drivers as 'contaminating' and 'inducing drunkenness and immorality', others argued that 'Afghans' treated their Aboriginal employees better than did white employers.[5] As with the official obsession with policing the trade between coastal Aboriginal people and indentured pearling workers from East and South-East Asia, it seems that the primary reason for the objections to economic exchange between Afghans and Aboriginal people was that it challenged the exclusivity of white control over the Aboriginal workforce. In a labour-scarce market such as the Kimberley, authorities and station owners would not tolerate competition for Aboriginal labour and implemented laws and police practices to prohibit them from working for anyone else (Skyring 2003:32–43). Records suggested that one of the objections to camel drivers' employment of Aboriginal people was that they sometimes paid them in cash,

---

5   Aborigines Department file, SROWA, 1907/0406.

rather than in food rations, which was the standard practice on the stations. One respondent speculated that the preference of Aboriginal workers for Afghan bosses prompted white employers to react with 'uneasiness' and 'jealousy'.[6]

Nevertheless, the department introduced measures to prevent camel drivers from employing Aboriginal people—and did so by expressly including them in the definition of 'Asians' who were already prohibited under the *Aborigines Act* from entering into work contracts with Aboriginal people. When the issue was raised again in 1915 in the eastern Kimberley, in relation to camel drivers who carted stores between Halls Creek and Wyndham, the response of the authorities was the same. Chief Protector Neville wanted to shut down the Afghan camp outside Wyndham (a camp known as 3 Mile) as a way of preventing 'sly grogging' and 'immorality' with Aboriginal women. As a local experienced policeman contended, however, the camel drivers were teetotallers and could attract women 'without resorting to the drink business', because they provided them with trinkets and dresses and generally better goods than women received from white men.[7]

While the settlers' often violent demands for their labour and lands created a massive upset in Kimberley Aboriginal social worlds, one of the more interesting aspects of the Karunjie research has been that some of the now senior men who were most involved in *Wurnan* exchange and the ritual ceremonial knowledge that accompanied it were some of those who worked most closely, and had some of the most intimate relationships, with white and 'Afghan' bosses. The tenor of these relationships is often described by Aborigines using idioms of emotional interdependency—very much in the vein of Hegel's master/slave dialectic. These idioms display how Aborigines thought of themselves as successfully making a boss into a 'good boss' who was compelled to acknowledge, in the end, his own need for his 'boy'. The white men involved expressed no such loyalties, reserving these for their former comrades-in-arms.

Paul Chapman and Campbell Allanbra, brothers from the main clan on which Karunjie was situated, both became prominent men in *Wurnan* exchanges and ritual life in the area. Their mother, Maggie, had been in a relationship with Sultan, who had also 'grown up' their father, before their father was shot by the whitefella Peter Reynolds in a fight over Maggie. Their mother and father had both, it seems, been able to accompany Sultan to Wyndham—where goods that became highly prized in the *Wurnan* could be obtained—to deliver loads of sandalwood. Sultan's brother, Sahanna, had as his wife a woman whom Chapman and Allanbra called a 'close mother'.

---

6   Officer in Charge, Port Hedland, 22 August 1907, in Aborigines Department file, 1907/0406.
7   Sergeant Buckland, in Police Department file, SROWA, 1915/4335.

The now senior man Nugget Tataya described what to all accounts sounds like a tender relationship with the white boss at Karunjie, Scotty Salmond, even though Salmond was renowned for his violent and abusive behaviour. Like the relationship of Left Hand Wundij and of his son Campbell to Sultan, Nugget described his ward-type relationship to Salmond as one in which he was Salmond's 'private boy'. This was a type of possessory human relationship that had been previously available only in the intimate (but also ambivalent) interactions between a boy and his initiatory 'boss', who would often become the initiate's father-in-law, and in husband–wife relationships in which 'jealousing', sometimes involving lethal conflict, seems to have been a strong feature. Salmond had taken a local Aboriginal woman, Dolly Nyamang, as his wife—someone whom Gudurr already called 'mother', thus entrenching the potential father–son relationship between these two men:

> Gudurr Tataya: Salmond—he cheeky old bloke, bad bloke, he had hearing aid, Orugudi [deaf one] we called him, policeman couldn't tell him anything, he grew me up and put me on a horse and he took me everywhere…this man bin grow me, I called him like my Dad, *idje*. When he was drunk he tell me 'come on' and I lay down on his guts,[8] he tell me you can lay down on my swag. When he go talking to other mob, drinking, he never hunt me out, he treat me like I was his son, my mother and father already passed away…

> When I was already grown up, this old fella, Scotty, chase the horse and tip over, he had a bridle and saddle and he fell on him and break his back and I had to tell Jack Campbell to come back, too bad…he [Scotty] told me to lay down on his guts and I cry for him…He was proper hard man when policeman tell him anything. One time Reggie Carbin [Wyndham police officer] bin come and ask for me to come with him, but he didn't know I was under Scotty, he wanted to make me a police-boy. I rolled my swag and getting ready to go with policeman but Scotty ask, 'Where you going? You not fucking police-boy, he my private boy you can't take him, he under me', he told im, I take my swag back and go back with Scotty. He never take me…finish, Dave wanted to put me on police job, but nothing…he said 'that my boy you not having him' [laughter]. (Redmond fieldwork notes, 2007)

---

8   In Ngarinyin correlations of bodily schemata, emotion and kin categories, the 'guts' (stomach) is the bodily site at which maternal feeling is said to be centrally located.

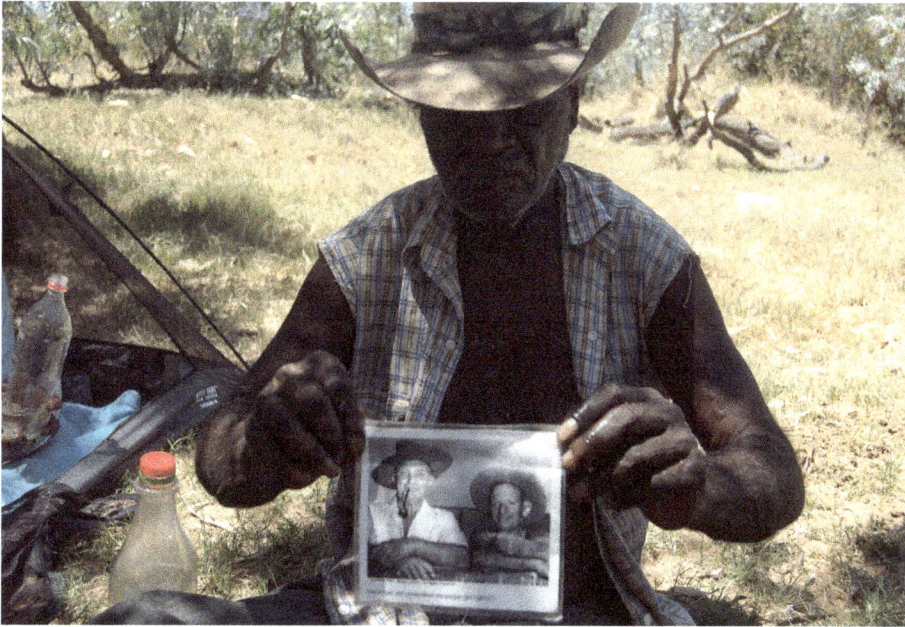

Figure 5.3 Gudurr with photo of Rust and Salmond 2008

Courtesy State Library of Western Australia image number 007852D.

In contrast with this description of these complex relationships provided by Aboriginal people such as Gudurr, in Salmond's and Rust's diaries of station life, their relationships with Aboriginal people seem strictly functional. While they hardly refer to the world outside Karunjie in these records, Aboriginal people are almost invisible. Some of the male workers such as Nugget, Campbell and Pompey are named, and Rust and Salmond seem to interact with the Euri-Aboriginal man, Jack Campbell, on a fairly equal basis. The other Aboriginal workers who made up their entire workforce are, however, referred to simply as 'boys' or 'blacks'. Women are mentioned only occasionally, as recipients of dresses. When Salmond was interviewed for a newspaper article in 1970, he presented Karunjie as a 'bachelor station', deleting his and Rust's Aboriginal wives from the picture. Indeed, except when Rust and Salmon got older and needed to rely on the help of neighbours and friends, women hardly figure at all in the written record of the lives of these returned soldiers. They saw their significant relationships as being with their 'cobbers' from the 10th Light Horse Regiment. Salmond made a list of the old regiment in one of his diaries, and when Rust started to recount his life story to Kandy Jane Henderson in Wyndham Hospital, she commented that 'he only wants to talk about the war' (Rust 1936–81).

Relationships with their station bosses appear to have had a very different meaning for Ngarinyin men such as Gudurr, however, who had lost both his parents as a young child. Allanbra and his brother, Chapman, developed strong capacities to form relationships with outsiders through whom they attained status and power in both the *Wurnan* and the pastoral economies. Allanbra became a head stockman on a number of regional stations and Chapman is still renowned as a ritual boss. Both were able to transfer objects between the *Wurnan* and the world of *almara* (whitefellas) in which they readily accepted their co-dependency on certain bosses, and through this their careers gained a prestige that eclipsed that of many of their countrymen, who preferred to stay in the bush rather than become attached to station bosses.

The country around Karunjie had long been a major centre of the *Wurnan* trade routes across the Kimberley, attracting large ceremonial gatherings during the early dry season when resources were abundant. The central roles that younger and middle-aged Aboriginal stockmen began to play in the *Wurnan* now depended heavily on their access to things that were obtainable only through their relationships with white patrons—relationships that gave them access to a range of desirable goods at the Wyndham stores when they drove cattle to market:

> Gudurr Tataya: They got red cloth from Wyndham, from Carleton, Ivanhoe, Rosewood, all the *Wurnan* mob, more further they come from Koolibah and Timber Creek, right through, they sell that bamboo, just like white man one but different…when I went droving some old people bin get em and bring em up here, they get wool and stuff from Chinaman shop. (Redmond fieldwork notes, 2007)

If not calculated in terms of wages for labour—something that became available to the majority of Kimberley Aboriginal station workers only in the 1960s—what gains became available within the pastoral economy to people such as Gudurr? While fear of police and settler violence against those living beyond the station homesteads, and access to desirable foodstuffs (particularly tea, tobacco and sugar) at those homesteads, must account for some of the motivation to become resident there, it does not seem sufficient to explain why up to 300 Aboriginal people were induced by a few white men to live and work around Karunjie Station from the late 1920s through to the early 1960s. The security and access to consumables provide an even less satisfactory explanation when we consider the narratives of the Aboriginal residents, which recount the constant movements of sectors of the station population, seemingly at will, back and forth between other settlements and the bush hinterland.

Figure 5.4 Roping cattle at Karunji Station ca. 1940-60

There were some positive aspects for Aboriginal people within the system of rations for labour, even when that system was underpinned by coercive practices, including racially discriminatory legislation that made it an offence for them to 'abscond' from their employment. Droving cattle to Wyndham meant that stockmen were constantly travelling over and 'look'em country' and could meet up with neighbours for ceremony, since it seemed cattlemen and police did not try to suppress the operation of *Wurnan* ceremonies. There are references in the records to people regularly going 'walkabout' and this was an accepted part of the station routine. For some Aboriginal men and women their relationships with violent whitefellas such as Salmond, and with marginal men such as Sahanna, provided a conduit to a set of goods (particularly red cloth), which replicated some of the ritual power associated with the red ochre that had been traded from this direction since time immemorial. Allanbra also noted that the sandalwood root they carted to Wyndham wharf had a strong red colour when it was cleaned, and that it returned as 'medicine', which seemed to avail it of the kinds of power associated with ritual healers.

Wurnan in the Kimberley was more formal than simple 'demand sharing' and partially shaped the way Ngarinyin people interacted with violent intruders. When people worked for white bosses, they gained very little materially but fairly quickly established ordered kin networks with the boss through local Aboriginal women and the kind of adoption Gudurr talks about—forms of exchange that were already familiar. Through their bosses, Aboriginal men also had access to prestige goods that were then incorporated into the *Wurnan* system, further consolidating the intersection between the two types of trade.

> When they sell all that thing from here from Derby, shell from saltwater come, they bin draw em, jaguli, they bin draw, like a wanjina, some from One Arm Point and some from Sunday island all that shell come from there, from [pearling] boat. *Wurnan* give me back to Kununurra mob… we gotta pass it on to nother bloke, if he hold em some fella might talk about you, growl you…

> GT: I come here for *Wurnan*…when we had *Wurnan* it start from, Pantijan country come to Gibb River then to Karunjie, nother one start from Tableland come to Karunjie, that the *Wurnan* they bin sell em they have big place there besides aerodrome, leave em in that cave there. When they come from Oombulgurri they split em out, one to Oombi, one to Fork Creek, nother one to Moonlight Valley, then Speewar station then to Doon Doon and Invanhoe station, nother mob get em from Fork Creek all the Carleton mob come and get em Mirriwung Gajerong *Wurnan* over there now. They sell em naga, red cock rag, or wool, red ochre sell em from there; that lot send em back *Wurnan* again. When that *Wurnan* come they bin spread em out to Tablelands and nother one to Gibb R[iver] then to Mt House and some to Pantijan, over, Pantijan send em straight to Derby now, they send naga, wool, sell, split em out everywhere right through, go right up, biggest *Wurnan* they bin have em, send em in cool weather, then hot time they sell all the thing all that *Wurnan*…

> Jigli Edwards: I started working there in Wyndham then came back Karunjie…up and down all the time, Oombi…My father carried *Wurnan*, went from this way, Mt House, straight through to Karunjie, then to Speewar…to Munja…we had all the people from Oombi going to Mt House…Dad was running it, biggest person now…then to Ellenbrae… We used to go to Mt House…Gibb River, Father Dad carried cloth and wool for present…

> People got cloth from *Wurnan* that red cloth, Father Dad carried it and hairbelt, *wanalan*, it went to Munja. After Father died, I worked on dog scalping with Edwards, help him, getting flour for damper…we used camels for carrying the things, helping im scalping dog…I met him in Wyndham that Edwards, camel bin carry tin to Munja from Wyndham, Afghans carried them to Mt House, Yulumbu, my sister rode camel, carting load. (Redmond fieldwork notes, 2008)

Through their client–patron relationship with station bosses, these Aboriginal men and women were able to travel away from the stations for long periods at the beginning of the wet season, meeting up with their bush-dwelling countrymen from neighbouring groups at the Fork Creek ceremony ground, 16 km south of Wyndham, where initiations and *Wurnan* exchanges were made. These ritual relationships appear to have quickly incorporated the Western goods that the travelling stockmen were able to purchase from Wyndham stores on the station account. This access to Western goods, and the right of safe passage they secured through their relationship to a known white boss, served to augment their power in local social and ritual worlds. Aboriginal people took what they could from an unfair exchange for their labour and funnelled the most desirable objects into their existing trade systems, injecting it with a new lease of life in the face of white domination in every other sphere. Because the *Wurnan* trade operated with some autonomy from the pastoral economy, Aboriginal people retained a control over it that they could not achieve within the labour-for-rations system.

The frontier economy's demand for Aboriginal labour provided an opportunity for some Aboriginal men and women to assert a degree of autonomy by gaining access to prized Western goods, which they then dispersed across the region as *Wurnan*. The power associated with ritual objects such as shells and hairbelts, the precursors of the new red cloth *naga*, which travelled through the Kimberley with performances of initiatory ceremonies, was seen to emanate particularly strongly from Western commodities with lustrous, colourful qualities bearing strong associations with women's sexual and reproductive power.

The emphasis in the *Wurnan* on fertility and ritual power seems to have played some role in the 'baby boom' in Aboriginal settlements across the region from 1960s onwards.[9] Akerman (1980) reported a heightened level of *Wurnan* activity in the Kimberley in the 1970s when working Aboriginal men began to access cash wages. This seems to be an example of intensified exchange as a strategy for social reproduction in the colonial situation—a dynamic that Andrew Strathern has called 'efflorescence' (Gregory 1982:115, 166).[10] By the mid-1980s, however, the *Wurnan* trade had again declined, suggesting that the ready availability of welfare and wages that had made Western commodities much easier to get eventually diminished the attraction of *Wurnan* as a means of gaining possession of highly prized objects such as cloth, dresses and *gardiya*

---

9   This was probably also an outcome of better diet afforded by cash wages and lower rates of leprosy, venereal disease and infant mortality as hospitals were gradually desegregated and Aboriginal people had access to better health care.

10   Here we can apply to colonial impacts on Aboriginal sharing practices a lesson from Gregory (1982:115), who, in analysing the efflorescence of the PNG gift economy under the influence of the colonial commodity economy, writes that 'the gift exchange of pre-colonial days…was very different from the gift exchange of today. Economic activity is not a natural form of activity. It is a social act and its meaning must be understood with reference to the social relationships between people in historically specific settings.'

(whitefella) tobacco. The *jaguli* continued to circulate but now in a sphere that became increasingly independent of the circulation of the desirable consumer items that accompanied them.

The operation of *Wurnan* helped sustain an uneasy accommodation between the original landholders and those who appropriated the country for cattle grazing. Even though the relationships between station bosses and Ngarinyin women sometimes started with violent kidnap or the murder of male relatives, the networks that developed between the station bosses and local clans became assimilated to Ngarinyin expectations about the obligations of kinship. The expectations of reciprocity integral to marriage exchange helped to shape the tenor of these relationships, incorporating the alien behaviour of the intruders into a local social reality that contained its destructive effects to some extent. The exchange relationships that were an integral part of *Wurnan*, and the prestige of introduced goods that were obtainable only by working for station bosses, promoted some stability in the decades following the extreme violence of invasion. The station bosses were largely oblivious to the importance of *Wurnan*, allowing it to continue as a relatively autonomous form of governance.

While Aboriginal workers received a poor exchange materially for their labour in the north-eastern Kimberley (see also White, this volume), their access to the whitefella goods that became incorporated into *Wurnan* meant that the rations-for-work system had some positive incentives for Aborigines of which the station bosses seemed to be unaware. For decades after white settlement at Karunjie, Aboriginal people maintained the prestige of a traditional system of trade, sustaining a parallel economy within a system designed to strip them of any economic power.

Bibliography

Aborigines Act No. 14 of 1905, 'An Act to make provision for the better protection and care of the Aboriginal inhabitants of Western Australia' [subsequently amended by the *Native Administration Act No. 43 of 1936*, and the reference to 'Aboriginal inhabitants' changed to 'Native inhabitants'].

Aborigines Department archival file, State Records Office of Western Australia (SROWA), Cons 255, 1907/0406, 'Chief Protector—re: employment of Aboriginals by Afghan camel drivers'.

Aborigines Department archival file, State Records Office of Western Australia (SROWA), Cons 993, 1943/1044, 'Employment of natives without permit by SAHANNA AND SULTAN of Moonlight Valley, Halls Creek'.

Akerman, K. 1980, 'The renascence of Aboriginal law in the Kimberleys', in C. H. Berndt and R. M. Berndt (eds), *Aborigines of the West: Their past and their present*, University of Western Australia Press, Nedlands.

Appadurai, A. (ed.) 1986, *The Social Life of Things: Commodities in cultural perspective*, Cambridge University Press, Cambridge, NY.

Blundell, V. and Layton, R. 1978, 'Marriage, myth and models of exchange in the west Kimberleys', *Mankind*, vol. 11, pp. 231–45.

Bottrill, A. M. and Sahanna, J. 1991, Sahanna: Sindhi camelman, soldier, sandalwooder, squatter, Typescript, Battye Library, Perth.

Godelier, M. 1999, *The Enigma of the Gift*, University of Chicago Press, Ill.

Gregory, C. 1982, *Gifts and Commodities*, Academic Press, London.

Jebb, M. 2002, *Blood, Sweat and Welfare: A history of white bosses and Aboriginal pastoral workers*, University of Western Australia Press, Crawley.

Lévi-Strauss, C. 1969, *The Elementary Structures of Kinship*. Eyre and Spottiswoode, London.

Mauss, M. 1954, *The Gift*, Routledge, London.

Moroney, F. 1970, 'Debbil-debbil of Karungie', *Countryman*, May, pp. 22–3.

Munn, N. 1970, 'The transformation of subjects into objects in Walbiri and Pitjantjatjara myth', in R. M. Berndt (ed.), *Australian Aboriginal Anthropology*, University of Western Australia Press, Nedlands, pp. 141–63.

Munro, M. 1996, 'Emerarra: a man of Merarra', in M. A. Jebb (ed.), *Morndi Munro Talks with Daisy Angajit [et al.]*, Magabala Books, Broome, WA.

Myers, F. 1988, 'Burning the truck and holding the country: property, time and the negotiation of identity among Pintupi Aborigines', in Tim Ingold, David Riches and James Woodburn (eds), *Hunters and Gatherers 2: Property, power and ideology*, Berg, New York.

Native Welfare Act No. 64 of 1954

Owen, C. 2003, 'The police appear to be a useless lot up there: law and order in the East Kimberley, 1884–1905', *Aboriginal History*, vol. 27, pp. 105–30.

Police Department archival file, State Records Office of Western Australia (SROWA), Acc. 430, 1915/4335, 'Depredations by Wyndham natives...sly grog selling'.

Redmond, A. 2001a, Rulug Wayirri: Moving kin and country in the northern Kimberley, unpublished PhD thesis, University of Sydney.

Redmond, A. 2001b, 'Places that move', in A. Rumsey and J. Weiner (eds.), *Emplaced Myth: The spatial and*

narrative dimensions of knowledge in Australian Aboriginal and Papua New Guinea societies, University of Hawai'i Press, Honolulu, pp. 120-138.

Rust, D. W., Papers 1936–81, MN 1781, Acc. 5354A, Battye Library Private Archives (includes Rust and Salmond diaries 1940–71 incomplete), Perth.

Sansom, B. 1988, 'A grammar of exchange', in I. Keen (ed.), *Being Black: Aboriginal cultures in 'settled' Australia*, Aboriginal Studies Press, Canberra, pp. 159–78.

Skyring, F. 2001, Wanjina-Wunggurr Wilinggin history report, filed re WAG 6016 of 1996 and WAG 6015 of 1999, *Paddy Neowarra & Ors v State of Western Australia & Ors*.

Skyring, F. 2003, Rubibi: history report, prepared for KLC and filed with the Federal Court re WAG 6006 and 6238 of 1998, *Frank Sebastian & Ors v State of Western Australia & Ors*.

6. Dingo scalping and the frontier economy in the north-west of South Australia

DIANA YOUNG

Introduction

Responding to the threat from the dingo to pastoral stock, in 1912, the South Australian Government passed the *Wild Dogs Act*. Later, in the 1920s, there were similar schemes introduced in Western Australia and the Northern Territory (Gara 2005). In reframing the dingo as a commodity, materialising its value through the presentation of its skin as a 'scalp' and offering a bounty for it, the legislation created specific conditions for encounters between Aboriginal people in the far north-west of South Australia and the settlers in the form of the bushmen who pursued that bounty and who came to be known as 'doggers'. For Aṉangu (Pitjantjatjara and Yankunytjatjara people), the term 'scalp' did not exist; it was and is still simply the skin of the dog: *papa miri*.[1]

Aṉangu did not wear animal skins on their bodies before contact with the settlers or utilise them in any systematic way except perhaps by using kangaroo skins as water bags (Young 2010). Instead it was the extrusions from skin—hair and fur—that every Aṉangu knew how to spin into string, which served to attach and reattach people and was one of a range of things used in exchange. My wider argument concerning skins points to the evidence that its potentiality was elaborated after contact with settlers and their goods and, as I argue here, in part by the commodification of dingo skin.

Through the colonists' bureaucratic reframing of dingo as vermin because of their threat to lambs (and to a lesser extent sheep), the lives of Aboriginal people still remote from the main areas of settlement would be changed. The commodification of the dingo's skin was in large measure responsible for the

---

1 *Aṉangu* means 'person' in Pitjantjatjara, and is used as a contemporary way of naming themselves by Pitjantjatjara and Yankunytjatjara people. It was not used in this way during the period under discussion here.

establishment of the Presbyterian Mission, for its siting at Ernabella and for the subsequent ability of Anangu to travel widely across country. The skin of the dingo was in summary an example of Webb Keane's exhortation to ask, 'what do things make possible?' Through the medium of the dingo skins, it is possible to discern specific distributions of power (Miller 2005:18).

Dogging and the getting of goods

Anapala was a place on Yankunytjatjara land nestled among ranges that the explorer Ernest Giles had named the Musgraves. It had a permanent waterhole and good run-off from the surrounding hills. It was a fecund, important place for Aboriginal people, rich in game and hence a good place for dingo, too. In the years of the Great Depression, it began to attract doggers. Here is Walter Smith, a bushman of some Aboriginal ancestry, telling Dick Kimber about a 1924 dogging trip:

> That Ernabella country was the best place, mate. God, talk about dingoes there. Caves there, you know and they go there mating time. All the dogs go there plenty of water about nice springs. Plenty of rabbits, wallabies and euros too for a feed for themselves and when the pups are born. (Kimber 1996:48–9)

On Walter Smith's 1924 dogging trip, all scalps—whether of pups, bitches or dogs—were worth 7s 6d. The doggers took steel axes and steel knives to exchange with Anangu for scalps: 'They just take that scalp for us, and cook him then' (Kimber 1996:48–9; see also Harney 1969:159; Tindale 1974:23).

In parting the dingo from its skin, Aboriginal people kept the meat for themselves and seem later to have concealed this consumption of dingo from the Ernabella missionaries.[2] Harney (1969:159) reported that the 'succulent pups' were cooked after their skin was removed to sell. I consulted Gordon Ingkatji on this point at Ernabella in 2009 (Field notes, 22 September 2009, 26, 4). He was at pains to point out that before white people came Anangu ate only *papa inyuru* (wild dogs), not camp dogs. Puppies, he said, are *kuka wiru*, 'lovely meat': 'You don't eat the really young ones but when they walk. You take the skins and cook him after, cut open the *tjuni* [stomach] and put *itara* [bloodwood] leaves inside—*salt wiya* [no salt].'[3] 'How did you skin them?' I asked. He ran a finger

---

2 Anangu stopped eating pups perhaps during the early 1950s. Certainly, the Ernabella Mission staff from this era did not seem aware that Anangu ate pups. See also Harney (1969), quoting Minyinderri (1963:160). Earlier accounts by visitors to the mission in the late 1930s noted that Aboriginal people ate pups.
3 Salt (*wiya*) applies to all the important *Tjukurpa* (Dreaming Ancestor) species of animal when Anangu consume them as meat.

across his upper lip: 'You cut across here or maybe above the eyes and round the neck and down the *witapi* [spine] and take the ears and tail.' In other words, the *papa miri* was the whole underside of the animal along with its tail.

Before the advent of the doggers, pups were a delicacy that Anangu cooked in their skins—as they did and still do with almost all other bush animals. The cook scorches off the fur and blackens the skin before the animal is cooked in a fire-pit oven. Yielding the dingo's skin to outsiders created cash and access to settler goods. The dingo had a far greater capacity when its surface and interior were made partible.

In 1920, the Pitjantjatjara country of the Petermann Ranges and the Uluru area were gazetted as the Peterman, North West and Central Australian Reserves (Layton 1986:72), but it was not policed by the authorities nor was there a ration station established inside it. Doggers were able to penetrate it with impunity. The reserve area was seen as a breeding ground for dingo that would harm the adjacent pastoral leases, and rather than shooting dingo or killing them with traps baited with strychnine, as was usual, the doggers found Aboriginal labour a better option (Gara 2005:1). Their hunting skills and habitat knowledge yielded a greater return of scalps and the doggers paid the hunters in goods: commonly flour, sugar and tobacco—the 'stimulants' that Stanner (1965) noted Aboriginal people 'craved' and would travel for. Obtaining clothing too was an incentive for Aboriginal people to engage in the dingo trade. H. H. Finlayson famously wrote that 'scalps were a sort of currency' (Rowse 1998:60); I return to the materiality of that currency later.

The doggers attracted large numbers of Anangu to their seasonal camps, desirous of the goods they could get for the dingo skins. Individual doggers often returned to the same base camp year after year, aiming to establish good relations with local Anangu. The police acted as the government agents who remunerated the doggers with cash. The local depot for such transactions was Oodnadatta to the east on the edge of the Simpson Desert, where there were pastoral leases already operating.

In 1933, the anthropologist Norman Tindale noted in his field journal that the doggers were exerting a huge attraction for Anangu, who were travelling and camping in large numbers with individual doggers. Tindale had difficulty finding natives to travel with him to Ernabella because of the draw of the doggers, although ironically he had employed as a guide and camel driver the dogger Alan Brumby (Tindale 1933). The incentive to travel with the anthropologist must have been, one can imagine, far less than the allure of staying with the dogger. Tindale (1933) wrote:

The doggers have runners out and are attempting to hold as many natives as possible; we may have an uphill go to get natives to Ernabella. (p. 567)

Propaganda by the dogger who has been competing for the services of the natives, has caused them to fear. (p. 605)

Jack Anderson, a dogger was camped at Konapandi [Kunapanti] and leaves for Ernabella accompanied by 27 natives. (p. 621)

The establishment of the mission at Ernabella

The confluence of desires—for scalps on the part of the doggers and for goods on the part of Anangu—gave rise to concern from parties who considered that the European doggers were ill-educated low-life corrupting the last intact natives on the continent. This perception was in reality not so easily defined. There were a number of men with Aboriginal ancestry (Walter Smith and Tommy Dodd, for example) who took up dogging. 'Contamination' of the native was by Afghans, too, as Albrecht noted (Redmond and Skyring, this volume; Rowse 1998). By 1930, the activity of doggers had transformed Ernabella Soak, as it was known in English, into a settler depot of sorts at the end of the Oodnadatta mail run. It was a place of organised contact between doggers and Anangu who came to barter their dingo skins (Elkin 1931:44; Hilliard 1968:95).

Visiting anthropologists, Elkin in 1930 and Tindale in 1933, the Hermannsburg missionaries, scout for the Presbyterian Mission Board J. R. B. Love and Charles Duguid all expressed concern to the Aborigines Protection Board and the South Australian Government. Duguid was a Scottish doctor of medicine who set out to visit the Musgraves in 1935 at the suggestion of Pastor Albrecht at Hermannsburg. One of the critical factors for Duguid in wanting to set up a mission in the area was the presence of doggers. Another was the steady drift of Aboriginal people from the region towards Oodnadatta. It is probable that Oodnadatta had become known among Anangu at least partly because of the doggers of 'the Musgraves and Great Central Aborigines reserve':

These people have all seen aeroplanes or motor cars and have come in contact with white men who, for years, have trespassed on the Reserve. They have become curious and are anxious to see beyond their old horizons. It is because they have been coming into the settled white civilization that we have gone out to meet them. (Duguid 1939)

After R. M. Williams made two dogging trips through the Mann, Musgrave, Rawlinson and Warburton ranges in 1928, returning to Oodnadatta with hundreds of scalps, he inspired other men working on the same pastoral station circuits north-west of Oodnadatta to do the same (Williams 1998:62). Among them were Harold Brown, Alan Brumby, Paddy De Conley and Charlie Lester. All these men went on to become pastoralists. They were the first non-Aboriginal people to really live with Anangu. Both Brown and Brumby had their names appropriated as last names by Anangu, as did De Conley as 'Connally'.[4] Harry Brumby, Alan's father, seems to have given his name to, or had it appropriated by, a Yankunytjatjara/Wirtjapakanja man who worked with Bill Harney and had his own camels.

Harold Brown and Alan Brumby had started out as partners in about 1929 making their first trip to the Musgrave and Mann ranges and Uluru (Gara 2005:3, quoting Terry 1932). Both had Aboriginal children with wives whom they subsequently abandoned (see also Gara 2005). As Redmond and Skyring note (this volume), 'white men's relationships with Aboriginal women were central to the operation of the frontier economy'. Harold Brown was killed with his non-Aboriginal wife when the bedroom roof of their mud house at Shirley Well (Officer Creek), near present-day Fregon, collapsed (Harney 1969:170; Hilliard 1968). Harney dates this event as 1939. Their house girl was Eileen Stephens, the Pitjantjatjara woman who recently found fame at the end of her life as a painter; she died in 2008.

In the 1940s, De Conley established a pastoral lease at Mt Conner (Layton 1986:67) after working as a stockman at Kulgera, where he was charged with owner, Bert Kitto, with murdering an Aboriginal employee; they were acquitted (Gara 2005:6). Among the drawings that Charles Mountford collected, made by Anangu at Ernabella in 1940, there are several concerning the poisoned flour episode. One by a young woman called Ada relates how the dogger Paddy De Conley left behind flour laced with strychnine. Ada said that two men and one boy died as a result of eating the flour, with this event taking place in about October 1936.[5]

In order to secure their rights to the dingoes and exclude others, the doggers purchased the leases on surrounding blocks of land, becoming putative pastoralists, using the proceeds of the skins. There was a government scheme that rewarded any pastoralist who sank a bore with £200 and 100 square miles (260 sq km) of land at peppercorn rent (Gara 2005:3). Brumby was the nephew of one Stan Ferguson, also a one-time dogger who had, in 1933, sunk a well at Ernabella Soak and stocked the new station with 2000 sheep and 200 goats (Hilliard 1968). Ernabella Station was thus officially established that year.

---

4 Cf. Toby Nganina on 'Paddy Connally' from Layton's fieldwork (1986:67) and the Connally family at Kalka/ Pipalytjara.
5 Ada, 6th October 1940 Ernabella, Mountford Collection Drawings, vol. 2, part 7, nos 101–16, State Library of South Australia, Adelaide.

Ferguson's son recalled his father's life in 1996. Ferguson had worked at Macumba Station, having migrated during the Depression years from Broken Hill in New South Wales to Oodnadatta. He married an Aboriginal woman there and set up Granite Downs Station with Charlie Lester, the father of well-known Yankunytjatjara activist Yami Lester. Next, Ferguson set up a station at Mooralinya—now the Anmuryinna Homeland, west of Indulkana on the Anangu Pitjantjatjara Yankunytjatjara lands. From there, Ferguson moved his family to develop Kenmore Park Station, selling it to George Fraser and moving on in 1933 to Ernabella. Here, according to his son, he wished to settle down, but eventually in 1936, the Presbyterian Church managed to negotiate a price with him and purchased the station as a going concern with its livestock and the homestead he had built.[6]

Ernabella was an excellent site for the mission with its potable waters and idyllic setting; also a draw were an existing well and a sturdily built homestead that remains to this day. The homestead was also just outside the reserve and Duguid intended it as a buffer for Aboriginal people between the pastoral world beyond it and the country to its west in the reserve. It was of course also intended as a gateway that kept 'unscrupulous whites' at bay.

In September 1936, Duguid (1963:52) finally persuaded the Presbyterian Church of Australia's Board of Missions to pass a motion to set up a mission at Ernabella. An important decision was made by the Mission Board to rid the area of the intrusive doggers (the doggers who were in effect using Aboriginal labour to dispossess those same people of their land). The natives would receive the full government subsidy for scalps either in the form of cash or exchanged for goods at the Ernabella Mission store.[7] Thus, by the time the Ernabella Mission was founded, Anangu were well acquainted both with white people and with their goods. The flow of novel goods was mediated by dingo scalping and the relationships it created. Love notes of the doggers in his journal of 1937 (p. 6) that 'the goods used in trade include flour, tea, sugar, tobacco, matches, shirts and trousers, and dresses. The question whether [they] ought to be clothed has been partly, and unfavourably, decided already by the doggers.'

The goods had to be desirable to Anangu otherwise they were useless as payment. If the 'question of clothing' was already decided in large measure by Anangu who had seen its capacities and potentials well before the Ernabella Mission began, so too was an idea of labouring for those goods; they were not the hand-outs for no labour that Duguid despised in government ration depots. Labouring for goods or for a combination of goods ('rations') and wages was the foundation of the Ernabella Mission ethic. Clothing had already become, even

---

6   Interview with Donald Ferguson, 1996, Ara Iritija Archive, m1015.
7   The mission did retain 2s as a handling charge in the mid-1950s to early 1960s (Sheppard 2004).

as rags, an essential exchange item among Aboriginal people themselves and one that was and is subject to 'demand sharing'—the practice of demanding a portion of resources that sustains or creates social ties, in the same way as food (Peterson 1993).

By 1940, there were still doggers in the reserve. 'Every main water I go there are deep camel pads, made by these doggers', notes Mountford (1940:1069). The doggers were flouting the law, not just by entering the land, but, knowing the difficulty of policing the reserve, by cohabiting with Aboriginal women (Gara 2005). Mountford fulminated in his field journal:

> I personally have told the Protector of Aborigines in Adelaide that doggers were going everywhere, and he said he did not want to know. The Anthropological Society wrote protesting, and the Protector replied 'that he had not been asked for permission to enter the reserve for the last 5 years'. (Mountford 1940:1069)

Although Duguid could boast in 1941 that the mission exerted control over the South Australian section of the Great Central Reserve, he wanted a camel patrol partly to police intruders, citing Laverton as the entry point for many doggers.[8]

Consumption

The Protestant Presbyterian Ernabella Mission, although exceptional in many ways, was like other such missions—and not only in Australia: intent on attempting to control discernment in consumption practices as an aspect of civilising and desirous of helping people to use those goods in particular ways, not least as personal property and as self-enhancement (Comaroff 1996). The point that cultures are constructed through consumption is a moot one here.

The new Ernabella Mission had an immediate problem—one that continued to haunt mission correspondence for decades to come—namely, that once Aboriginal people came into the mission, they had to want to use it as their preferred base, to make it their *ngura*/place or home. There was no compulsion to stay. As the missionaries knew, especially at the start, the gospel teachings alone could not hope to anchor people to the place. Wages were paid largely in goods; these commodities had to compete with those at the surrounding depots, stations and missions—goods that would make Ernabella desirable to Aboriginal people.

---

8 Letter, Duguid to Chinnery, 1 August 1941, BOEMAR records, Mitchell Library, Sydney.

In 1948, a mission report suggests that the Ernabella Mission cash store should maintain a wider range of goods than at present, 'so as to encourage the scalp trade and more frequent visits by bush natives'.[9] Clothing could now be bought in the Ernabella Mission store either with wages or with the proceeds of the scalps. The cash subsidy for a scalp was now £1.[10] In 1946, Haasts Bluff—formerly a pastoral lease but then a new reserve and an outstation of the Hermannsburg Mission—received '853 dingo scalps' but had also traded '3171 kangaroo skins'. At Areyonga, another Hermannsburg outpost, 748 dingo scalps and 571 kangaroo skins were received, with a 6d handling charge on the scalps being deducted. According to Harney, the bounty price for dingo differed between Western Australia and the Northern Territory; it was worth 10s in the latter, 'but three times that amount in WA'.

Sheep and dingo

Kimber (1996:48) notes that the linkage in Aboriginal thought between sheep and dingo is evinced by the fact that the southern Arrernte at first used the term for dingo ('*unguina*') for sheep, as the dingo has a bushy tail similar to the woolliness of sheep.[11] Sheep went inexorably together with dingo since no use was made of fences (Rowse 1998). Where there were sheep or goats there had to be 24-hour shepherding to protect them from the depredations of dingoes. Rowse discusses how scalping and shepherding were interlinked occupations for Aboriginal people around the Central Desert stations Tempe Downs, Loves Creek and Henbury. This pattern was reproduced around Ernabella. Long before there were 'outstations', there were sheep camps around Ernabella. By 1940, there were many livestock run on the mission; 'sheep counted 29/1/40, 1441, goats plus kiddies 202, camels 8'.[12]

The mission instituted a well-sinking program that augmented those already existing from the doggers' efforts as pastoralists.[13] Sheep camps were made around wells. Shepherding was an ideal occupation for people who had just 'come in' from the bush. Here, a family group could live together for several months at a time with a reliable supply of water, augmenting their rations as wages of flour, tea and sugar with bush foods and perhaps with dingo scalping.

---

9   Ibid.
10   Ernabella Mission, General Secretaries' Visit, 2 November, V. W. Coombes 1948, BOEMAR records, Mitchell Library, Sydney.
11   Harney (1969:155) writes that camels were given the name for dogs: 'we call camel Puppanarri.'
12   Letter, Mr Ward to Dr Duguid, 7 February 1940, Ernabella, BOEMAR records, Mitchell Library, Sydney, p. 1. Ward's list concludes: 'Horses. Not seen here regularly but all here I think except the stallion which I shot and the people ate.'
13   Cf. Ian Dunlop (1962), showing an Ernabella-based man, Louis, with a well-sinking business. Earlier wells were dug out by hand.

When I lived on the Anilalya Homelands in 1997 and 1998, my constant companions—Anangu then in their sixties, seventies and eighties—unfailingly pointed out the old wells and sheep camps to me, naming then as we passed, as doubtless they had to other incomers. Turners Well, for example, is a favourite honey ant hunting location and Youngs Well remains a homeland. One of the last conversations I had with Billy Wara (d. November 2008), whose portrait features in Hilliard's book as a boy who gave figs to Lasseter (the lost white explorer who died of starvation because he refused the food offered by local people), was about the sheep camps and the shearing *iriti* ('in the old days') (Hilliard 1968). In tandem with the recollection by older Anangu of the sheep camps ('use sheep shit for your garden', people told me, 'it's the best', even though there were no sheep left in 1997, nor had there been since the mid-1970s) was that of pupping—*papa miri* time.

Sheep wool was the economic basis of the mission, sent through the Finke rail stop to Adelaide, but two sheep a day were butchered for meat since there was no refrigeration and the skins from these were also sold (Edwards interview, 1 July 2008). It was also by spinning the sheep fur/*inyu*—analogous to the spinning of other animal fur and human hair pre-contact—that the Ernabella women provided the basis for the Ernabella craft room. This is another aspect of frontier economy that began in 1948 but one that I am unable to explore here.

By 1958, when the Ernabella store was still receiving scalps and selling supplies, better provision was required for the storage of both dingo and sheep skins.[14]

Spatio-temporal dingo skins

When the *piriya*—a warm wind that has been loosely equal to 'spring time'—blows and the Seven Sisters appear again in the eastern sky at dawn with their lascivious male pursuer, *Wati Nyiru*, or in non-Aboriginal terms, Orion and the Pleiades, Anangu know that the dingo pups are being born. Harney (1969:158) calls the Pleiades the 'dog stars', as the dingo has seen them before Anangu. This is a rewarding time to be out collecting food from the bush, after winter rains. The mission sheep shearing also took place at this time, employing local men. At the close of shearing, the shearers were paid off, each receiving a little extra cash (Edwards interview, 1 July 2008).

Anangu then went travelling—indeed, were encouraged by the mission to do so, in order that they used the reserve. Anangu refer to this time, when talking about it now, as 'holidays' (also Harney 1969:159). They left the mission to hunt

---

14   Australian Presbyterian Board of Missions Report of Inspection of Ernabella Mission by Rev. G. Anderson and Rev. H. M. Bell, September 1958, BOEMAR records, Mitchell Library, Sydney.

for dogs and perhaps visit their own country (see White, this volume, for a similar seasonal pattern among Aboriginal people in New South Wales). It was a way of showing country to children. Successfully hunting for dingo skins enabled the travel, providing both the means and the end.

At this time, the missionaries would close up the craft room and the school since they were governed not by the Education Department calendar but by the mission calendar. Bill Edwards was then acting mission superintendent. In 2008, he recalled:

> [T]hey [Anangu] could buy a big bag of flour and sugar and distribute it and they would get on their camels and head out and we would arrange to meet them before they left…they might say, 'look in two weeks can you be at Amata [then Musgrave Park Station]?' or somewhere west of Amata so we would arrange to take flour, sugar, tins of things and we would meet them. 1958—[my] first year—we went west of Amata and people would line up on the road with their dingo pup skins and trade these for things we had such as tins of powder[ed] milk for the babies and so on.

> …The people would go about their own business and so forth and gradually come back and we would open the school and the craft room again. We might come back with 150 to 200 scalps.

> …People might work for a month (for example as shepherds) and get £1 10s and for five dingo pups…£5 so that was a lot of money. You could get a 60 lb bag of sugar or a 150 lb bag of flour for £5 at the mission store. So that was a precious commodity. (Edwards interview, 1 July 2008)

> During that period of three months' shepherding contract men got a shirt and a pair of trousers, and women [who were paid less] got printed material every six weeks or three months two and a half yards or, if they were a little larger, three yards and they would make their own dresses with that. (Edwards interview, 1 July 2008)

The establishment of a camp for tourists at Uluru in the late 1950s provided work for Anangu, cooking and making beds and enabling further such employment for Aboriginal people along the tourist route in from Alice Springs (Interview with Amanyi [Dora] Haggie [Okai], Ernabella, August 2008). Barbara Nipper's mother made beds for the tourists in Bill Harney's time (late 1950s to early 1960s). Barbara Nipper's husband (Nipper Winmati) worked cutting firewood. At weekends, they would go out using one camel to Kata Tjuta, Titirarra Rockhole, Impumpu, Mantarur, Puta Puta, Tjunti or Docker River, hunting dingo skins. Two dingo skins were worth £1. They received 2s from tourists for camel rides. Peter Severin of Curtin Springs pastoral lease paid them money for the scalps. Some places would buy the skins only with rations—golden syrup, jam, sugar, and so on—not with money (Barbara Nipper, Peter Sutton field book, 88:230–1).

Figure 6.1 Sorting dingo skins at Ernabella 1957

Ara Irititja Project, Collection Uniting Church (Vic), photographer Bruce Edenborough, Ernabella 1957.[15]

The film *Camels and the Pitjantjatjara* was made at Curtin Springs and shows people setting off to get dingo skins (Sandell 1969). In 1954, the Ernabella Choir, a group of young people, went to Adelaide to see the Queen. They sold dingo scalps to finance their own trip (Carell and Dean 1955).

So, between the 1940s and the 1960s, pupping was a perfect occupation for Anangu. There was no 'boss' as there was in pastoral and mission work. To a large extent, you could choose to whom you surrendered the skins and thereby what you received in return. The number of dingoes was still expanding and the bounty went up accordingly. There was some complaint that Aboriginal people were 'farming dingo' by only getting the pups and not the adults (cf. Sheppard 2004:39). As Sheppard notes, the 'farming' accusation was almost certainly true. To address this, in the mid-1960s, the bounty was changed to £2 ($4) for a big scalp and only 10s ($1) for a pup (Edwards interview, 1 July 2008).

---

15   The man with the red headband is Ngulitjara, the father of Robert Stevens. The other Pitjantjatjara man is the father of Munti Smith.

The materiality of dingo skin as commodity

Although for some decades the dingo skin was a currency common to doggers, missionaries, station owners and Aboriginal people alike, the effectiveness of that currency and people's attitudes to its materiality varied between them.

The dingo is, according to the women who taught me, a *'watiku miilmiilpa Tjukurpa'*—a secret, sacred Dreaming that belongs to men. According to Ingkatji in 2009, it is a *Tjukurpa*, which belongs to both men and women. This variation in who tells what and how is ubiquitous in Western Desert cultures where men's and women's roles in ceremony are complementary. One can extrapolate from these two statements that the dingo is a *Tjukurpa* belonging to men and thus women cannot speak directly about it although an individual may be knowledgeable (*ninti*), and that there are non-secret aspects to the Dreaming (Wallace 1990:89). A more delineated case of taboo is that of the kangaroo. In the 1960s, when the craft women made shoes from kangaroo skins to sell to the settler market, they were forbidden by their men to use local kangaroo skin (Hilliard 1968). *Malu* (kangaroo) is, however, more definitely *watiku* ('belonging to men'). For the dingo to be skinned was, however, acceptable; both men and women could handle the skins.

For the mission staff, the dingo skins were not dense enough in their materiality; they were easily counterfeited or recycled. It is said that corrupt police, who were the handlers of the skins, could with a certain amount of ingenuity claim them twice and double the money. Anangu too tried this, according to the then mission superintendent: 'you had to watch this—you lined up the scalps and someone could come along and sell them back again from the other end of the line' (Edwards interview, 1 July 2008). The pup skins were accepted for payment if the whole thing from the ears down to the tail was presented—a small scalp fully materialised. For the mature dogs, the police would accept the two joined ears and the tail as separate—a rather more immaterial version of a dingo. Anangu could manufacture dingo 'ears' by sewing up pieces of skin (Edwards interview, 1 July 2008). This playfulness or trickster element in creating 'ears' in the scalp trade is analogous to certain contemporary woodcarving amendments. For example, spear throwers' timber and quartz blades are joined together using a resin made from spinifex grass—a resin that is labour intensive to produce. Nowadays, the resin can be creatively imitated by melting black rubbish sacks to produce a similar-looking, though not similar-smelling, substance.

During the 1960s, *punu* (artefacts) replaced dingo skins as the principal source of independent income for Aboriginal groups (Layton 1986:80)—due in part to the Uluru tourist trade. Rose (1965:68) notes that in the early 1960s the Angas Downs artefact trade, where Anangu were trading directly with tourists, made about £2 a week whereas a four-week dogging trip yielding 14 scalps provided 5 guineas a week (Rose 1965:71, cited in Layton 1986:81). Both were seasonal, since tourists came mostly during the cooler winter months and pupping took place in the spring.

Conclusions

Dogging was important for several reasons. It provided the impetus to begin the mission at Ernabella to protect Anangu from exploitation by the doggers. It was, however, mostly through the doggers that Anangu first gained access to non-Aboriginal goods, and the Presbyterian Church had the foresight to understand how this could be used to fulfil the mission's aims. Going out for dingo skins, west into the reserve, stopped Anangu travelling to settled areas, justifying the reserve's existence, and at the same time fulfilled the desire of Anangu to acquire European things. Collecting dingo skins enabled people to travel back to their own country, earning money, acquiring food and other goods as they went along. The dingo skins were wealth in many ways and it is no wonder that *papa miri* is remembered with such fondness by older people now.

I want to emphasise here the importance of the dingo trade in the development of a 'frontier economy' where it was far from a marginal activity but one that lasted for 40 years, but also the materiality of the skins as a mediating currency that contributed to different forms of objectification for Aboriginal people.

In more recent (and erudite) accounts of Indigenous central Australians, settler goods remain secondary in a large part because they have been understood by anthropologists as being in the service of relatedness and ultimately disposable in that service. Working with Indigenous consultants at Hermannsburg, Austin-Broos (2006:29, 2009) concludes that 'money is…rendered as a thing in the service of relatedness'. In Peterson's (1993) influential paper on demand sharing in Indigenous Australia, she writes that Aboriginal people 'tend to assimilate the meaning of commodities and cash to this mode of social relations'. Myers (1988), writing of the community outstation truck, also concludes that the truck for Pintupi is just a thing in the same service and could thus be disposed of by burning it to prevent further demands on the person who held its key. Others have argued that Aboriginal societies are economies in which services are the things exchanged, so that the materiality of the objects is not crucial (Merlan 1991). There is an idea that things themselves carry a capitalist and colonial ideology within them, following Lukacs (1971; Redmond 2006; Rowse 1998; Stotz 2001), but that somehow the materiality of those things is irrelevant or at the very least secondary to their role as mediators. Critiques of materialism, as Daniel Miller (2006:343) has pointed out, often assume that such an approach imposes 'a mistaken emphasis on objects as opposed to persons'—that is, to focus on materialism denigrates the attachment of persons rather than in fact serving to reattach them in creative ways through the specific qualities of things.

The dingo skin, once separated from the flesh of the dingo, achieved a seemingly neutral liminal status that enabled it to become currency between Aboriginal people, between settlers and across cultures. Yet it cannot have been a neutral thing that had the same meaning for all the trading parties. With the skins, Anangu acquired settler commodities and through these began to remake their world just as those goods remade them. Dingo skins were locally produced and became the outward flow of trade networks whose incoming goods included foodstuffs, axes and clothing. The socio-temporal life of things in motion, linking people and contexts, requires also a 'critical fetishism' to help elucidate the nuances of value creation of both things and people (Appadurai 1986, 1990; Foster 2006; Kopytoff 1986; Munn 1986). Addressing the dingo's skin in various contexts is inadequate in the task of teasing out its value to Aboriginal people. The skins were derived from a very animate source: an important Dreaming animal that was part of country, not an imported commodity. Did Anangu understand dingo scalping to be 'giving' an objectification of their culture to the various settlers: doggers, missionaries, pastoralists? Was this an act that was 'at once a declaration of one's own value and an engagement with the recipient' (Myers 2002:5), as the woodcarvings and paintings that they later made became?

Some time during the early period of contact with the settler economy, cloth, ready-bought yarns and clothing became valuable to Aboriginal people. Accumulating clothing is now, and has been since at least the 1950s, a means of accumulating wealth; it is used as payment in ritual throughout many areas of Aboriginal Australia. I am not suggesting that trading dingo skins for clothes, as Anangu often did, was conceived by them as a tight symbolic connection, exchanging surface for surface, although this could have been the case. I am arguing that the surface of things and persons—and thing-like persons and person-like things—became increasingly important after contact when the means to elaborate surfaces became available. Attwood (1989:20), writing of the colonisation of an Aboriginal group in New South Wales, finds that there was an 'early Aboriginal perception that clothes and bodies of whites were inseparably joined'.

Among Anangu in the Western Desert, the same moment occurred—50 or so years later. Cloth quickly becomes conceived of as skin-like and is valued for that reason since it is a material that easily makes bodies mutable (Young 2010). Clothes became an aspect of personhood. Western Desert Aborigines reconfigure themselves through wearing coloured cloth that materialises their connections both to one another and to their country, whose surface is mutable, especially chromatically mutable (Young forthcoming). Clothing is, however, also a partible aspect of personhood. Hair-string becomes reserved for specialist ritual use and although it continues as an exchange item it is too labour intensive to compete with the imported cloth and yarns. At the same time, the skin of the dingo becomes routinely separated from its body and circulates, attracting other goods in return. These skins that served as currency were also the adornment of the dingo.

For hunter-gatherer people concerned with the minutiae of practices and appearances, it is likely that Anangu found similarities between the outbound dingo skins and the incoming cloth and the possibilities of political power that each could exert. This might be termed an economy of surfaces—one that leads to new forms of objectification among Aboriginal people.

Acknowledgments

I have used a combination of recollection and archival documents in this essay. I wanted to include the recollections of those who lived through this era—an era that is on the cusp of being conjured only through media.

Thank you to Anangu for teaching me since 1996, especially the Stanley and Windlass families and to Gordon Ingkatji. Warm thanks to Bill Edwards for generously allowing me to tape an interview with him and for his comments on the essay. Thanks to Peter Sutton for access to his research for the Yulara Native Title claim. Thanks to John Dallwitz at the Ara Irititja Archival Project and to BOEMAR for allowing me access, in 2003, to the records of the Uniting Church on the Ernabella Mission and for permission to quote from them. The British Academy funded this research trip from the United Kingdom to Australia in 2003.

References

Appadurai, A. 1986, 'Introduction: commodities and the politics of value', in A. Appadurai (ed.), *The Social Life of Things: Commodities in cultural perspective*, Cambridge University Press, UK.

Appadurai, A. 1990, 'Disjuncture and difference in the global economy', *Public Culture*, vol. 2, no. 2, pp. 1–24.

Attwood, B. 1989, *The Making of the Aborigines*, Allen & Unwin, Sydney.

Austin-Broos, D. 2006, '"Working for" and "working": the Western Arrernte in kin-based and market-based society', *Oceania*, vol. 76, no. 1, pp. 1–15.

Austin-Broos, D. 2009, *Arrernte Present, Arrernte Past: Invasion, violence, and imagination in Indigenous Central Australia*, University of Chicago Press, Ill.

Carell, Victor and Dean, Beth 1955, *Dust for the Dancers*, Ure Smith, Sydney.

Comaroff, J. 1996, 'The empire's old clothes, fashioning the colonial subject', in D. Howes (ed.), *Cross Cultural Consumption*, Routledge, London and New York, pp. 19–38.

Duguid, C. 1939, *The Medical Patrol*, Pamphlet, Ernabella Mission, South Australia.

Dugiud, C. 1963, *No Dying Race*, Rigby, Adelaide.

Dunlop, I. (dir) 1962, *The Aborigines of Australia*, Film, Commonwealth Film Unit (Screen Australia), Sydney.

Elkin, A. P. 1931, 'The social organisation of South Australian tribes', *Oceania*, vol. 2, pp. 44–73.

Foster, R. 2006, 'Tracking globalisation. Commodities and values in motion', in P. Spyer, C. Tilley, S. Kuechler and W. Keane (eds), *The Handbook of Material Culture*, Sage Publications, Thousand Oaks, Calif., pp. 285–302.

Gara, T. 2005, 'Doggers in the north west', *History Matters*, vol. 15, no. 2, pp. 8–10.

Harney, B. 1969 [1963], *To Ayers Rock and Beyond*, Rigby Ltd/Seal Books, Adelaide.

Hilliard, W. 1968, *The People In Between*, Hodder and Stoughton, London.

Kimber, R. G. 1996, *The Man from Arltunga. Walter Smith Australian bushman*, The Arltunga Hotel and Bush Resort and Hesperian Press, Alice Springs, NT, and Carlisle, WA.

Kopytoff, I. 1986, 'The cultural biography of things', in A. Appadurai (ed.), *The Social Life of Things: Commodities in cultural perspective*, Cambridge University Press, UK, pp. 64–91.

Layton, R. 1986, *Uluru: An Aboriginal history of Ayers Rock*, Aboriginal Studies Press, Canberra.

Love, J. R. B. 1937, Diary of a visit to Ernabella to establish a Presbyterian Mission, 24th May to 24th October 1937, Manuscript, State Library of South Australia, Adelaide.

Lukacs, G. 1971, *History and Class Consciousness: Studies in Marxist dialectics*, Translated by R. Livingstone, Merlin Press, London.

Merlan, F. 1991, 'Women. Productive roles and the monetisation of the service mode in Aboriginal Australia: perspectives from Katherine, Northern Territory', *Australian Journal of Anthropology*, vol. 2, pp. 259–92.

Miller, D. 2005, 'Introduction', in D. Miller (ed.), *Materiality*, Duke University Press, Durham, NC, and London, pp. 1–50.

Miller, D. 2006, 'Consumption', in P. Spyer, C. Tilley, S. Kuechler and W. Keane (eds), *The Handbook of Material Culture*, Sage Publications, Thousand Oaks, Calif., pp. 341–54.

Mountford, C. P. 1940, Journal of an expedition to the north west of South Australia, [2 vols], State Library of South Australia, Adelaide.

Munn, N. 1986, *The Fame of Gawa. A symbolic study of value transformation in a Massim (Papua New Guinea) society*, Duke University Press, Durham, NC, and London.

Myers, F. 1988, 'Burning the truck and holding the country: property, time and the negotiation of identity among Pintupi Aborigines', in T. Ingold, D. Riches and J. Woodburn (eds), *Hunter Gatherers Today*, Berg, Oxford, pp. 52–74.

Myers, F. 2002, *Painting Culture. The making of an Aboriginal High Art*, Duke University Press, Durham, NC, and London.

Peterson, N. 1993, 'Demand sharing: reciprocity and the pressure for generosity among foragers', *American Anthropologist*, (NS) vol. 95, no. 4, pp. 860–74.

Redmond, A. 2006, 'Further on up the road: community trucks and the moving settlement', in T. Lea, E. Kowal and G. Cowlishaw (eds), *Moving Anthropology: Critical Indigenous studies*, Charles Darwin University Press, Darwin, pp. 95–114.

Rose, F. G. G. 1965, *The Wind of Change in Central Australia. The aborigines of Angas Downs*. Akademie Verlag, Berlin.

Rowse, T. 1998, *White Flour, White Power: From rations to citizenship in Central Australia*, Cambridge University Press, UK.

Sandell, R. (dir) 1969, *Camels and the Pitjantjatjara*, Film, Australian Institute of Aboriginal Studies, Canberra.

Sheppard, N. 2004, *Sojourn on Another Planet*, Nancy Sheppard, Collinswood, SA.

Stanner, W. E. H. 1965 [1958], Continuity and change, Presidential address to Section F. (Anthropology), Australian and New Zealand Association for the Advancement of Science, Adelaide, 1958, [Reprinted in Stanner, W. E. H., *White Man Got No Dreaming*, University of Chicago Press, Ill., and London].

Stotz, G. 2001, 'The colonizing vehicle', in D. Miller (ed.), *Car Cultures*, Berg, Oxford and New York, pp. 223–44.

Tindale, N. B. 1933, Journal of an anthropological expedition to the Mann and Musgrave ranges north west of South Australia May–July 1933 and a personal record of the anthropological expedition to Ernabella 1933, Manuscript, South Australia Museum, Adelaide.

Tindale, N. B. 1974, *Aboriginal Tribes of Australia: Their terrain, environmental controls, distribution, limits, and proper names*, University of California Press, Berkeley.

Wallace, N. 1990, 'The religion of the Aborigines of the Western Desert', in M. Charlesworth, R. Kimber and N. Wallace (eds), *Ancestor Spirits: Aspects of Australian Aboriginal life and spirituality*, Deakin University Press, Geelong, Vic., pp. 48–92.

Williams, R. M. 1998, *A Song in the Desert*, Angus and Robertson, Pymble, NSW.

Young, D. 2010, 'Clothing in the Western Desert', in Joanne Eicher (ed.), *The Encyclopaedia of World Dress and Fashion*, Berg, Oxford.

Young, D. (forthcoming), 'Mutable things: colours as material practice in the north west of South Australia', *Journal of the Royal Anthropological Institute*.

7. Peas, beans and riverbanks: seasonal picking and dependence in the Tuross Valley

JOHN WHITE

The Tuross River Valley is one of six major estuarine systems along the South Coast region of New South Wales. Today, the valley falls within the boundaries of the Eurobodalla Shire. The Yuin people are acknowledged as the traditional owners and custodians of the region. The township of Bodalla is located on the northern elbow of the Tuross River and the major nearby towns are Moruya in the north and Narooma to the south. While Bodalla achieved renown as a major dairying centre in the late nineteenth century, the forestry and horticultural industries have also made significant contributions to its economic development. The important roles that Aboriginal people have played in the expansion of the rural economy have, however, been largely neglected in the local histories of the South Coast. This chapter is part of a broader effort aimed at correcting the lack of acknowledgment of the contribution of Aboriginal labour to the local economy and, more generally, in the wider Australian context. The Tuross River farms at the 'back of Bodalla' hold vivid memories for present-day Aboriginal people living in the Eurobodalla Shire, many of whom spent much of their childhood years in and around the bean and pea fields. Bean and pea production began in the valley in the 1930s and provided work for Aboriginal people through to the constriction of the industry in the 1970s. The oral history record confirms that the majority of pickers were Aboriginal people, with South Coast families being joined in the picking fields by itinerant workers at the height of the season due to the large labour force needed to ensure that crops were picked in the best condition.[1]

Studies by Bell (1955) and Castle and Hagan (1978) have documented the relationship between Aboriginal people and the economy of the South Coast during the mid to late twentieth century. Both studies conclude that Aboriginal

---

1   This chapter draws on three publications arising through the Eurobodalla Aboriginal Cultural Heritage Study. For an extensive study of Aboriginal history in the region, see Goulding and Waters (2005). For oral accounts relating to cultural heritage, see Dale Donaldson (2006, 2008).

people were dependent either on the employment offered by settler society or on hand-outs and rations provided by the state. At first glance, the use of the word 'dependent' appears to mean a state of reliance by Aboriginal people on settler society for the means of survival. The notion sits within a more pervasive trope, however, which questions the viability of heterogeneous social and economic forms in Aboriginal communities. In 1951, A. P. Elkin outlined what he considered to be culturally determined stages relating to the response of Aboriginal people to white settlement along a continuum ranging from a pre-colonial stasis to full assimilation (Elkin 1951). Elkin's notion of assimilation was based on the total adoption of white culture by Aboriginal people and was influential in shaping the terms of reference used in both anthropological and broader public discourse during the debates of the time.[2] As part of a longer legacy, this paradigm heavily informed Bell's study of the economic conditions of 'mixed-blood' Aboriginal people between Port Kembla and the Victorian border along the South Coast of New South Wales. Bell (1955:186) identified the importance of seasonal picking to the livelihood of Aboriginal people in the Bodalla and Bega districts and described the level of their involvement in the horticultural industry as being a 'monopoly'. Interestingly, Bell (1955:198) concluded that this pattern of employment illustrates 'the lack of any successful economic assimilation…into the general Australian economic system, and, hence, their economic dependence upon the white community'. Aboriginal involvement in seasonal work (as opposed to continuous employment) was seen as lacking the kind of syncretism espoused by Elkin and, therein, impeding the process of assimilation.

In a later study, Castle and Hagan also trace the rise of Aboriginal involvement in the picking industry of the Bega Valley and conclude that engagement in the sector situated Aboriginal people in a position of structural dependence that, through processes of industry decline and increasing involvement in the political sphere, presaged a transition to 'independence' in the mid-1970s (Castle and Hagan 1978). This cycle, they argue, was constituted by an annual oscillation between seasonal picking and what Elkin (1951) classed 'intelligent parasitism'. While stating that the resident Aboriginal families were descendents of a dispossessed and displaced people whose 'former way of life had since then become impossible', and whose 'customs and law had broken down', the idea that assimilation had failed is not explicated (Castle and Hagan 1978:159). Castle and Hagan argue that by the 1920s only a very small proportion of Aboriginal people were engaged in the workforce and even less had consistent contact with the cash economy. This pattern is presented as being continuous through to the

---

2   For an examination of the assimilation policy debates between Elkin, Strehlow and Hasluck, see McGregor (2002).

1960s and caused in part by the policies of the Aborigines Protection Board (and its successor, the Aborigines Welfare Board). Castle and Hagan's understandings of this period are clearly presented in the following passage:

> In all aspects of life they were subject to white authority. They were socially segregated and dependent for their welfare on white charity and benevolence. They accepted these relationships. There was among them no movement to change or alter the world in which they found themselves. If they had a consciousness of themselves as Aborigines, then it was a fatalistic one which held that what had occurred was inevitable, and that the future could bring no change. Those of them who were Christians knew of the Ten Tribes of Noah. For them, salvation came in the next world. For the unregenerate, there was no hope. (Castle and Hagan 1978:164)

According to this reasoning, regardless of whether Aboriginal people were engaged in wage–labour relationships or not, the failure of assimilation through the perceived inability of Aboriginal people to blend into the broader social and economic milieu established a mire of hopelessness and dependence. The transition to 'independence' in the 1970s, brought about through processes of industry decline, increasing political agency for Aboriginal people, greater provision of town housing and broadening employment opportunities, could then be rationalised as successful cultural syncretism (and hence, successful assimilation).

While converging on the same conclusion of dependence, neither Bell nor Castle and Hagan pays attention to the non-monetised value of resource use for Aboriginal people working in seasonal employment. The continuation and reconstitution of a fishing tradition among South Coast Aboriginal people remain defining aspects of Yuin identity today, and (in terms of providing an independent avenue for economic activity) should be addressed in a re-examination of twentieth-century seasonal picking. Moreover, neither study acknowledges the long record of engagement between Aboriginal people and the expanding settler economy. I argue that the use of the notion of 'dependence' (as unsuccessful assimilation) obfuscates the innovative and socially meaningful ways in which Aboriginal people interact with the economy. In light of these two studies, this chapter aims to trace the historical trajectory of settler colonialism and governmental control in the Tuross Valley and its surrounds, detailing the rise of Aboriginal engagement with the picking industry, and will conclude by make some comments on the usefulness of the term 'dependence' in this historical context.

Expansion of colonial capitalism

Congruent with the experiences of Indigenous communities throughout south-eastern Australia, the expansion of colonial capitalism on the South Coast of New South Wales was accompanied by increases in governmental intervention in the process of colonisation, particularly the exercise of control over its original population through the use of rationing, surveillance and institutionalisation (see Morris 1989; Rowse 1998). In contrast with the establishment of Christian missions in other parts of Australia, the station at Wallaga Lake on the NSW South Coast was a secular, government-run institution. The creation of the stations (and the Aborigines Protection Board for that matter) was part of a concerted effort by the state to contain the situation that had arisen through the initial period of colonisation. As Long (1970:26) notes: 'Government activity until 1881 had been confined to desultory efforts to moderate conflict with the nomadic Aborigines as the frontier of White settlement expanded and then to mitigate the effects of contact on the Aborigines within the limits of settlement.' While it was assumed that increasing state intervention would help to reduce frontier violence, the need to 'mitigate the effects of contact' was underlined by conservative racial discourses that demanded that the state control and 'civilise' Aboriginal people both within the limits of settlement and elsewhere on the frontier.

The formalisation of administrative control over Aboriginal people in New South Wales can be traced to the concerns of missionaries regarding the vulnerability and penury of Aboriginal people who had survived the initial invasion. Prominent missionary figures argued that renewed effort should be given to the 'task of civilisation' or, in the words of the Reverend J. B. Gribble, 'to wipe out that long-standing disgrace, viz. the unjustifiable neglect of the heathen in our midst' (cited in Long 1970:26). The successful petitioning of the church led to the establishment of missions at Maloga on the Murray River in 1874 and Warangesda on the Murrumbidgee River in 1880. Linked to Gribble's concerns was a second, secular rationale, described by Morris (1989:90) as a desire to render Aboriginal people governable by reducing them 'to the status of colonial wards'. The aspiration of missionaries to protect (and indoctrinate) Aboriginal people was translated into legalistic custodianship on the creation of the office of Protector of Aborigines in 1880 (Morris 1989:90). In 1881, the colonial administration appointed George Thornton as Protector of Aborigines, whose initial charge was to commission a comprehensive enumeration and survey of the condition of Aboriginal people throughout the state.

Thornton's preliminary conclusion was that assistance should be given only to Aboriginal people living on-country and he argued that all efforts should be made to prevent their presence 'about the metropolis' (Long 1970:27). As Morris notes, the rationale behind this move was twofold. First, it was hoped that communities would be largely self-sufficient with the provision of opportunities for collective agricultural cultivation. Second, according to the 'commonsense' view that Aboriginal people were going to disappear entirely, the creation of reserves as segregated havens away from the rigours and confusions of settler society was thought to have provided 'the soothing pillow of a dying race' (Morris 1985:93–4). In an assessment that must have frustrated Gribble and his contemporaries, Thornton also concluded that secular administration would be far more effective than religious instruction, and urged that young Aboriginal people should be taught manual skills appropriate for entry into the colonial workforce (Long 1970:27). Soon after, in 1883, a Board for the Protection of the Aborigines was appointed under the direction of Thornton, though it lacked the legislative muscle needed to control the movement of Aboriginal people. The first station in New South Wales was created when the board reserved a portion of land at Wallaga Lake for the use of Aboriginal people in 1891. In 1909, the *Aborigines Protection Act* was passed, granting the board the powers it needed to segregate the Aboriginal population. The location of the Wallaga Lake station—16 km from Bermagui, 24 km from Narooma, 40km from Bodalla and 64 km from Bega—was ideally placed to suit the board's goal of isolating Aboriginal people from the regional centres (Long 1970:62). The Act was, as Morris (1989:90) argues, 'the pivotal point…which prefigured a change in the nature of control over Aboriginal communities in the latter decades'.

Early engagement with the settler economy

Chris Lloyd's chapter in this volume argues that a critical determinant of economic growth in the Australian settler economy was the availability of labour. In the case of the Eurobodalla region, the evidence suggests that the shortage of available labour was alleviated to some degree by the incorporation of Indigenous workers during the initial period of economic expansion and diversification in the settler economy. By the time the board had passed the 1909 Act, Aboriginal people on the South Coast had already been actively engaged with the settler economy for at least 70 years. Aside from early records documenting the involvement of Aboriginal people in the whaling industry at Twofold Bay, several sources provide evidence of Indigenous labour with the initial European settlers in the Eurobodalla region (Brierly 1842–43, 1842–48, 1844–51). One of the earliest written records identifying individual Aboriginal workers was by John Hawdon, who, along with Francis Flanagan, had taken up land in the Moruya area by 1830. In one of his letters, Hawdon refers to an Aboriginal man known as Benson as a 'faithful servant for many years'. He refers to two other men called Campbell and Walker in a similar way. On the advice of Aboriginal people who showed him the location of 'good grass and water', Hawdon later expanded his landholdings to include parcels in the Bodalla area (Buck n.d.). Further north at Broulee, Flanagan observed:

> Those who choose to work can obtain plenty of food and clothing, and they seldom have of necessity to depend upon fishing or hunting for subsistence…Both males and females are employed by the settlers in gathering the maize and potatoe crop, and some of them in reaping. They have commonly been remunerated in provisions, clothes, tea, sugar, tobacco, &c., but many of them now insist upon being paid in money. They are always employed for stripping bark…They will only work when the fancy seizes them, and always go off without warning. (Flanagan 1845; see also Gibson, this volume on attitudes to employment)

After less than a decade of contact with the first settlers, Aboriginal people in the Eurobodalla region were already engaged in reciprocal relationships of labour and in-kind or cash payment. Their extensive knowledge of the coastal hinterlands and the correct timing for stripping bark made them valuable to the tanning industry. Wattle bark was the first legume cash crop in Australia and provided an extract used for tanning throughout the colonies. By 1823, the tannin yielded from the bark-stripping labour of 'bush workers' was being shipped to Britain (Davidson and Davidson 1993:215). It appears that transactions were taking place on a negotiated, contract basis, as a journalist's account of a journey along the South Coast in 1871 implies:

> About five miles from Moruya we met a blackfellow carrying a long straight stick. He recognized Mr Flanagan with a grin, and pointed to the notches—about forty in number—quite triumphantly. On enquiry I discovered that the blackfellow is employed bark-stripping, and gets so much per sheet, for all he strips. The notched stick was his account of the number of sheets. (Anon. 1871)

These relationships were, to some extent, forged through hardships experienced by the early settlers and kindness on the part of Aboriginal people. While violence was common on the frontier, as Goulding and Waters (2005:37) note, 'conflict between Aboriginal people and Europeans in the early period of European intrusion into an area is only one part of the story'. For example, Mrs Celia Rose, who arrived in Moruya as a young child in the early 1830s, recorded the local Aboriginal people providing food to the settlers: 'There was only one sailing vessel…that called at Broulee about once a month, bringing provisions from Sydney, and the shortage was at times acute. Aboriginals saved the settlement several times from starvation by supplying fish and oysters' (Rose 1923). A similar encounter occurred in 1841 when several Aboriginal men swam out into rough seas and rescued the survivors of the wrecked schooner *Rover*. Soon after, gorgets (or brass plates) were presented to the men in recognition and reward for their efforts (Oldrey 1842).

The Commissioner for Crown Lands, John Lambie, recorded European farmers in 1845 being assisted by Aboriginal labourers in a range of activities, with labour being rewarded with food and clothing (Lambie 1846). Lambie (1851) lamented that the Aboriginal workers could not be depended on, but were 'well treated, and well paid by those who employ them'. Lambie's replacement, Commissioner Manning, contradicted Lambie's observation, stating that 'quiet and orderly in their deportment, when not ill used, they are willing to labour for wages so small that their services are in general demand' (Manning 1852). While the reason for this discrepancy is unclear, Manning's observation resonates with the historical record of the use of Aboriginal labour throughout the nineteenth century.[3] Importantly, as Goulding and Waters (2005:41) point out, Manning realised that Aboriginal people were motivated to work for the settlers on a seasonal basis, preferring to wander off in warmer months when resources were plentiful along the coast. Clearly, Aboriginal people had been able to successfully modify their pre-existing patterns to their changing economic circumstances and incorporate the presence of Europeans into their seasonal movements (see Cameron 1987; Organ 1990; Rose 1990). Further, as Cane (1992:8) remarks, the exchange of material goods and services between Aboriginal people and settlers 'is probably consistent with traditional methods of reciprocal exchange and could be readily incorporated into the new Aboriginal economy'. Similarly, Cameron's (1987) examination of the documentary record relating to South Coast Aboriginal people in the nineteenth century implies socioeconomic transformation, arguing that both customary and newly acquired skills enabled Aboriginal people to carve an important, though undervalued, place in the regional economy.

Following incremental changes to legislation between 1861 and 1905 designed to open up the large pastoral leases to small selectors, Aboriginal people along the South Coast were increasingly forced off their country (Goulding and Waters 2005:48). Prior to land being rapidly taken up in smaller allotments in the Tuross Valley (and vast networks of post and wire fencing being laid to delineate boundaries of title), there was still scope for the purchase of large estates. In 1860, Thomas Mort purchased more than 13 000 acres (5300 ha) at Bodalla and shortly after added another 4000 acres (1600 ha) for the Comerang farm. Mort's vision was to create an integrated, privately owned estate and included the construction of a general store, bakery, butchery, hotel and blacksmith's workshop (Whiteford 1985:14). This period of rapid dispossession and displacement of Aboriginal communities on the South Coast gave rise to a range of initial responses on the part of Aboriginal people. Some travelled

---

3   For a regional comparison, see Bennett (2003).

hundreds of kilometres to Sydney to petition for land, boats and fishing rights while camping at Port Jackson (Goodall 1996:75). Others fought for land to be reserved through correspondence with the Aborigines Protection Board. Close to Bodalla, 'Permissive Occupancies' that had been granted to three Aboriginal men in 1872 were gazetted as Aboriginal reserves in 1878 (Goodall 1996:79). Other Aboriginal people continued to live in camps in the vicinity of Wallaga Lake until the station was established in 1891 (Anon. 1879). The location of these camps and reserves was important in enabling the continuation of connections to the estuarine and marine environments and the maintenance and transformation of customary fishing practices (see Cane 1992; Cruze et al. 2005; Goodall 1982).

Aborigines Protection Act 1909: transitions in socioeconomic conditions

As the legislation laid down in the *Aborigines Protection Act* was being rolled out across the state, the intensity of state intervention into the lives of Aboriginal people at Wallaga Lake increased dramatically. It was understood that all adult men who were fit to work should leave the station to find employment or risk penalty under the 'work test' regulation in the Act, although this pattern appears already to have been established. In 1903, H. M. Trenchard was sent by the Aborigines Protection Board to inspect the conditions at Wallaga Lake and he reported that:

> The young men on the Station are not encouraged to remain on the Station, and they are able to obtain suitable employment at certain times of the year at the farms in the district, and from one of the Managers' monthly reports it appeared that forty-seven men from the Station were engaged in work of various kinds off the Station, earning from 15s. to 30s. per week. (Trenchard 1904)

On a return visit seven years later, Trenchard wrote:

> The people appear fairly contented, and not doing too badly in spite of bad accommodation, the numbers on the Station being much reduced in consequence of there being plenty of work obtainable, and fear of possible action by the Board under the new Act, which has been much exaggerated...It was made very plain to the residents that in future, men must work or leave the Station. (Trenchard 1911)

Another aspect of the Act had profound impacts on the stability of family life for Aboriginal people throughout New South Wales. The Act provided the board legal sanction to remove Aboriginal children from their families—a situation exacerbated by increasing powers being granted by way of the 1915 amendment. The process of 'apprenticing' Aboriginal children, as Goodall (1990) argues, 'sought systematically to remove as many Aboriginal children as possible and never to allow them to return to their communities'. This shift in emphasis from segregation to assimilation was in essence a policy of dispersal with the aim of breaking up family groups (Read 1982). The constant movement of Aboriginal families brought about by successive governmental interventions prescribing where and how they should live also, however, broadened the geographic range of kinship networks throughout the South Coast region of New South Wales.

The rise of the manufacturing industry following the application of the protective tariff of 1908 brought it into direct competition for labour with primary producers. The tariff stipulated that the manufacturing industry was required to pay 'fair and reasonable wages'. In the words of The Bodalla Company's director in 1912, the protective tariff had 'drawn a large proportion of the labour required in the country into the towns' (Whiteford 1985:17). The labour shortage, which had hamstrung the expansion of the primary sector, was alleviated to some degree by the 'work test' stipulations of the *Aborigines Protection Act*, even though the legislative aim (in terms of revenue) was reducing the cost of government rations. While there were Aboriginal milkmen working at Wallaga Lake, there is little evidence to suggest that Aboriginal people were similarly employed in the Tuross Valley, reflecting what Morris (1985:99) describes as segmented employment patterns based on an 'ideology of pollution'. Aside from labour devoted to 'improving the land', Aboriginal people were not widely employed by dairying producers in the region. Racialised divisions of labour were consistent with the policies of the board that sought to 'train the Aborigines and make them fit for gradual assimilation' (Long 1970:31). Divisions of labour also occurred along gendered lines within this schema: Aboriginal girls were apprenticed and trained as domestic maids or servants while Aboriginal boys were taught skills appropriate for labourers, farmhands or timber workers. As Goodall (1990) notes, the removal and training of Aboriginal children were a complex 'interaction between prevailing anxieties about race and gender, labour market needs and pre-existing administrative precedents'. As such, the policy of assimilation was not intended to produce an egalitarian outcome but, rather, a socially stratified one that conformed to the conservative discourses of the time.

Racial attitudes were manifested not only in stratifying the type of work available to Aboriginal people, but also in competition for lower-paying jobs and through contestations over land. The end of World War I resulted in pressure being placed on the Protection Board to revoke reserved land for the use of returned servicemen. As Cane (1992:11) notes, by 1926, 75 per cent of reserved land in the state had been revoked, including the revocation of two reserves at Bodalla in 1920. As Goodall (1982:227) describes, however, the major pressure on Aboriginal communities living on reserves was from town expansion, with the viability of several reserves being disputed for residential development. Contestations over reserved land were followed by the Great Depression of the 1930s, which impacted heavily on the lives of Aboriginal people. This is reflected by a 200 per cent increase in the number of people living at the Wallaga Lake station between 1921 and 1939 (Long 1970:62). After hitting rock bottom in 1932, the employment situation slowly improved. Long (1970:31) notes that World War II created a labour shortage, rapidly reducing the unemployment rate of Aboriginal people in reserves from 36 per cent in 1940 to less than 4 per cent by 1944. The unemployment rate for mainstream Australia then stabilised, and between 1945 and 1974, it fluctuated about an average of 2 per cent (Commonwealth of Australia 2005). The return of servicemen after the war combined with the economic recovery to create a highly competitive labour market in which Aboriginal people were consistently relegated to lower-paying jobs.

World War II also caused a rise in the production of beans and peas, which nearly doubled to meet the demands of the armed forces (Davidson and Davidson 1993:351). In the Tuross River Valley, more than 15 farms diversified to include the production of legume cash crops. The farms at the 'back of Bodalla' were mostly family-owned operations, with the exception of The Bodalla Company (formed after Thomas Mort's death in 1879), which had also included horticultural acreage. The Bodalla Company kept fastidious records of payments made to individual bean and pea pickers between July 1959 and June 1962, corresponding with three financial years or growing seasons. The picking season began in the Tuross Valley in October and ran until March, and farmers would want to get two picks off the crop during each season. The following reminiscence of a local farmer gives a good indication of the nature of the industry:

> After planting the beans or peas on the rich river flats in Eurobodalla or Cadgee…there was a lot of labour involved later in picking the fresh crop, usually only a first or second pick…A number of Aboriginal people were always employed during the picking season. A good strong back was needed and a fast picker would pick up to 8 bags of beans in a day (80lbs per bag)…It was important to work the long hours otherwise the crop would spoil with beans becoming too old and stringy. (O'Toole 1997:30)

Importantly, The Bodalla Company's wage cards show that picking work was not always continuous, but rather it involved targeted increases in labour in order to harvest the crops in the best condition. Further, as Figure 7.1 illustrates, the availability of work was not consistent for each growing season. Depending largely on climatic conditions, the variability in crop production was erratic and workers employed in picking therefore needed to be highly flexible about when and where their labour would be required. (While the oral record illustrates that other farms paid regularly on Saturdays, there is no evidence suggesting that this was regularly the case on The Bodalla Company farm.)

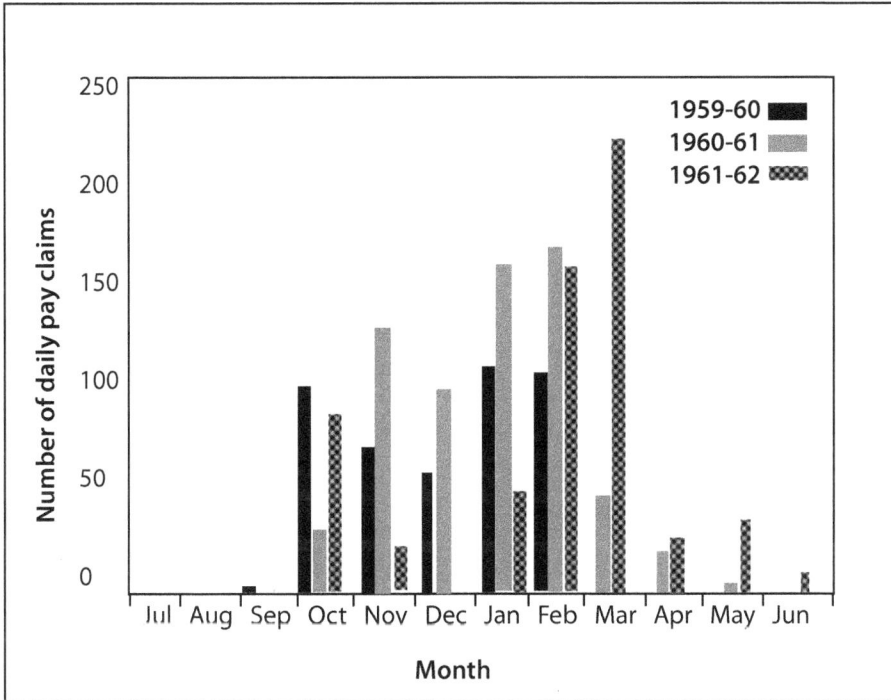

Figure 7.1 Number of pay claims per month for bean and pea picking, The Bodalla Company, 1959–60

Source: The Bodalla Company, Wages and summary cards for bean and pea picking, 1958–62.

In 1961, the Aborigines Advancement League conducted a survey of the living and working conditions of Aboriginal people in the South Coast region. At a property near Eurobodalla they noted that pickers were allowed to stay on the farm permanently and that 'the people are quite pleased with relations with their employer' (Anon. 1961). This pattern is consistent with oral accounts of picking life, in which Aboriginal families were welcome to live in farm sheds or to set up camps on the properties so that they could work when required. In many cases, men were holding down continuous employment in the nearby sawmills while women and children would work together in the picking fields. Many families from Wallaga Lake moved over to the Tuross Valley temporarily during the picking season. Others who continued to live on the station were rounded up by farmers who needed labour and ferried to and from the Tuross Valley on the back of trucks. The Bodalla Company wage cards show clustering around family names and illustrate that whole families were working together when their labour was needed. As Dale Donaldson (2006:84) remarks, 'picking work was hard work, but paid off because a lot of time was spent amongst one's family'. The condition of mainstream 'full employment' that existed throughout this period also drew hundreds of itinerant Aboriginal workers to the Tuross Valley looking for work during the picking season. The banks of the Tuross River were the sites of temporary camps for travelling seasonal pickers and local families alike. While most itinerant workers moved on at the end of the main season, some stayed and made strong connections to the Eurobodalla region that last through to the present day.

Conclusions: critique of the notion of dependence

Through this brief examination of the historical record, it is clear that the expansion of the settler economy was concurrent with governmental intervention into the lives of Aboriginal people. Early engagement with the settler economy was characterised by the transformation of existing social and economic practices and an independent and viable economy based primarily on fishing. Contra to Castle and Hagan's (1998:25) argument that 'Aboriginal people neither sought nor were given the opportunity to adapt to or participate in the white economy', the archival record on the NSW South Coast points to the active participation of Aboriginal people accompanied by rapid transformations to incorporate the settler economy into pre-existing practices and seasonal movements. Through the post-frontier period, this engagement was characterised by seasonality and constrained by government policy prescribing where and how Aboriginal people should live. The policies of assimilation, while initially aimed at breaking up Aboriginal intra and trans-familial groups, also sought to create a racially stratified underclass that preserved the status quo. These policies were accompanied by extremely low mainstream unemployment after World War II in which Aboriginal people filled a structural niche in low-paying jobs. Bean and pea production involved heavy manual labour with poor working conditions, but was a desirable alternative for people because it enabled families to work together. In light of the historical record, I will now discuss some aspects of the use of the term 'dependent' in previous studies to describe Aboriginal bean and pea pickers.

The studies by Bell (1955) and Castle and Hagan (1978) both neglect the importance of economic activities occurring outside the paradigmatic 'real' economy, thus placing the emphasis on the role of employers as 'patrons' and on the welfare state. Bennett's recent study of Aboriginal responses to the colonial economy in the Shoalhaven and Illawarra regions of New South Wales between 1770 and 1900 concluded that Aboriginal people maintained 'a viable and independent economy in articulation with an expanding capitalist economy' (Bennett 2003:270). Throughout the post-frontier period, Aboriginal people lived what Cane (1992:12) describes as a 'difficult and precarious socio-economic existence' and consistently turned to fishing as an avenue for self-sufficiency. The success of Aboriginal fishers also drew them into conflict with white fishermen, reaffirming conservative racial delineations. As Goodall notes:

> While employment opportunities for Guris [Kooris] were remarkably more limited on the south coast than in the other regions, Guris' self-sufficiency was enhanced not only by subsistence fishing but by fishing for the market, at which they were successful enough to cause local fishermen to protest to the Protection Board through the Fisheries Department in 1914 and 1918. (Goodall 1982:115)

As an opportunity for self-sufficiency, fishing also provided an avenue for a certain kind of autonomy—one that has been eroded by the successive revocations of reserves and increasing restrictions placed on Aboriginal fishers through the regulation of commercial and recreational fishing. The oral history record describes fishing activities as being an important aspect of seasonal work, with families setting up temporary camp at nearby beaches and estuaries when they were not needed in the picking fields. Fishing also provided a vital means of subsistence for Aboriginal people who were camped on the banks of the Tuross River when picking was on. Rather than describing the involvement of Aboriginal people in the horticultural industry in terms of a seasonal work cycle sustained by 'intelligent parasitism', it would be more appropriate to see picking work and fishing in terms of seasonal responses to changing economic circumstances. Thus, the record suggests that historical engagements between Aboriginal people and the settler economy have been mutually constituted as a result of complex historical processes.

Reflecting a broader trend in Aboriginal studies throughout much of the twentieth century, the term 'dependency' has been used ubiquitously to describe the economic status of Aboriginal people living on the South Coast to such an extent that it has obscured the importance of Indigenous contributions to the region's economic development. Bell's (1955) study concluded that South Coast Aboriginal people were dependent on either the employment offered by the white population or the financial assistance provided by the government. This conclusion was supported in Castle and Hagan's (1978:163) study in the Bega Valley, where bean picking and pea picking were rendered as dependent activities. The conflation of seasonal employment with a state of dependence is inappropriate given that the horticultural industry was largely dependent on Aboriginal labour. In Bell's words:

> Seasonal work (crop picking) claims the largest number of Aborigines engaged in primary production, with casual work on dairy farms and in grazing, forestry and fishing completing the picture. Accustomed down through the years to performing seasonal work, the South Coast Aborigines now consider it their chief occupation. Indeed, they have a monopoly. Whites do not offer for it, partly because it is identified with the Aborigines, and partly because it is temporary. (Bell 1955:186)

The reasons for the decline of seasonal horticulture on the South Coast in the 1970s are also pertinent here. Some people cite increasing mechanisation and competition in bean and pea production from farmers in Queensland and New Zealand driving down prices and making manual, cool-climate horticulture simply unsustainable. Others point to changes in the Aboriginal workforce (Castle and Hagan 1978:167). Increases in the political agency of Aboriginal people throughout New South Wales resulted in more and more strikes and walk-offs due to poor pay rates and labour conditions. Moreover, increasing opportunities for regular employment accompanied by the greater provision of both town housing and welfare benefits meant that Aboriginal people had a broader range of options available to them. In all likelihood, the decline of seasonal horticulture on the South Coast was a combination of these two factors, which, nevertheless, highlights the importance of Aboriginal labour to the sector. In the case of the South Coast, the interdependence that existed between Tuross Valley farmers and seasonal pickers has been subsumed under a racially motivated delineation between the structural position of Aboriginal workers and their non-Indigenous counterparts. An Aboriginal worker's employer was a patron; a whitefella's employer was simply their boss.

References

Anon. 1871, 'A tour to the south: from our special correspondent: no. 10—the Broulee district (continued)', *Town and Country Journal*, 7 October 1871, pp. 522–3.

Anon. 1879, 'The Tilba Tilba district', *Bega Standard*, 29 November 1879, p. 2.

Anon. 1961, *Aborigines Advancement League: Survey into living and social conditions of Aboriginal people from Wollongong to the Victorian border*, South Coast Labour Council, Wollongong, NSW.

Bell, J. H. 1955, 'The economic life of mixed-blood Aborigines on the South Coast of New South Wales', *Oceania*, vol. 26, p. 181.

Bennett, M. 2003, For a labourer worthy of his hire: Aboriginal economic responses to colonisation in the Shoalhaven and Illawarra, 1770–1900, Unpublished PhD thesis, University of Canberra, ACT.

Brierly, O. 1842–43, Journal of a visit to Twofold Bay, Dec. 1842 – Jan. 1843, Mitchell Library, Sydney.

Brierly, O. 1842–48, Diaries at Twofold Bay and Sydney, Mitchell Library, Sydney.

Brierly, O. 1844–51, Reminiscences of the sea: about whales, Mitchell Library, Sydney.

Buck, M. n.d., *Old Colony Days: John Hawdon's letters. Volume II*, Moruya and District Historical Society, NSW.

Cameron, S. 1987, An investigation of the history of the Aborigines of the far South Coast of New South Wales in the nineteenth century, Unpublished B. Letters thesis, The Australian National University, Canberra.

Cane, S. 1992, Aboriginal fishing on the South Coast of New South Wales: a report to Blake, Dawson and Waldron and the NSW Aboriginal Land Council, Unpublished typescript.

Castle, R. and Hagan, J. 1978, 'Dependence and independence', in A. Curthoys and A. Marcus (eds), *Who are Our Enemies? Racism and the Australian working class*, Hale & Iremonger in association with the Australian Society for the Study of Labour History, Neutral Bay, NSW, pp. 159–71.

Castle, R. and Hagan, J. 1998, 'Settlers and the state: the creation of an Aboriginal work force in Australia', *Aboriginal History*, vol. 22, pp. 24–35.

Commonwealth of Australia 2005, *Budget 2004–2005*, Department of Treasury, Canberra.

Cruze, B., Stewart, L. and Norman, S. 2005, *Mutton Fish: The surviving culture of Aboriginal people and abalone on the South Coast of New South Wales*, Aboriginal Studies Press, Canberra.

Dale Donaldson, S. 2006, *Stories about the Eurobodalla by Aboriginal People: Eurobodalla Aboriginal Cultural Heritage Study. Stage two*, Susan Dale Donaldson Environmental and Cultural Services, Eurobodalla Shire Council, Moruya, NSW.

Dale Donaldson, S. 2008, *Aboriginal Men and Women's Heritage: Eurobodalla*, Eurobodalla Shire Council, Moruya, NSW.

Davidson, B. R. and Davidson, H. F. 1993, *Legumes, the Australian Experience: The botany, ecology, and agriculture of Indigenous and immigrant legumes*, Research Studies Press, Brisbane.

Elkin, A. P. 1951, 'Reaction and interaction: a food gathering people and European settlement in Australia', *American Anthropologist*, vol. 53, pp. 164–86.

Flanagan, F. 1845, 'Response to circular letter from Francis Flanagan. Report from the Select Committee on the Condition of the Aborigines with appendix', *Minutes of Evidence and Replies to a Circular Letter*, Government Printing Office, Sydney.

Goodall, H. 1982, The history of Aboriginal communities in NSW 1909–1939, Unpublished PhD thesis, Department of History, The Australian National University, Canberra.

Goodall, H. 1990, '"Saving the children": gender and the colonisation of Aboriginal children in NSW, 1788 to 1990', *Aboriginal Law Bulletin*, vol. 2, no. 44, p. 9.

Goodall, H. 1996, *Invasion to Embassy: Land in Aboriginal politics in New South Wales, 1770–1972*, Allen & Unwin, Sydney.

Goulding, M. and Waters, K. 2005, Eurobodalla Aboriginal Cultural Heritage Study South Coast New South Wales. Stage one, Goulding Heritage Consulting Pty Ltd.

Lambie, J. 1846, 'Annual report on the state of the Aborigines for the year 1845, Commissioner of Crown Lands Lambie to Colonial Secretary Thomson', *Historical Records of Australia*, Series 1, p. 25.

Lambie, J. 1851, Annual report on the Aborigines of the Maneroo district for the year 1850, Commissioner Lambie to the Chief Commissioner, Crown Lands Office Cooma, Colonial Secretary Papers, Special bundles, Annual reports on state of the Aborigines in the various districts, 1851–53, State Records of New South Wales, Sydney.

Long, J. P. M. 1970, *Aboriginal Settlements: A survey of institutional communities in eastern Australia*, The Australian National University Press, Canberra.

McGregor, R. 2002, 'Assimilationists contest assimilation: T. G. H. Strehlow and A. P. Elkin on Aboriginal policy', *Journal of Australian Studies*, vol. 75, pp. 43–50.

Manning, C. 1852, 'Report on the state of the Aborigines in the Maneroo district', Commissioner Manning, 23 March 1852, Colonial Secretary Papers, Special bundles, *Annual Reports on State of the Aborigines in the Various Districts, 1851–53*, State Records of New South Wales, Sydney.

Morris, B. 1985, 'Cultural domination and domestic dependence: the Dhan-Gadi of New South Wales and the protection of the state', *Canberra Anthropology*, vol. 8, nos 1–2, pp. 87–115.

Morris, B. 1989, *Domesticating Resistance: The Dhan-Gadi Aborigines and the Australian state*, Berg, New York and Oxford.

Oldrey, W. 1842, Return of Aboriginal natives taken at Broulee the 6th day of May 1842, Colonial Secretary special bundles: Aborigines 1837–44, Papers dealing with the issue of blankets, and including returns of the native population in the various districts, State Records of New South Wales, Sydney.

Organ, M. 1990, *A Documentary History of the Illawarra and South Coast Aborigines*, Aboriginal Education Unit, Wollongong University, NSW.

O'Toole, C. 1997, *Beyond Bodalla: Recollections from my life*, Moruya and District Historical Society, NSW.

Read, P. 1982, *The Stolen Generations: the removal of Aboriginal children in New South Wales 1883 to 1969*, Occasional Paper No. 1, New South Wales Ministry of Aboriginal Affairs, Sydney.

Rose, C. 1923, 'Recollections of the early days of Moruya', *Journal and Proceedings of the Royal Australian Historical Society*, p. 8.

Rose, D. B. 1990, *Gulaga: A report on the cultural significance of Mt Dromedary to Aboriginal people*, Forestry Commission of NSW and NSW National Parks and Wildlife Service, Hurtsville, NSW.

Rowse, T. 1998, *White Flour, White Power: From rations to citizenship in Central Australia*, Cambridge University Press, Melbourne.

The Bodalla Company 1958–62, Wages and summary cards for bean and pea picking, Noel Butlin Archives Centre, Canberra.

Trenchard, H. 1904, *Aborigines Protection Board. Report for the year 1903*, Second Session, Legislative Assembly of New South Wales, Sydney.

Trenchard, H. 1911, Letter of report from Mr. H. Trenchard to the Chairman, Aborigines Protection Board, 18th August 1911, as an attachment to a letter from the Secretary of the Aborigines Protection Board to the Under Secretary of the Department of Public Instruction, 8th September 1911, Wallaga Lake School File 1876–1939, State Records of New South Wales, Sydney.

Whiteford, D. 1985, *An Economic History of the Bodalla Company 1900 to 1920. Student research essays in economic history*, Department of Economic History, Faculty of Economics and Commerce, The Australian National University, Canberra.

8. 'Who you is?' Work and identity in Aboriginal New South Wales

LORRAINE GIBSON

Ideas and practices relating to work, productivity and leisure are a source of much disagreement and ill feeling between Indigenous and non-Indigenous people in Australia. For dominant Western cultures, labour in its most common guise of 'work' offers a cogent means through which people come to know themselves and become known to others (Crawford 1985). How does this notion translate to Indigenous social realms? This chapter offers an ethnographically grounded examination of the intersections between work, employment and identity for Indigenous people living in a country town in far western New South Wales, Australia.[1] What does it mean to be a productive and valued person within Aboriginal society and in what ways is this tied to and/or antithetical to participation in the mainstream economy? How are Aboriginal people figuring ideas of work and productivity as a means to forging a particular identity? This chapter explores the tacit and reflexive cultural import of these questions and some of their lived effects.

Attitudes to work

This chapter offers some personal accounts of the various functioning of notions and practices towards work, culture and identity within, and across, black and white segments of the Australian population. In so doing, differing values and attitudes towards work, identity and Aboriginal culture are seen for their role in black and white relationships and for Aboriginal socioeconomic engagement. Importantly, the chapter shows the ambiguity, ambivalence and slipperiness pertaining to these categories as they are differently and reflexively experienced and interpreted, and how ideas and attitudes towards work and employment are tied in complex ways to belonging and to identity politics. In so doing, it points to the challenges for effective policy and practice in areas

---

1 'A longer version of this paper appears in Oceania Vol. 80 entitled 'Making a life: getting ahead and getting a living in Aboriginal New South Wales'.

of education, vocational training and sustainable employment. In many parts of settled Australia, stereotypical relations between blackfellas and whitefellas are constantly being played out in damaging and unproductive ways. When whites talk of 'lazy black bastards' who sit on their 'fat arses' all day, and blacks respond by asking if whites want them 'to work like white cunts—24 hours a day', these judgments make for easy rhetoric yet mostly go unanalysed. In these ways, the ground is laid for cultural differences that are often unexplored for their complexity and effects.

Based on ethnographic fieldwork in Wilcannia between July 2002 and the present, the chapter only scratches the surface of this complexity, as it is limited to the particular circumstances of Wilcannia—a small town with a fluid population of between 550 and 650 residents of whom at any given time the substantial majority are Aboriginal. Having said this, my current research in Moree, Kempsey and in Glebe in Sydney over the past two years demonstrates that many of the economic and social circumstances and attitudes of Wilcannia can be extrapolated out to other NSW country and urban locations.

Who you is?

In the dominant culture of Australia and indeed in Western cultures more generally, there is a tendency to conflate a person's social value and worth with their occupation and to socially position them accordingly. 'What do you do?' is often one of the first questions asked in social situations in the way of making small talk (itself arguably a dominant cultural predisposition of the dominant culture). The inferences made from this small talk are, however, not so insignificant. A person is often located and marked within the social structure by occupation as well as by the perceived nature of the work undertaken. *What* a person *does* has become increasingly conflated with *who* a person *is*, both for the self and others. The question 'What do you do?' is not, however, in the main, part of Aboriginal discourse in far western New South Wales. Instead people ask, 'who you is?'[2] The question 'who you is?' performs a function similar to the dominant-culture question 'what do you do?' in that it operates as a two-way process that serves to locate interlocutors in the social structure. The

---

2   Discussion with the linguist Paul Monaghan provided the following explanation for the form of 'who you is?' 'There are many varieties of Aboriginal English that defy the norms of Standard Australian English. In many varieties the copula (i.e., the various forms of the verb "to be") is omitted, and this is a feature shared by pidgin varieties of English and creoles. Examples are "who that", "where she". My guess in this case, which is concerned with personal identity, is that it serves a useful function. What other resources are there to express this concept? The syntax—the order of the words—probably just reflects the non-standard variety of English being spoken. It does, however, seem to capture the emic or in-group aspect. So it is most likely a useful phrase that carries local character and marks the speaker accordingly' (Personal communication, Dr Paul Monaghan, Adelaide University, 11 May 2010).

kind of information fed back and its implications differ in the two cases. While the question 'who you is?' is regularly asked of any new white face in town, whites do not approach blacks to seek out this kind of information. Blacks also do not voluntarily or regularly identify themselves in these terms to whites. The answers being elicited by Aboriginal people are not related to job title or perceived income. Here, my experience in Wilcannia reflects that of MacDonald's work with the Wiradjuri around Cowra in central New South Wales—namely, that their ontology remains to some extent 'a *relational ontology* [that] sees people defined through *relationships* rather than roles' (2004:15).[3] When an Aboriginal person in Wilcannia asks 'who you is?' of another Aboriginal person, the response being sought locates a person relationally—for example: 'I'm X's nephew' or 'my Mother is A' or 'Y is my cousin'. In responding to questions such as this, Aboriginal people explore kin relationships and social networks across towns and cities. This serves to socially and geographically locate the people being met, thereby positioning them within recognised frameworks and the kind of social intercourse that may or may not be entered into. An example of this process took place one night in the Wilcannia golf club. An Aboriginal woman in her mid-twenties came over to the table where I was sitting with four Aboriginal people having a drink. She asked one of the men, 'Remember me, Uncle Brian—you used to nurse me?' Uncle Brian said, 'No, what your name?' The woman replied by giving her name and saying who her mother and father are. Those present then linked these kin connections to other kin connections and events. Uncle Brian then went on to tell everyone at our table that when the woman was a little girl he used to nurse her on his knee. The woman was quite large and Uncle Brian went on to say, 'I wouldn't wanna fucken nurse you now.' This produced gales of laughter and the story, building up to the punchline, was retold again and again to every person who joined the table. At the end of the evening, all the people who sat at our table throughout the night knew who the woman was (if they did not before) and had shared in past events of her life and the lives of related kin. It is incidents such as this that strengthen, highlight, renew and expand kin and social networks and sociality. They locate people within the social strata in ways that are grounded in knowing and being known in relation to others, to place, to events and in time.

The question 'who you is?' when asked of a white person may not necessarily have as its *preferred* purpose the elicitation of an occupation, but, in the experience of the Aboriginal people of Wilcannia, most non-Aboriginal people respond to this question with an occupational answer. This is to a great extent

3   After I gave this paper at the AAS conference in 2008, Diane Austin-Broos approached me to say that my observations in western New South Wales resonated with, and echoed, her observations on social roles and introductions in relation to her work with Arrernte people in the Central Desert. We were excited that we had come up with these observations independently of one another, taking into consideration the very different histories and structures of the communities in which we work. She has written about her observations in her excellent (at that time upcoming but now published) book (Austin-Broos 2009).

how the people responding perceive what is in fact being asked. 'I'm a teacher at the school' or 'I'm a nurse at the hospital' is *who* as well as *what* these white professionals perceive themselves to be. Occupation is often their *purpose* to *being* in Wilcannia (double entendre intended). Occupation is what white people for the most part are *doing with*—*doing for*—Aboriginal people in Wilcannia. This is a world of whitefellas ostensibly doing things for blackfellas through work. Indeed, blackfellas' contact with whitefellas 'at work' is often blackfellas' main experience of whitefellas. According to Austin-Broos (2003:124), blacks and whites 'meet only at the point of service delivery in a highly bureaucratised welfare economy'. These primarily work-defined relationships shape interaction as they also create perception. This point of meeting and coming together is also, however, a point of separation and difference.

Willis (1977:2) considers Western societies' mode of identification with work to result from the fact that 'labour power…is the main mode of active connection with the world: the way *par excellence* of articulating the innermost self with external reality'. The self is expressed through work and working relations as these are understood. As Willis (1977:2) goes on to say, this active connectivity with the world through labour power is 'the dialectic of the self to the self through the concrete world'. For the dominant culture, labour in its most common guise of 'work' offers a cogent means through which those in the West come to know themselves and become known to others. Personhood in this model is in part defined through '"badges of ability", achievement, and the symbols of consumption that only success at work can buy' (Crawford 1985:78).

In the Wilcannia labour context, non-Aboriginal people hold most of the better-paid and more permanent positions. Therefore, Aboriginal experience of who whitefellas are—that is, job-holders and town service providers—meets the self-perception of the white job-holder. In other words, white people *are* nurses, police, managers and administration/office workers; black people, for the most part, *are not*. Of the few Aboriginal people employed in Wilcannia, these include teacher's aides, health workers, a police liaison officer and a shifting handful of cultural site officers and trainee site officers with the National Parks and Wildlife Service (NPWS). Two positions administer the Community Development Employment Projects (CDEP) program, one the Job Network office and one the Local Aboriginal Land Council.[4] The State Aboriginal Land Council, which purchased Weinteriga sheep station outside town also has an Aboriginal manager. These account for approximately 16 positions. During school holidays and busy tourist times, there are also a few casual jobs for tour

---

4   The Community Development Employment Projects (CDEP) program is a government initiative. Until changes introduced in 2008 that saw its reach reduced, the CDEP sought to generate sustainable employment opportunities for Aboriginal people. Known colloquially as 'work for the dole', the program requires people to work, on average, two to three days a week and receive 'top-ups' to their welfare payments. In 2004, 42 people were registered to work with the CDEP in Wilcannia.

guides at Mutawintji National Park. These, and the 16 positions mentioned, are all Aboriginal designated jobs. In terms of mainstream positions, during 2005, Aboriginal men held six out of eight jobs on the outdoor staff for the Central Darling Shire Council (CDSC General Manager, September 2005).[5] The two motels each employed Aboriginal women as casual room cleaners; the golf club employed two women part-time behind the bar; one woman worked casually at the local food store; one woman worked part-time as a lifeguard/caretaker at the shire-run swimming pool; and two white local builders each employed two particular Aboriginal men on a fairly regular basis as general labourers. The experience that Aboriginal people form the majority of the population, yet hold a fraction of the mainstream and more skilled jobs, elicits and further ingrains cultural differences; these are a source of much ill feeling as well as misunderstanding between Aboriginal and non-Aboriginal people in Wilcannia.

When a white policeman comes to work in town and his wife is appointed as a shire clerk; when a local white farmer whose farm is suffering a downturn, and who is known by most Aboriginal people in town as a bigot, is appointed as a 'Cultural Sites Supervisor' over Aboriginal workers, when his wife is appointed as a clerk at the shire; when a new-to-town white is appointed as the town's Community Development Facilitator and subsequently appoints his wife as a 'mentor' for Aboriginal people paid at consultancy rates; when these things happen, Aboriginal people note and remark on them: 'Why don't our own people get these jobs?' There is little awareness of the training and skills required for certain jobs, and the allocation of jobs to whites is not rationalised in these terms. It is seen as giving a preference to whites, which is undoubtedly sometimes the case. The reasons for this preferencing, however, which are much more complex, are reduced to consolidating the Aboriginal experience of who fills these kinds of jobs and why.

It might be argued that if few Aboriginal people are employed (in what is overall a relatively small pool of available jobs) then identification with an occupation is not possible or is, at best, a limited option. By looking historically to a time in Wilcannia when employment was, relatively speaking, quite readily available (cf. John White, this volume) and in comparing it with the uptake of contemporary available employment in Wilcannia, a sense of the place accorded to work as a part of life can be more fully expressed. Before the 1960s, many Aboriginal men in Wilcannia were employed within the pastoral industry. From the late 1960s, the pastoral industry declined across the far west and indeed the nation (Beckett 1958). There remains for those local Aboriginal people aged from their forties, however, a strong verbally expressed connection between identity and jobs held in the past. Older people said things such as, 'I was a ringer' (a

---

5   Outdoor staffers are those who, as the title suggests, work outdoors in mostly general labouring positions. For Central Darling Shire Council (CDSC), there are no Aboriginal workers among the 16 'indoor staff'.

stockman) or 'I was a concreter with the DMR' (Department of Main Roads), when talking about their past.[6] These kinds of statements were not responses to questions or discussions about work; they were an unsolicited part of everyday talk as people walked around town with me pointing out such things as gutters, concrete culverts and tarred roads that they had helped to construct. In the case of Wilcannia, 'things' such as concrete culverts invoke a sense of place as they also reinforce relatedness. When telling stories such as this, people indicate who was present, who the people were in relation to themselves and significant others, where these people are now, if they have 'passed away', who did what on the job and some of the laughs and incidents they shared.

They are stories about people, place and activities, more than work-related stories. They involve a sharing and a reliving of experience, which reinforce and/or remind the self and others of important aspects of social relations (cf. Austin-Broos 2006 in relation to the Arrernte of Central Australia). I contend, however, that, even though jobs in the pastoral industry were a source of pride, the extent to which a sense of self—cultural identity proper—was, and is, currently linked to being in employment or a particular occupation remains limited. Beckett's work in the 1950s and my own work in Wilcannia from 2002 suggest that then, as now, being employed (or more specifically, being regularly employed) as a particular way of looking at life is, for most, at once peripheral to, irrelevant to and resistant to the 'business' at hand—that is, the 'business' of being Aboriginal (cf. Peterson 2005). Beckett writes of the far west in 1958 that

> even when regular jobs are to be found in the locality, many aborigines [sic]—particularly those from Murrin Bridge and Wilcannia—find the regular working week irksome…Aboriginal workers go home for a weekend and fail to return until Tuesday or Wednesday—or not at all! A family illness, the hangover from a drinking spree or some petty distraction has kept them back. (Beckett 1958:194–5)

This appears to suggest a 'take it or leave it' attitude to employment as well as a prioritisation of other things. Beckett (1958:195) goes on to state, 'Men will say "I don't want to work all the time like some people do". Leisure is something for which they are ready to forego the money they could otherwise be earning.' MacDonald (2004:12; cf. Eades 1994:99) also asserts that financial considerations are not a priority and 'Aboriginal understandings of relatedness often take precedence over working for the sake of work or for the pay packet'. The situation in the 1950s that Beckett (2005:114) describes whereby Aboriginal people made little effort to go out and find work, and where 'some quite literally wait for it to come to them', is one that resonates in Wilcannia today. This is

---

6 The Department of Main Roads employed Aboriginal people as labourers until it moved its operations to Broken Hill in 1987.

despite a strong Aboriginal rhetoric that having a job is the answer to the social ills, including alcohol abuse and alcohol-related violence. What is done in terms of the low uptake of available jobs seems to contradict this. The taking up or rejection of employment is, however, no simple equation; jobs and job prospects appear at face value to be available, yet many factors work against the taking up of these opportunities.

If one feels that the only jobs available to you are the 'shit jobs' that Aboriginal people say whitefellas would not take, the tendency to 'knock them back' is understandable. Why strive for the shitty jobs of the white working class?[7] High unemployment and the offer of what are perceived to be lesser-valued, lesser-paid, often short-term government-funded jobs and work programs that do not lead to employment encourage neither a strong work ethic nor any sense of personal worth in relation to mainstream regular 'work'.[8] Good jobs are seen to be the domain of the whites or those who are *like* whites. Here, we enter the territory of the 'coconut': those Aboriginal people who are said to be black on the outside and white on the inside—people who are charged with keeping 'a white house'; people who, 'don't sit down with us', 'who don't share', who 'big note' themselves and whose patterns of work, consumption and communication leave them open to the charge that they are not Aboriginal enough. A Koori from Sydney who was teaching a part-time Technical and Further Education (TAFE) art course for Aboriginal people in a neighbouring town said that the students had taken exception to his manner. Although Aboriginal, he was seen to be acting like a 'white boss'. He told me that the people in the art course responded to him by calling him 'a fucken coconut'. He said he took out his payslip and showed it to the class, saying: 'See this, this is what I take home every week, I'll be a fucken banana if it means I take this home.' In saying this, he was telling the class that it did not matter what names the class called him, in the end he took home a sizeable pay packet, which we can read as something he valued and which allowed him to live the way he wanted to live. Yet, this is precisely part of what the class was criticising. There was a clear difference in values operating, which indirectly inverted the meanings of the class/teacher interaction. By demonstrating his worth and values in his own terms, the teacher for his part thought that he had 'got one up' on the people calling him a coconut. For those naming him a coconut, however, his actions simply confirmed the label.

Whereas coconut status and behaviour are generally agreed on and some people never seem to be free of the title, it is not a fixed title or status. One may shift

---

7   While fruit picking used to be a popular means of earning income without a constancy of work, this form of work has fallen out of favour with younger people. They say the work is too hard and that there is little financial recompense. It is seen as a lesser job (cf. White, this volume).

8   The 'counter-culture' of the 1960s, when Timothy Leary exhorted people to 'tune in, turn on and drop out', is one example of the rejection of the Protestant work ethic and its values by many young (and not so young) non-Aboriginal people.

in and out of the status as behaviour is modified and/or a situation is perceived. Although having a job is never specified as being the cause of coconut status, and not all who hold jobs are named coconuts, it is often the prerequisite of having a job, and therefore access to certain resources, which enables coconut behaviour and naming.

The much promulgated pan-Aboriginal trope of caring and sharing is implicated here in ways that have become increasingly complex as a changing cultural dynamic has led to unequal access to social, political and cultural resources and authority. This in turn has seen a great deal of ambivalence and ambiguity in what it means to be a culturally successful and productive blackfella in Wilcannia today. Systems of sharing that used to operate on the basis of more basic needs are being reworked as greater access to, and desires for, material goods has entered the informal economy, and as networks increase in number and across areas. This situation of change has destabilised some longer-standing hierarchies and more understood patterns of sharing (cf. Peterson 1993).

While the threat of social ostracism is ever present for those who do not participate in the sharing economy (Beckett 2005:108), a small but increasing number of people are nevertheless choosing this position with varying degrees of reticence or assertion. Some are feeling torn in ways that have little precedent as people negotiate their chosen path of higher education, a more nuclear-style family and the accumulation of the material that generally requires leaving town, and often means cutting certain kin ties and perceived obligations. These forms of intra-cultural social and economic change have created a realm of much intra-cultural misunderstanding, anger and confusion. The contradictions and impossibilities are, here, at times a double bind and a double burden.

Asserting blackness often means positioning oneself against whiteness and against white ways of working and being, by means of particular identificatory practices, relations and alliances. Such attitudes and practices can, however, entail a continuation of subjection in certain terms—a self-damnation of sorts (Willis 1972). For some, and at some level, the recognition of this situation causes degrees of ambivalence, bitterness, anger and envy, as well as laughter and irony. Such responses may or may not be subject to any cognised examination and are directed towards both white and black. Yet, for those who resist this subjection, regular employment and associated choices have other effects and connotations. Intra-cultural divisions and attitudes towards employment and those employed are indicative of an increasing reflexivity and raised consciousness about differing social and economic expectations and positions. Through the trope of caring and sharing differing expectations, desires and actions feed into a complex system that shapes ideas and practices relating to kinship and relatedness, social obligation, personhood, morality, and goods and services (cf. MacDonald 2003, 2004; Schwab 1995:3). Despite increasing social divisions in relation to jobs and material goods, one cannot, I believe, speak of classes in the Marxist sense of a relationship to the capitalist division of labour—nor are Aboriginal people asserting such a class position. Certainly, while most unemployed and low-paid employees are aware of differences between themselves and those with better-paid jobs and higher living conditions, there is little in the sense of a working-class consciousness whereby people are aware of their 'interests and of their predicaments as a class' (Thompson 1980:781).[9]

Most Aboriginal people in Wilcannia have a different subjectivity altogether in relation to mainstream employment—not harnessed, not subject to self-surveillance and not defined in terms of work and leisure. Subjectivity in Wilcannia is connected (if not always in practice, then ideologically) to different domains such as kinship and the pan-Aboriginal trope of 'caring and sharing', which have their own economic and moral values. For many Aboriginal people, work and its rewards sit uneasily with the upholding of a distinct identity. They recognise that regular employment affords some of the material things that many would like to have, but are not prepared to forfeit other culturally perceived and culturally attributed values, social obligations and desires (as well as the time to fulfil these). Family illness, a hangover from 'a big night on the drink', Nana's need to do some shopping, the arrival of family or friends from out of town or an unexpected occurrence of interest continue to be the causes of much non-attendance at 'work'. I was talking one day to an Aboriginal woman about my two sisters in Scotland and she told me about her two sisters who live in South Australia and Sydney. She said that one of her sisters and her immediate family visit Wilcannia two or three times a year and stay for two or three weeks. She said that during these visits she did not go to her work as a teacher's aide at the local school. This woman was highlighting to me the *importance* of family, not the *unimportance* of work. Non-attendance at work by virtue of these kinds of reasons is, for whites, however, a sign of irresponsibility, if not laziness.

Some Aboriginal people oppose and resist the identifying link of whiteness and work more directly. A white workplace supervisor who works for an Aboriginal housing service told me about an incident that took place between himself and one of four Aboriginal workers fixing up a house. According to the supervisor, the workers had arrived late and then proceeded to make a cup of tea and have a smoke and a yarn. The supervisor indicated that the work being done was spasmodic and often delayed while the workers talked with people they knew

9   These are big issues and cannot be explicated fully here. My current research is exploring the notion of social placement, class and class consciousness for Aboriginal people in a comparative study across Moree, Kemspey, Glebe, Wilcannia and Alice Springs. During the 1940s, Reay and Sittlington (1948) asserted an argument for class and status among 'mixed-blood' Aborigines in Moree. They divided the town into four classes—two highest and two lowest—which were, in part, designated in terms of dwelling types and location. My early research impressions show distinct differences in what could be termed class awareness between Wilcannia and more regional centres where greater work opportunities exist, such as Moree and Kemspey.

passing by. After lunch, one of the Aboriginal workers said that he was leaving. The supervisor asked him where he was going and the man replied that he had a doctor's appointment. The supervisor then asked him why he had made the appointment on a day he knew people had been organised to come together in order to complete the job. The supervisor told the worker that his presence was required for the job to be completed that day. According to the supervisor, the worker 'went off' at him, saying he had to look after his health and that he had diabetes. The supervisor said that he did not mean that the man should not to go to the doctor, but that it might be better if he could plan his visits around work. The worker asked the supervisor if he wanted him 'to work like a white cunt'. When the supervisor asked him what he meant, he replied, '24 hours a day'. Inhering within this dialogue is an assertion of differentiation, as well as a mutual assertion of 'rights', with inter-cultural overtones. In voicing his rights to good health, and in not wanting to work 24 hours a day, the man is asserting his difference from whites as well as his perceived rights as a worker. The supervisor, on the other hand, is asserting what he sees as his 'right' to expect a worker to account for time considered to be work time, *paid* time, time *owned* by the employer. The cultural characteristics of attitudes to work here are, in Cowlishaw's (2004:118) words, 'a kind of companion to racial identity'.

It is not unreasonable to say, echoing Weber (1976:182), that for most people in mainstream society, 'the idea of duty in one's calling prowls about in our lives like the ghost of dead religious beliefs'. For the dominant culture, paid work continues to be a moral obligation and St Paul's dictum that 'he who will not work shall not eat' still resonates, albeit in less specifically religious terms. Although some whites also reject this view, it remains a view of 'moral agency vested in white identity' (Cowlishaw 2004:100). When white people in Wilcannia talk about 'lazy black bastards', this statement is not unconnected to the fact that whites perceive most Aboriginal people to be doing quite well by virtue of unemployment benefits and other perceived government 'hand-outs'. They eat, but 'they don't fucken work'. There is a sense of outrage and not a little jealousy.

The majority of Aboriginal people in Wilcannia are unemployed and are seen by whites to have no desire to work in the way that the majority of employed whites do. Aboriginal people have a way of living and a perceived attitude to 'work' that the majority of whites condemn. The fact that Aboriginal people say that they do not want to work 'like those white cunts' is an assault on whitefellas' way of life and their moral values. Not only do whitefellas consider that it is 'our taxes' paying for the blackfella to 'sit on his black arse', but welfare payments are seen to support a way of life that encourages what is seen as a lack of self-discipline and social responsibility.[10]

Conclusion

In small towns such as Wilcannia there is a justification of white moral values that finds its power and persuasiveness through discourse that gives force to the 'alleged 'transgressions by Aborigines of mainstream social patterns' (Morris 1997:166). It is *not* work in Western definitions to 'look after country', 'go huntin' an' get the old people some wild meat', to take Nana shopping, to nurse children, look after sick family or stay with family or friends who have come to visit rather than attend work. For many Wilcannia Aboriginal people, hunting, fishing and spending the day along the riverbank with kin and friends are as, Povinelli (1993:26) remarks (in the case of the Belyuen mob), 'a form of production in the fullest cultural and economic sense of this term, generating a range of sociocultural meanings'. To say that Aboriginal people do not consider regular work a social responsibility is to miss the importance and nature of what 'work' is.

The overall point to be made is that for most Aboriginal people in Wilcannia, you are who you are, not by virtue of what you have 'become' in any economic, professional or educational sense. In a particular sense, 'who you are' is not a becoming; it is established at birth. A person does not become somebody, a person already has become, is somebody by virtue of being born into a family: 'People enjoy the complete acceptance of belonging by birth and of right' (Keen 1994:13). The person is a Hunter girl or a Bugmy boy, or one of the Bates, Clarks, Johnsons, Kings, Lawsons and Whymans, and in so being is inextricably linked to all others within these wider family networks. This sense of self, for most, is not determined by engagement in the capitalist division of labour; indeed, the greater the engagement in the capitalist economy, the more problematic and fraught a sense of self and of belonging can become.

---

10   Although not framed in quite the same way, some Aboriginal people (including leader Noel Pearson) also express concern about the detrimental effects of welfare dependency, which has killed 'the will to work' (Pearson 2000).

Bibliography

Austin-Broos, D. 2003, 'Places, practices, and things: the articulation of Arrernte kinship with welfare and work', *American Ethnologist*, vol. 30, pp. 118–35.

Austin-Broos, D. 2006, '"Working for" and "working" among Western Arrernte in Central Australia', *Oceania*, vol. 76, no. 1, pp. 1–15.

Austin Broos, D. 2009, *Arrernte Present, Arrernte Past: Invasion, violence and imagination in Indigenous Central Australia*, University of Chicago Press, Ill.

Beckett, J. 1958, A study of a mixed-blood Aboriginal minority in the pastoral west of New South Wales, Unpublished Master's thesis, University of Sydney, NSW.

Beckett, J. 2005 [1958], *A study of Aborigines in the pastoral west of New South Wales*, Oceania Monograph 55, University of Sydney, NSW.

Cowlishaw, G. 2004, *Blackfellas, Whitefellas and the Hidden Injuries of Race*, Blackwell Publishing, Malden, Vic.

Crawford, R. 1985, 'A cultural account of "health": control, release, and the social body', in J. McKinlay (ed.), *Issues in the Political Economy of Health Care*, Tavistock Publications, New York.

Eades, D. 1994, 'They don't speak an Aboriginal language, or do they?', in I. Keen (ed.), *Being Black: Aboriginal cultures in settled Australia*, Aboriginal Studies Press, Canberra, pp. 97–116.

Keen, I. 1994, 'Introduction', in I. Keen (ed.), *Being Black: Aboriginal cultures in settled Australia*, Aboriginal Studies Press, Canberra.

MacDonald, G. n.d., A man's wage for a man's work: the dynamics of equality and respect in the lives of Aboriginal working men, Unpublished Paper presented to The Individual in Labour History Conference, University of Sydney, November 2003.

MacDonald, G. 2003, Sustaining Wiradjuri meanings in a changing world of work, Unpublished paper presented to the Centre for Aboriginal Economic Policy Research (CAEPR) seminar, The Australian National University, Canberra, November 2003.

MacDonald, G. 2004, *Two Steps Forward, Three Steps Back: A Wiradjuri land rights journey—letters to the Wiradjuri Regional Aboriginal Land Council on its 20th anniversary, 1983–2003*, LhR Press, Canada Bay, NSW.

Morris, B. 1997, 'Racism, egalitarianism and Aborigines', in B. Morris and G. Cowlishaw (eds), *Race Matters*, Aboriginal Studies Press, Canberra.

Pearson, N. 2000, *Our Right to Take Responsibility*, Pearson and Associates, Cairns, Qld.

Peterson, N. 1993, 'Demand sharing: reciprocity and the pressure for generosity among foragers', *American Anthropologist*, vol. 95, pp. 860–74.

Peterson, N. 2005, 'What can the pre-colonial and frontier economies tells us about engagement with the real economy? Indigenous life projects and the conditions of development', in D. Austin-Broos and G. MacDonald (eds), *Culture, Economy and Governance in Aboriginal Australia*, [Published workshop proceedings, University of Sydney, 30 November – 1 December 2004], University of Sydney Press, NSW.

Povinelli, E. 1993, *Labor's Lot: The power, history, and culture of Aboriginal action*, University of Chicago Press, Ill.

Reay, M. and Sittlington, G. 1948, 'Class and status in a mixed-blood community (Moree, NSW)', *Oceania*, vol. 18, p. 3.

Sansom, B. 1988, 'The past is a doctrine of person', in J. R. Beckett (ed.), *Past and Present*, Aboriginal Studies Press, Canberra, pp. 147–61.

Schwab, R. G. 1995, *The calculus of reciprocity: principles and implications of Aboriginal sharing*, CAEPR Discussion Paper, no. 100, Centre for Aboriginal Economic Policy Research, The Australian National University, Canberra.

Thompson, E. P. 1980, *The Making of the English Working Class*, Victor Gollancz, London.

Weber, M. 1976, *The Protestant Ethic and the Spirit of Capitalism*, Allen & Unwin, London.

Willis, P. 1972, *The motorbike within a subcultural group*, Working Papers in Cultural Studies 2.

Willis, P. 1977, *Learning to Labour: How working class kids get working class jobs*, Saxon House, Farnborough, UK.

9. Sustainable Aboriginal livelihoods and the Pilbara mining boom

SARAH HOLCOMBE

Introduction[1]

Recently referred to as 'recreational lifestyles' (Johns 2009:22), the various socioeconomic choices that some Aboriginal people make, in remote areas especially, are often contrasted with how these same people should be operating in the 'real economy'. There is considerable debate about the value of the 'real economy' as a term, given that neo-liberalism tends to be the reference point (Altman 2009; Pholi et al. 2009). Nevertheless, if we think in terms of the 'mainstream'—as this term tends to be understood—the mining industry can readily be typified as the 'real' economy. Pilbara Iron, a business arm of Rio Tinto, has had mixed success in engaging Aboriginal people in this economy. Through a range of strategies, however, such as pre-employment programs, 11 per cent of their workforce is now Aboriginal (Rio Tinto 2007:90), though not necessarily all are local native titleholders from the region of the mine.[2] The focus in this chapter is on the Pilbara Iron Ore operations generally and the activities of Gumala Aboriginal Corporation (Gumala) more specifically.

Gumala was set up in 1998 as one of four structures to manage the *Yandicoogina Land Use Agreement* (*YLUA*). As the Aboriginal organisation based at Tom Price, Gumala was developed to act as the voice of the agreement's beneficiaries in developing, researching and preparing proposals for investments and community projects for submission to Gumala Investments Proprietary Limited

---

1   In the earlier stages of drafting this chapter, I was pursuing the path of co-authorship with Don Gordon, who was at that time Gumala Project's Coordinator. He very helpfully provided some up-to-date information about the 'new generation' Gumala and details of research they were undertaking. He left the employ of Gumala in July 2009, however, so the co-authorship plans were necessarily terminated. Along with Gordon, I also acknowledge the discussions held with the then new CEO, Steve Mav. Although one of the aims of this chapter is for it to be of value to Gumala, the views and opinions expressed remain the responsibility of the author.

2   Disaggregating this 11 per cent figure for Aboriginal employment into Aboriginal language affiliation and usual residence would be a very useful exercise.

(GIPL). Apart from managing and maintaining the capital base of the General Foundation, GIPL considers Gumala project-funding requests. Gumala is the sole shareholder of GIPL as trustee, while GIPL has ultimate decision-making power in all matters relating to the foundation. As an independent body, GIPL consists of six members: three non-Aboriginal experts and three Aboriginal beneficiary representatives. The annual meetings are held in Perth. Gumala also operates its own business arm, Gumala Enterprises Proprietary Limited (GEPL). This business arm includes Gumala contracting, ESS Gumala (a hospitality venture) and Gumala tourism, which operates the Karijini Eco-Retreat. Gumala also operates a range of community development programs and business start-ups, some of which operate through their recently established Member Services Unit. Gumala also has contractual responsibilities to ensure that heritage clearances are undertaken within the area of the *YLUA* with a unit to expedite such clearances. They now have more than 750 beneficiaries of the agreement, though they began with less than 350.

In a recent paper (Holcombe 2009), I explored the issue of entrepreneurialism and the possibilities and limitations the *YLUA* offered for opportunities for individuals. The key question considered was 'how individuals could benefit', especially given the pervasive paradigm of 'community' that structured the agreement's 'community benefit package'. In that paper, I touch on the redevelopment of Gumala as a new-generation organisation that had been restructured and refocused. This was principally as a result of the unsuccessful liquidation attempt of GIPL by Gumala in 2007 and the subsequent 'fallout' from this, which included the loss of senior staff (see Holcombe 2009). That paper also briefly touched on the issue of mine closure, and in this chapter I give further consideration to the post-agreement and post-mine regional economy and the implications this has for Gumala. As noted by Scambary (2007), Gumala 'has become both a focus for the attainment of mainstream economic development in the form of business development *and* also the attainment of aspirations associated with customary livelihood pursuits' (p. 167, emphasis added).

In 2004–05, Taylor and Scambary (2005) were commissioned by Rio Tinto to profile outcomes of regional participation by Aboriginal people in the Pilbara mining industry. They note that previous research elsewhere in remote Australia had indicated that, despite major agreements,

> for a complex set of reasons, Indigenous economic status had changed little in recent decades—dependence on government remains high and the relative economic status of Indigenous peoples residing adjacent to major long-life mines is similar to that of Indigenous people elsewhere in regional and remote Australia. (Taylor and Scambary 2005:1)

The Taylor and Scambary monograph indicates that this pattern has continued in the Pilbara region. Despite massive mineral development and the signing of significant agreements such as the *YLUA*, which have been operating for more than 10 years, there is little evidence that the majority of members are better off than their non-member neighbours (Taylor and Scambary 2005:1). In light of these findings, Gumala has a strong interest in developing initiatives that look to ensuring that existing initiatives and any new ones enhance the possibility of their members benefiting from the *YLUA*. Thus, they have an investment in considering ways to improve services to their beneficiaries. To this end, a recent survey by Gumala—although not directly about employment, but rather about members' housing needs—suggests that Aboriginal employment rates in the Pilbara are significantly higher than Taylor and Scambary (2005) found.

While survey respondents were not asked about their employment directly, they were asked what their main source of income was and what their secondary source was—out of a choice of wages, Centrelink payments, self-employed, sitting fees or heritage surveys, and home duties or none. More than one-third indicated that wages was their main income and about half said Centrelink. Gumala notes (Gordon, Personal communication, 1 June 2009) that as this included people who would not be regarded as being in the workforce (for example, pensioners and mothers caring for young children), it could be that more than half the members who could be regarded as available for work are in fact in the workforce. Gumala notes, however, that this estimate is still tentative as the analysis is not yet completed and respondents were not asked specific questions such as 'Who is your employer?' and 'How long have you been working there?' These questions might be the focus of a future survey.

Although this potentially higher rate of employment is indeed encouraging and suggests that more Gumala members are in mainstream employment than previously recorded, the Gumala organisation notes that it is still significantly less than the general population. An avenue considered in this chapter for developing new employment initiatives is the possibilities that the sustainable livelihoods approach could offer Gumala, and by extension other Aboriginal organisations set up to manage land-use agreements. In Altman's (2009:14) view, the attraction of exploring such alternative approaches to economic development seems 'highly appropriate at this moment in Australia's history, when neoliberal economic rationalism and globalism are under challenge'.

Situating the sustainable livelihoods approach in wider policy

I am drawn to exploring the sustainable livelihoods approach, as it offers a suite of systematic engagement tools in an approach that develops social as well as economic sustainability. The sustainable livelihoods approach as used internationally in rural development (Carney 2002; Scoones 1998) has been little applied to development in remote Australia, although this is changing (see Davies et al. 2008; Fisher 2002a). This approach has been central in the international effort of poverty reduction and environmental management in countries throughout Africa, Asia and Latin America, although it has its critics (Brocklesby and Fisher 2003). I will provide some detail about the framework in the next section. Taking a lead from Davies et al. (2008:55), I will consider its potential value in 'illuminating possibilities for new livelihood systems... and local strategies that are adaptive and resilient to the ongoing risks and vulnerabilities faced by desert Aboriginal people and the regions where they live'. The power of this approach to community development lies in its flexibility of application and its people-centred nature, as driven by a responsive and participatory paradigm.

The concept of 'development' is itself, however, a major challenge to policymakers in Australia and has not been engaged with as a policy approach to working with Indigenous Australians (see Holcombe 2006a, 2006b). If one types 'development Australian government' into the Google search engine, the international AusAID program will top the list. The development concept in Australia is only loosely applied to specific programs (which have very little do with development) such as the Community Development Employment Projects (CDEP) program (see Langton 2002). Indeed, Dodson (2009) recently observed that although the Australian Government has received a tick for implementing the Paris Declaration on its international aid effectiveness, the ethos endorsed by this declaration on 'partnerships and participation' is not transferred to Indigenous policy development in Australia.

Rather than delving into the legacy of policy approaches to Aboriginal affairs (see, for instance, Altman and Rowse 2005; Dillon and Westbury 2007; Chapter 1, this volume), it might be useful to consider instead the potential value of the livelihood approach to shift this ground and unsettle this legacy. Fisher, who introduced the sustainable livelihoods approach to Australia, 'argued that there was little understanding among support agencies of the aspirations of remote Aboriginal people, and very little attention to sustainability when agencies make investment decisions affecting remote communities' (cited in Davies et al. 2008:56). Further, Fisher 'proposed that applying a sustainable livelihoods approach in partnership with remote communities would greatly improve understanding of the complex factors that impact on settlement viability, bring greater rigour to investment decisions and promote community members' capacity to express and work towards outcomes they are seeking' (cited in Davies et al. 2008:56).

In light of this, it is useful to reflect on Taylor and Scambary's Pilbara baseline profile, as they observed that:

> Policy development involving Indigenous populations has typically been reactive to needs as they become revealed (e.g. in terms of post-facto responses to housing shortages or employment needs), as opposed to being proactive in seeking to anticipate and plan for expected requirements. However, being proactive requires a measure of future requirements for infrastructure, programs and services—a practise that is standard procedure for mainstream regional planning, and not least for the mining industry business units. However, it is something that is rarely achieved, or even attempted for Indigenous communities. (Taylor and Scambary 2005:18)

Similarly, in a recent paper (principally a literature review) on the social dimensions of mining in Australia, Solomon et al. (2008) outline a number of 'research and practise gaps'. One of these is 'community and regional development...such as knowledge of specific regional development such as the impact on the resources boom on other activities in regions, on social cohesion, on infrastructure and the long-term legacy of mining activities and closure' (Solomon ct al 2008:146).

As a locally based Aboriginal organisation operating regionally, Gumala is potentially in an ideal position to address these gaps and be reflective of its role in addressing the needs of regional development. Implementing and utilising elements of the livelihoods framework could be a means to do this. Gumala already operates responsively through a participatory paradigm and it has recently developed a member's services unit and a women's advocacy unit. Like any Indigenous organisation, however, it has resource constraints and a constituency that is highly mobile and dispersed, and highly politicised. There are some members of the Gumala constituent beneficiary group (750 plus) who could usefully be re-enfranchised by the collaborative methods the sustainable livelihoods approach advocates. Underlying the value of this approach is the recognition that the agreement offers a range of opportunities that Gumala is becoming increasingly responsive to, in its recognition that for its beneficiaries it is not an either/or situation of 'culture or capitalism'. Before discussing this issue in more detail, however, it seems important to briefly overview the recent regional economic history of the Pilbara to provide some background context.

As examined elsewhere (Edmunds 1989; Holcombe 2006b), mining tenements in the Pilbara region were taken up by large companies from the 1960s, beginning with Mt Tom Price, and escalating to 11 major open-cut iron-ore mines in the Hamersley Ranges region alone.[3] Local Aboriginal people were not party to this development and any social development was ceded to economic development as the state government took a back seat to the minerals industry.[4] In the industry development of closed towns for workers (such as Tom Price), Aboriginal people as non-workers were marginalised. Many had already moved away to the coast— to Onslow, Roebourne and Port Hedland—after the 1967 referendum that led to the demand for children's schooling. Work in the pastoral industry had also dried up for a range of reasons, such as the granting of equal pay and increased mechanisation (Brehaut and Vitenbergs 2001). Indeed, although local Aboriginal people had been active in alluvial mining in the region for many years (McLeod 1984; Wilson 1961) or had worked in the pastoral industry, such work readiness was not recognised by the incoming industry, although there were exceptions (Peter Stevens in Olive 1997:81). Likewise, a generation of stockwork expertise was never established, as Aboriginal people were moved off the stations from the late 1960s (Brehaut and Vitenbergs 2001; Olive 1997). This same generation was also the first to systematically receive formalised schooling (see Smith 2002). Today, the Indigenous population of this region thus exhibits many of the traits of the Third World in the First (Young 1995).

The sustainable livelihoods approach

The sustainable livelihoods approach has only recently gained currency in Australia, although it has been credibly used as a tool in development programs in relation to poverty alleviation internationally since the late 1980s. This approach dates back to the work of Robert Chambers (1987) in the shift away from a technology-centred interventionist approach to a people-centred approach. It incorporates much of what is considered 'best practice' in development when working with marginalised groups. A core strength of the approach is that it focuses on the existing capabilities and strengths of individuals, families and households, rather than their needs and deficits. By analysing these strengths— partly through the framework of an 'asset pentagon'—those that have the potential to reduce poverty are revealed. This pentagon, as a tool, comprises the five forms of capital: human, social, natural, physical and financial (Figure 9.1). This approach understands the conventional economic focus on market

---

3   These are: Hope Downs, Area C, Yandicoogina (RTIO), BHP Yandi, Channar, Eastern Ranges, Paraburdoo, Tom Price, Marandoo, Brockman and Pannawonica.
4   Interestingly, however, a significant number of Torres Strait Islanders moved to the Pilbara to work establishing mining infrastructure, such as the railway (see the 2006 documentary film *Island Fettlers* at <http://australianscreen.com.au/titles/island-fettlers/>).

production, salaried employment and cash income as the key elements of wellbeing as ethnocentric, reductionist and inadequate to account for the ways in which people really make a living (Chambers and Conway 1992). Rather, the approach recognises the often transient, dispersed and diverse nature of such activities when pursued by marginalised people and the importance of reflecting local conditions, priorities and social structures in approaches to development.

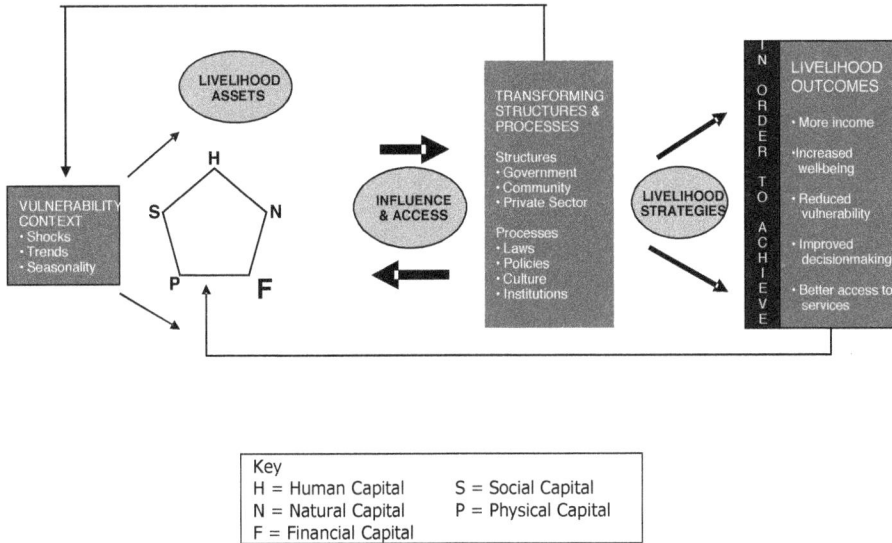

Figure 9.1 Sustainable livelihoods framework

From Davies et al. (2008:57)

The asset pentagon as a tool could be accused of being over-simplified and too predictable for Aboriginal people, and one could also ask where culture fits in. In remote regions far from market economies, such as most settlements in Central Australia and Arnhem Land, the predominance of assets tends to fall towards social and natural capital, with typical deficits in human, financial and physical capital. Certainly, this was the case in research using this framework in the Central Australian community of Engawala, with participants making the subjective assessment that their natural and social capital stocks were more significant than the other three (Moran et al. 2007:54). In mining-intense regions such as the Pilbara, however, the asset pentagon is likely to take quite a different shape. Without having undertaken field research specifically using this framework in the Pilbara, it seems likely to reveal a far more diverse range of assets, so that such an exercise would reveal more than it elides in the Pilbara region. Nevertheless, I agree with Hinselwood (2003:243) that we should show a 'staunch lack of respect for rigid diagrams' as these can be charged with 'enticing people into simplicity and rigidity'. If used flexibly, however, the framework, including the asset pentagon, can be an effective tool for organising and analysing ideas.

A brief overview of the preliminary findings from research in the Anmatyerr region (Ti Tree) of Central Australia is useful here, as it could offer some early insight into the potential value of utilising the framework. The research by Measham et al. (cited in Davies et al. 2008) suggested that social capital was the most important asset engaged when local Aboriginal people made decisions about livelihood strategies. The key example of this was that 'many Aboriginal people reported that they began to work in a particular job, or undertook particular activities in the care of land or people, because they were nominated or "picked" by someone else as the person who should do that job' (Davies et al. 2008:60). The implications of this form of job-placement facilitation suggests that a systematic focus on building intra-Aboriginal networks and linkages, as well as focusing on engaging mentors, could be a valuable means of ensuring that available job vacancies are filled.

The sustainable livelihoods framework also promotes a systems perspective by drawing attention to the dynamic nature of people's interactions with government policy and the range of institutions that enable or constrain decisions. It can be understood as a holistic tool in its multi-factoral approach as this attempts to also locate the 'influence' that people have on institutions and the relations of power between them. In this schema, Gumala is understood as an institution that has the power to influence people's assets and strategise outcomes.

As a tool for improving community development practice, the approach was introduced to Australia by Fisher (2002a) through the Centre for Appropriate Technology (CAT) in the Central Australian office in Alice Springs. More recently, it has been taken up by researchers at the Desert Knowledge Cooperative Research Centre (CRC)—notably those working in the Livelihoods in Land project (led by Davies), which aims to 'examine the opportunities for Aboriginal people living in remote locations to manage natural and cultural assets on behalf of Australians and create a livelihood around this activity' (*Livelihoods in Land Fact Sheet* 89, Core Project 1).[5]

The sustainable livelihood approach, however, is not directly transferable to Australia for a range of reasons outlined by Fisher (2002a). He lists the characteristics that distinguish Australia from the rural communities for which the approach was originally developed in Africa, and so on. The Australian differences include: the remoteness of many communities from main service

---

5 See the web sites: <http://www.desertknowledgecrc.com.au/research/livelihoods.html> and <http:// www.desertknowledgecrc.com.au/http//www-desertknowledgecrc-com-au/publications/factsheets/DKCRC_ FS.Livelihoods%20inLand.web.pdf>

centres and markets; the access of most communities to welfare support or CDEP; the strong connection that Aboriginal people feel to the land; their marginal status within a prosperous liberal economy; and their tradition and culture of hunting and gathering as opposed to sedentary production or enterprise (Fisher 2002b). Likewise, Australia is a 'First World' economy that has allocated the status 'unemployed' to Aboriginal people and they might be marginal to the prosperous liberal economy, but importantly they are a part of it.

Nevertheless, much of the value of the framework lies in its flexibility, its bottom-up methodology and the fact that the approach can be used as a research heuristic, as has been done by Davies et al. (2008). The approach is used in their desert research 'as the basis for systems modelling, as a tool for collaborative planning by families and communities, and for improving cross-cultural communication' (Davies et al. 2008:55). The value of the approach for this research chapter lies in its potential to assist the Gumala Aboriginal Corporation to consider a wider range of approaches to delivering benefits to its members. Gumala has an obvious interest in ensuring that its 750-plus beneficiaries under the *YLUA* do indeed benefit from membership and in exploring new and innovative ways to achieve this. Shifting the focus away from singular outcomes, defined purely by economic drivers, to multiple outcomes that include health and wellbeing, is a value of this approach.

In a previous paper (Holcombe 2009), I utilised the concept of 'community economies' (Gibson-Graham 2002) to give voice to alternative economies that Aboriginal people were attempting to develop—nascent as some of these were. These included bush products, eco and cultural tourism and small-scale pastoralism. Some of these same enterprises are of course still 'on the table' or have been further developed, such as tourism. It seems to me that the sustainable livelihoods approach goes beyond the community economies concept by providing an overarching framework and a language. For instance, the board of CAT adopted a sustainable livelihoods approach for the organisation as a whole. Using the framework as a community planning tool, they see it as a means of understanding the complexities of people's lives by incorporating key elements that have been overlooked by conventional planning, such as the importance of social networks and access to land (*Our Place*, 3/2002:16).[6] CAT defines a sustainable livelihood as 'the range of activities that support improved well-being through work, enterprise and trading and that can be maintained into the future' (*Our Place*, 3/2002:16).

An important principle of the sustainable livelihoods approach, according to CAT, is its emphasis on

---

6   *Our Place* is the CAT triannual magazine featuring articles produced by CAT about people and technology in remote communities. It is available online at <http://www.icat.org.au/default.asp?action=article&ID=3>

the strengths of people, rather than their needs. In particular it aims to achieve an analysis of those strengths which have the potential to reduce poverty. These include the ability of a social group to influence policy, their access to technologies or markets and the resources available to them. (*Our Place*, 3/2002:16)

Such an approach could work to extend the community-planning repertoire of Gumala to incorporate those beneficiaries who are not employed and who might have remained outside the orbit of engagement with the mining industry or the existing opportunities that Gumala has to offer. Thus, it is not inconsistent with Gumala and the foundation's charter as 'a public benevolent institution for the objects of the relief of poverty, sickness, suffering, distress, misfortune or destitution of the Traditional Owners, particularly those Traditional Owners in the Pilbara Region'. Likewise, this planning approach can operate in tandem with existing successful business-development programs. Working with such an approach is, however, an acknowledgment that a broader set of parameters is required to work effectively, in a long-term way, with a people who have a specific socio-demographic profile at significant variance to the mainstream (Taylor and Scambary 2005) and often very different cultural priorities. As Trigger observes:

> Sustainable economic development in Aboriginal communities involves a wide range of matters beyond the essential first steps of making available certain types of jobs, training and business enterprise opportunities. Both the inclinations of individuals to take up such opportunities and, when they do, the subsequent impacts on communities' socio-economic well being, are matters intimately connected to deeply enculturated dispositions and life-practises. (Trigger 2005:51)

'Deeply enculturated dispositions and life practices'

In his paper on mining projects in remote Australia, Trigger (2005) both problematises the 'culture concept' and details the implications these different dispositions have for Aboriginal engagement with the mining economy. He is careful not to elide 'culture' as the catch-all concept that is blamed for the lack of uptake of development 'opportunities' or engagement with the mainstream economy. This relationship between Aboriginal culture and economic development has been explored in detail by Peterson (2002) through what he has termed the 'domestic moral economy', building on his earlier work on 'demand sharing' (1993). Peterson notes that as 'with all societies, "sedimented dispositions" among Aboriginal people are only partly articulated in any conscious fashion—a point of some relevance to those carrying out "consultations" with regards to planning employment, training and related programs' (in Trigger 2005:51). It seems to me that the sustainable livelihoods approach can also enter here as a tool that attempts to articulate the impacts these different dispositions have on economic engagement through its participatory approach to planning.

It is pertinent here to revisit the four elements that Peterson proposes as constituting the 'domestic moral economy', as these impact on mainstream economic engagement (in Trigger 2005:51, paraphrasing a 2002 conference paper of Peterson's). These are

1. an ethic of generosity informed by a social pragmatics of demand sharing
2. embedded in a system of kin classification that requires a flow of goods and services to produce and reproduce social relationships
3. personhood constituted through relatedness but valuing egalitarian ideology
4. an emphasis on polite indirectness in interaction because open refusal is a rejection of relatedness.

The value, for those in the industry, of learning to recognise and thus acknowledge 'culture' is that it gives voice to Aboriginal economic practices and acts to provide some explanation for behaviours that could appear incomprehensible to non-Aboriginal observers. The need to articulate how the Aboriginal economy operates drove the WA Department of Consumer and Employment Protection and the Department of Community Development to fund a research project on the 'Strategies Goldfields Aboriginal people use to manage in the Aboriginal economy and the mainstream economy at the same time' (Centrecare 2005). This project, entitled 'Living in Two Camps', was underpinned by the 'idea that there were two separate economies that were operating alongside each other at the same time, sometimes reinforcing each other but more often in conflict'. The research found that 'many Aboriginal people, no matter what their material and personal resources, are conscious of how fragile and unpredictable their economic lives can be, and involvement in the Aboriginal economy was a kind of mutual insurance which would guarantee survival if times got tough' (Centrecare 2005:5).

This important point also underscores the value of engaging in multiple economic activities as an effective strategy for survival in highly variable environments, particularly deserts. Indeed, Stafford-Smith (2008) outlines an argument for a 'desert syndrome', which includes managing economically for a stochastic— that is, a highly variable and unpredictable—environment. Although there is increasing evidence that local economies in any region built on a diverse economic base are more resilient in the face of crises, it could be argued that this trait is a tendency that underwrites desert survival.

On a larger, regional scale, Stafford-Smith (2008:8) notes that the variability and unpredictability of desert economies are driven by distant markets where desert enterprises are usually only a small part of the production system and subject to the vagaries of what is happening elsewhere. Thus, they are price takers, rather than price makers. He further observes that mineral prices are set globally and desert Australia has limited influence over this, and that there have been mining booms before, just as there have been pastoral booms that have, however, left many Aboriginal people unemployed. Thus, a reliance on one form of economy—as a regional economic driver—can be risky in the desert.

Indeed, transferring this logic to a mining economy reminds us that the immensity of regional mining activity has been termed a 'monopsony', whereby industry is virtually the sole buyer of goods and services in their area of operation (Saleem and Behrendt 2001:1).[7] As the major regional socioeconomic intervention, the scale of the remote mining economy can be demonstrated by Rio Tinto's level of commercial activity alone. In 2001, $235 million dollars in taxes and royalties were paid to the WA Government and $1 billion spent in goods and services—the majority in Western Australia (Rio Tinto 2002). This brings us to the question of the sustainability of this mining activity.

Sustainable mining, mine downsizing and mine closure

The concept of sustainability—as now applied to the triple bottom lines of the social, environmental and economic—is not usually comfortably applied to the extractive-resource industries. As the Pilbara Regional Sustainability Strategy notes, 'it is not possible to sustainably use a non-renewable resource and thus in this sense of the word mining is not sustainable' (Newman et al. 2005:17). Nevertheless, the annual reporting criteria of major corporations, such as Rio Tinto and BHP Billiton, now include the triple bottom line. And interestingly, the *Sustainable Development Report* for 2007 for Rio Tinto Iron Ore (RTIO) has the 'economic' update as the last section, preceded by sections on governance, social, employees, community and environment. As Newman et al. (2005:18) note in relation to the disjuncture between the sustainability concept and mining, it 'is not whether [mining] can be sustained forever but how can the process the business is using simultaneously improve other social, economic and environmental value[s]'. This is, of course, where a diversity of regional opportunities needs to be considered and where the sustainable livelihoods framework could prove its value.

---

7   The term 'monopoly' applies to the sole seller of goods and services.

Planning for mine closure begins in the early stages of project development (Moller et al. 2006:4). In a paper outlining Pilbara Iron's approach to sustainable development in relation to the closure of the Tom Price mine (the oldest of their mines) and Paraburdoo (see Figure 9.2), a set of potential post-closure land-use options was considered as possibly viable. These included such economic activities as 'tourism, environmental and heritage conservation, native title and pastoralism' (Moller et al. 2006:6). No figures, however, were given on when such closure was anticipated or how these alternative economy plans could be realised (and what does 'native title' mean as an economic activity?). This section, however, necessarily touches only on the issue of downsizing or closure and I have not as yet been able to locate specific closure plans for the Rio Tinto Yandi mine.

The *Yandi Agreement* was originally set to be active for 20 years (1997–2017). With the 'ramp up' or increase in production, this operating period was reduced (as of 2004) to 16 years, and possibly less today. According to this time frame, the *YLUA* now has only another four years of life. Obvious questions exist around 'what happens to the income stream when the agreement comes to an end? Can it be renegotiated if the mine continues?' And 'what arrangements are there to ensure that the trusts keep generating an income stream?' Such questions direct Gumala to consider whether the organisation and the Aboriginal capacities built to manage it are being built to outlast the agreement.

Compared with gold or zinc mining, for instance, iron-ore mining is long term. This in itself creates a range of issues. When the mining industry is gone from the region in perhaps 20 to 50 years it will doubtless be Aboriginal people who remain, especially given the predominance of 'fly-in/fly-out' workers. Roles for them in rehabilitation seem obvious, utilising the natural resources that remain. Local Aboriginal people would seem to be strategically placed to manage mine-closure issues—as Solomon et al. (2008:147) note: 'the value of a place of capitalist enterprises such as mining is commercial, whereas for Aborigines the value may be both economic and cultural, and for some Aborigines it will be mainly the latter.'

RTIO in the Pilbara operates and maintains a network of 10 mines, three ports and the largest privately owned railway in the world (Milli Milli Magazine 2007). It also manages six pastoral stations in the Pilbara. The cattle barons no longer exist. Though the pastoral leases could be viable, they are essentially valuable to the industry only for the availability of the land they represent. Symbolically and practically, the cattle industry has been marginalised by the mining industry. Not surprisingly, health and safety have apparently 'improved significantly as pastoral employees are now subject to the same requirements as those on the mine site' (Stanton-Hicks 2007:10).

Environmentally, the footprint of the industry is extremely significant and there clearly has been very significant and, in some cases irreparable, damage to country. For instance, an MA thesis in applied geology on the impacts of mining and mine closure on water quality for the Yandi iron-ore mine notes that there are four possible closure models for the mine pit (Gardiner 2003). Each model has one or two extensive lakes, although none of the scenarios has the lakes with potable water. Indeed, the salinity of the pit lakes would not be expected to stabilise for 1000 years. All models note varying degrees of adverse affects on the downstream creeks. The 2007 RTIO *Sustainable Development Report* does note, however, that for the Yandi mine, unlike all others in the region, the issue of de-watering is being managed in a more sustainable way.[8]

In the vast areas of 'no-go zones', a number of major access roads require driver awareness training, where the community will be issued a permit and people with a valid driver's licence will be given a driver's awareness card (Milli Milli Magazine 2007). The complex network of roads and the safety requirements of the mine culture have institutionalised and circumscribed people's movements. That some Aboriginal people might feel 'boxed in' by the enormity of the mining footprint is no surprise. The intensity of the environmental footprint and the highly institutionalised mine culture present significant challenges for operating outside it. Perhaps ironically, although the benchmark for gaining work in the industry is extremely high, even given the range of pre-employment programs, the industry is so pervasive that it is difficult to disengage and pursue economic alternatives.

Figure 9.2 goes some way to illustrating the vast areas iron-ore mining incorporates geographically and environmentally; moreover Paraburdoo mine is one of many mines in the region. This picture also shows infrastructure, in the form of roads, which was constructed solely for Pilbara Iron's use.

Skills developed by local Aboriginal people are transferable to other industries and other locations. This assumes, however, that Aboriginal people are migratory and prepared to relocate for work out of their home region. This could be a greater possibility for some, especially in future generations; however, little is known about the extent to which skills acquired by Aboriginal mine workers contribute to the human and social capital of their respective communities (see Barker 2006). Nevertheless, there is little debate that employing local people— Aboriginal and non-Aboriginal—in the mining industry is a more sustainable approach for the region than the current majority approach of fly-in/fly-out (FIFO) (see Armstrong 2004, in Newman et al. 2005). This contentious issue of

---

8   Ore bodies form a significant aquifer. It is industry and regional practice to discharge water into existing waterways, creating the risk of altering the ephemeral ecosystem. To reduce this risk, Rio Tinto developed a trial aquifer re-injection system, returning the water to the aquifer at an appropriate distance from the mine site (Rio Tinto 2007:59).

rostering the majority of mining staff as FIFO from large cities such as Perth is a significant sustainability issue indicative of mining revenue leaving the region (see Armstrong 2004, in Newman et al. 2005:40).

Landscape rehabilitation, both during the mine life and post-mine, is an obvious area for Aboriginal employment, if not potentially a livelihood activity. RTIO, however, notes in its 2007 *Sustainable Development Report* that 'progressive rehabilitation is constrained by the need to maintain ore access and set land aside for future waste dumping sites. Areas are rehabilitated when they are no longer required by operations. Due to rapid expansion in 2007, fewer areas became available for rehabilitation' (Rio Tinto 2007:40). Although it could appear that these significant environmental issues, combined with the regional dominance of the industry, compromise the viability of applying the sustainable livelihoods framework, it seems to me, rather, that it becomes all the more imperative to consider it as a means of economic diversification. Nevertheless, the framework sits most comfortably in remote areas with ample access to natural resources.

Figure 9.2 Paraburdoo mine looking north-west

Source: Jason Brennan Senior advisor, Communications & External Relations, Rio Tinto Iron Ore

Homelands

A strength of the *YLUA* has been the encouragement for and establishment of outstations or 'homelands', as they are known in the Pilbara. With little state investment in homeland infrastructure, the agreements, notably the *YLUA* discussed here, have been the drivers of homelands, under the aegis of 'community development'. According to Gumala, about 120 people (most of whom are Gumala members) live on the three homelands and three 'blocks' that they assist. These three homelands or formal communities are Youngaleena, Wakathuni and Bellary; the three 'blocks' are Wirrilimarra, Windell Block and Ngumee Ngu. Although the majority of Gumala members live in towns in regular houses, Gumala notes that 'the symbolism of homelands is potent' and 'their importance extends well beyond those actually living there' (Gordon, Personal communication, 1 June 2009).

Guerin and Guerin (2008) consider remote communities or homelands as 'spiritual hubs'. They note that although clearly not all people who have rights to live on a homeland are able to, as they might live elsewhere for education or employment, the sustainability of them is dependant on this wider network. Thus, when discussing the sustainability and importance of homelands the issue is not just about how many people live there, but about how wide the influence of all members who live there is (Guerin and Guerin 2008:13). For instance, the homelands in the Pilbara provide a base for important cultural activities, such as annual initiation ceremonies, and a ready departure point for customary economic activity. The value of living on one's country and the more ready access to customary harvest activity have not to my knowledge been explored in this region, as they have in Arnhem Land, for instance (see Altman 1987). Mapping the mobility of Aboriginal residents of towns to homelands to which they have right of access would be a useful exercise in this context. How geographically extensive is the catchment of these homelands?

The Pilbara Regional Sustainability Strategy found that 'the natural environment is a key local advantage of the Pilbara, being the physical basis of resources, tourism, pastoralism and fishing industries, a conservation asset and intimately linked with ongoing Indigenous cultures' (Newman et al. 2005:116). The homelands are clearly at the centre of this resource and thus, in some ways, best placed to capitalise on it.

According to Gumala, in the past decade, it has provided considerable assistance to the six homelands and blocks. It has been the sole developer of the three 'blocks', while it has provided less support than the government for the three homelands. This is, however, set to change, with, according to Gumala, 'the government rethinking its support for homelands and likely to provide less for them' in the future (Gordon, Personal communication, 1 June 2009). At the same time, 'Gumala is conducting a review of its role with the blocks and homelands and this may lead to some increases in support and the establishment of a capital works program' (Gordon, Personal communication, 1 June 2009).

Heritage clearances as a livelihood strategy

Perhaps paradoxically, the work that local Aboriginal people, as cultural custodians, undertake for mine expansion and development could be understood in terms of a livelihood approach. This is because it values, or at least purports to value, the existing knowledge and skills that Aboriginal people have in the cultural and environmental values of their land. This work undertaken under the WA *Aboriginal Heritage Act* (1972) entails groups of Aboriginal people being taken out to areas of proposed mining activity or infrastructure development to ensure that any sites of archaeological and/or spiritual significance are not damaged. Hence, it could be understood as 'harvesting heritage' (see Holcombe 2009).

Acknowledging the pitfalls of this work—such as the politics of ensuring that the right Aboriginal people are invited, and that the gender balance is addressed and that some sites are inevitably sacrificed or compromised—it nonetheless offers some insight into the value of considering this sort of work as a livelihoods strategy. This is because of the possibilities such work affords to regenerating or consolidating the social capital that people have through extended family networks. Indeed, an analysis of how people are chosen for the work could prove telling in light of the work of Measham et al. (cited in Davies et al. 2008) in the Anmatyerr region discussed earlier.

The flexibility the work affords to being out and learning on country can be highly valued, including keeping engaged with the expanding footprint of the mining industry. For instance, in 2004, RTIO 'paid for more than 1000 days of mainly Aboriginal elder time undertaking cultural heritage across the 12 native title groups' (RTIO 2006a:V). This was 'ramped up' in 2006 to 2578 days over 96 surveys (RTIO 2006b:32). Thus, a market value is assigned to this work and it is a routine aspect of Pilbara Iron's (and most other mining companies') work practices.

Nevertheless, it has to be acknowledged that there is a certain tension between the 'ramping up' and hence the need to clear more land, and the knowledge of the land and environment that this work is promoting. One would imagine that the process would become more valuable for the Aboriginal groups involved if there was a standard approach to ensuring that there was opportunity for intergenerational knowledge transmission. That is, to ensuring that younger people always accompanied the 'elders'. It could also be the case, however, that the work is politically volatile for traditional owners. On what basis are people chosen to participate? There are invariably issues around the personalities of the participants—Aboriginal and non-Aboriginal—on both sides. This issue of handpicking participants appears, however, to have been managed largely through the development of 'working groups' for each native title claimant group.

It is noteworthy that the RTIO Aboriginal Training and Liaison (ATAL) unit has developed an Archaeological Assistants' Training Course (AATC). ATAL notes that it gives Aboriginal people the opportunity to enhance their skills and knowledge in archaeological theory and practice, including the identification, recording and management of archaeological sites and artefacts. The course was developed following numerous requests from members of the Aboriginal community to gain more training in the field of archaeology. On completion of the AATC, participants receive a Statement of Attainment for partial completion of Certificate II in Metalliferous Mining—Open Cut, with an emphasis on Archaeological Assistant. Certificate II is a nationally recognised qualification under the Australia Quality Training Framework (Pilbara Iron, ATAL 2006).

Conclusion

This chapter has been a speculative consideration of the sustainable livelihoods strategy as a framework and language for Gumala, and potentially other Aboriginal organisations set up to manage agreement flows. Considering the sustainable livelihoods approach in the context of a regional mining boom recognises that not all Aboriginal people are either able or willing to seek employment in the industry. Employment parity between Aboriginal and non-Aboriginal people might never be reached or, indeed, if we assume that it can, it could take several generations. This also assumes, however, that assimilation is inevitable and that the mine economy is somehow infinite or ongoing, which of course it is not. What does appear to be ongoing is Aboriginal people's attachment to homelands and the country on which they are situated.

So it seems that the Pilbara region at least, with its access to a mine economy, has a relative advantage in the support that Aboriginal native titleholders receive for homeland or outstation development. Likewise, the leverage that Gumala is able to gain from the state and commonwealth governments from already having a certain baseline of funding is also crucial for their continuing support. There is also evidence, albeit from Gumala, that there are more Aboriginal people employed in the mining industry than was found by Taylor and Scambary (2005). The extensive pre-employment programs that Rio Tinto and others such as Ngarda Civil and Mining have implemented appear to be making their mark.

The possibilities for sustainable livelihoods are clearly compromised by the pervasiveness of mining in the Pilbara region and the footprint of the industry, as this encompasses not only the actual mines, but also the complex network of infrastructure, water requirements, and so on. Likewise, mining cannot sit comfortably with the concept of sustainability, unless there is directed focus on developing the region's other capital—the social, cultural, human and environmental. As Armstrong (in Newman et al. 2005:40) argues, 'a sustainable solution to FIFO in the Pilbara is about increasing the positive benefits of mining to local communities whilst reducing their dependence upon it'. Gumala is in a strategic position in the region to do this and deliver sustainable outcomes.

Trigger (2005:54) notes that 'the research literature squarely suggests that a form of fundamental cultural change is implicated in economic development-based solutions to Indigenous disadvantage. To frame this positively, new ways must be found of articulating market participation with a number of key Indigenous values.' In engaging with the sustainable livelihoods approach and engaging with Gumala—as an Aboriginal organisation set up to harness benefits from the *YLUA*—this chapter has gone part of the way to finding such alternative forms of articulation. Likewise, whether we use the language of 'sustainable livelihoods' or 'community economies' is not necessarily the point. Rather, the point of this chapter has been to articulate the value of alternative frameworks for economic engagement from the mainstream against the backdrop of mine downsizing or mine closure, the broader issues of sustainability and the 'deeply enculturated dispositions' of Aboriginal people. Nevertheless, the consideration of mine closure issues has been preliminary only and international comparative research could usefully be undertaken, specifically on the Brazilian iron-ore mining industry—one of the largest competitors with the Pilbara.

Bibliography

Ah Mat, R. 2003, The moral case for Indigenous capitalism, Address to the NTRB Native Title on the Ground Conference, Alice Springs, NT, 5 June 2003, <http://ntru.aiatsis.gov.au/conf2003/papers/ahmat.pdf>

Altman, J. C. 1987, *Hunter-Gatherers Today: An Aboriginal economy in north Australia*, Australian Institute of Aboriginal Studies, Canberra.

Altman, J. C. 2009, *Beyond closing the gap: valuing diversity in Indigenous Australia*, CAEPR Working Paper No. 54/2009, Centre for Aboriginal Economic Policy Research, The Australian National University, Canberra.

Altman, J. C. and Rowse, T. 2005, 'Indigenous affairs', in P. Saunders and J. Walter (eds), *Ideas and Influence: Social science and public policy in Australia*, UNSW Press, Sydney, pp. 159–77.

Barker, T. 2006, *Employment outcomes for Aboriginal people: an exploration of experiences and challenges in the Australian minerals industry*, Research Paper No. 6, Centre for Social Responsibility in Mining, University of Queensland, St Lucia, <http://www.csrm.uq.edu.au/docs/t06.pdf>

Brehaut, L. and Vitenbergs, A. (eds) 2001, *The Guruma Story. Told by Guruma Leaders Group, led by Peter Stevens*, IAD Press, Alice Springs, NT.

Brocklesby, M. A. and Fisher, E. 2003, 'Community development in sustainable livelihoods approaches—an introduction', *Community Development Journal*, vol. 38 (3 July), pp. 185–98.

Carney, D. 2002, *Sustainable Livelihoods Approaches: Progress and possibilities for change*, Department for International Development, United Kingdom.

Centrecare [Sercombe, H.] 2005, Living in two camps: the strategies Goldfields Aboriginal people use to manage in the Aboriginal economy and the mainstream economy at the same time, Unpublished report of a research project funded by the Department for Consumer and Employment Protection and the Department for Community Development, Government of Western Australia.

Chambers, R. 1987, *Sustainable livelihoods, environment and development: putting poor rural people first*, Institute of Development Studies Discussion Paper 240, University of Sussex, UK.

Chambers, R. and Conway, G. 1992, *Sustainable rural livelihoods: practical concepts for the 21st century*, Institute of Development Studies Discussion Paper 296, University of Sussex, UK.

Davies, J., White, J., Wright, A., Maru, Y. and LaFlamme, M. 2008, 'Applying the sustainable livelihoods approach in Australian desert Aboriginal development', *The Rangeland Journal*, Special Issue: Desert knowledge, vol. 30, no. 1, pp. 55–65.

Dillon, M. and Westbury, N. 2007, *Beyond Humbug: Transforming government engagement with Indigenous Australia*, Seaview Press, South Australia.

Dodson, M. 2009, Communities in control: the real Australian experience, 2009 Community Leadership Oration, Communities in Control Conference, Moonee Valley Race Club, Vic., June 2009.

Edmunds, M. 1989, *They Get Heaps: A study of attitudes in Roebourne Western Australia*, Aboriginal Studies Press, Canberra.

Fisher, S. 2002a, 'The sustainable livelihoods approach: a path well travelled', *Our Place*, vol. 3, no. 19, pp. 16–17.

Fisher, S. 2002b, *A livelihood less ordinary: applying the sustainable livelihoods approach in the Australian Indigenous context*, Centre for Appropriate Technology Paper, viewed 23 February 2009, <http://www.icat.org.au/media/Research/work%20and%20livelihoods/Livelihood-less-ordinary.pdf>

Gardiner, S. J. 2003, Impacts of mining and mine closure on water quality and the nature of the shallow aquifer, Yandi iron ore mine, Unpublished Master of Science thesis, Department of Applied Geology, Curtin University of Technology, WA, viewed 22 May 2009, <http://espace.library.curtin.edu.au:1802/view/action/nmets.do?DOCCHOICE=15728.xml&dvs=1245809919322~725&locale=en_US&search_terms=000012589&usePid1=true&usePid2=true>

Gibson-Graham, J. K. 2002, 'Beyond global vs. local: economic politics outside the binary frame', in A. Herod and M. Wrights (eds), *Geographies of Power: Placing scale*, Blackwell Publishers, Oxford, pp. 25–60.

Guerin, B and Guerin, P. 2008, Mobility and sustainability of remote Australian communities: community issues, Desert Knowledge Symposium and Showcase, Alice Springs, NT, 3–6 November.

Hinselwood, E. 2003, 'Making friends with the sustainable livelihoods framework', *Community Development Journal*, vol. 38 (3 July), pp. 243–54.

Holcombe, S. 2005, 'Indigenous organisations and miners in the Pilbara, Western Australia: lessons from a historical perspective', *Aboriginal History*, vol. 29, pp. 107–35.

Holcombe, S. 2006a, The challenge of sustainability in remote settlements, Paper presented at the Desert Knowledge CRC Symposium, Alice Springs, NT, November, <http://www.desertknowledgecrc.com.au/socialscience/downloads/DKsymposiumabpapFRD.pdf>

Holcombe, S. 2006b, 'Community benefit packages: development's encounter with pluralism in the case of the mining industry', in T. Lea, E. Kowal and G. Cowlishaw (eds), *Moving Anthropology: Critical Indigenous studies*, Charles Darwin University Press, Darwin, pp. 79–94.

Holcombe, S. 2009, 'Indigenous entrepreneurialism in the context of mining land use agreements', in J. C. Altman and D. F. Martin (eds), *Power, culture, economy: Indigenous Australians and mining*, CAEPR Monograph 30, ANU E Press, Canberra, pp. 149–69.

Johns, G. 2009, *No Job No House: An economically strategic approach to remote Aboriginal housing*, The Menzies Research Centre Ltd, Canberra, <http://www.mrcltd.org.au/research/indigenous-reports/No_Job_No_House.pdf>

Langton, M. 2002, A new deal? Indigenous development and the politics of recovery, Dr Charles Perkins AO Memorial Oration delivered at the University of Sydney, Sydney, October 2002, <http://ses.library.usyd.edu.au/bitstream/2123/1634/1/Langton%20Perkins%20Oration%20USyd%20Oct%202002.pdf>

Levitus, R. 1999, 'Local organisations and the purpose of money', in J. C. Altman, F. Morphy and T. Rowse (eds), *Land rights at risk? Evaluations of the Reeves Report*, Research Monograph No. 14, Centre for Aboriginal Economic Policy Research, The Australian National University, Canberra.

Levitus, R. with Altman, J. C. 1999, *The allocation and management of royalties under the* Aboriginal Land Rights (Northern Territory) Act: *options for reform*, CAEPR Discussion Paper No. 191, Centre for Aboriginal Economic Policy Research, The Australian National University, Canberra.

McLeod, D. 1984, *How the West was Lost: The native question in the development of Western Australia*, D. W. McLeod, Port Hedland, WA.

Milli Milli Magazine 2007, 'Rio Tinto iron ore', *Milli Milli Magazine*, 27 July 2007, <http://www.riotintoironore.com/documents/Milli_Milli_27.pdf>

Moller, M., Flugge, R. and Murphy, D. 2006, Pilbara Iron's approach to sustainable development during mine closure—the case study of greater Tom Price and Pannawonica operations, Unpublished report, Sinclair Knight Merz, Australia.

Moran, M., Wright, A., Renehan, P., Szava, A., Beard, N. and Rich, E. 2007, *The transformation of assets for sustainable livelihoods in a remote Aboriginal settlement*, Desert Knowledge CRC Report 28, Desert Knowledge CRC, Alice Springs, NT.

Newman, P., Armstrong, R. and McGrath, N. 2005, *Pilbara Regional Sustainability Strategy: A discussion document*, Institute for Sustainability and Technology Policy, Murdoch University, Perth.

Olive, N. (ed.) 1997, *Karijini Mirlimirli: Aboriginal histories from the Pilbara*, Fremantle Arts Centre Press, Perth.

Peterson, N. 1993, 'Demand sharing: reciprocity and pressure for generosity among foragers', *American Anthropologist*, vol. 95, no. 4, pp. 860–74.

Peterson, N. 2002, From mode of production to moral economy: sharing and kinship in fourth world social orders, Paper presented to the Ninth International Conference on Hunting and Gathering Societies, Edinburgh, Scotland, 9–13 September.

Pholi, K., Black, D. and Richards, C. 2009, 'Is "Close the Gap" a useful approach to improving the health and wellbeing of Indigenous Australians?', *Australian Review of Public Affairs*, vol. 9, no. 2, pp. 1–3.

Pilbara Iron, ATAL 2006, Working with us: Aboriginal Training and Liaison (ATAL), web content, <http://www.pilbarairon.com/SiteContent/working/atal.asp>

Rio Tinto 2002, *Future Matters Newsletter*, Winter 2002, Rio Tinto, Perth.

Rio Tinto 2007, *Annual Report 2007*, Rio Tinto, Perth.

Rio Tinto Iron Ore (RTIO) 2006a, *Breaking New Ground: Stories of mining and the Aboriginal people of the Pilbara*, Quality Press, WA.

Rio Tinto Iron Ore (RTIO) 2006b, *Pilbara Operations Sustainable Development Summary Report: More value with less impact*, viewed 3 July 2008, <http://www.pilbarairon.com.au/sd/RTIO%20Sust%20Dev%20Summary%20(FA).pdf>

Saleem, A. and Behrendt, L. 2001, 'Mining and Indigenous rights: the emergence of a global social movement', *Cultural Survival Quarterly*, vol. 25, no. 1, p. 5.

Scambary, B. 2007, My country, mine country: Indigenous people, mining and development contestation in remote Australia, Unpublished PhD dissertation, The Australian National University, Canberra.

Scoones, I. 1998, *Sustainable rural livelihoods: a framework for analysis*, Institute of Development Studies Working Paper 72, Institute of Development Studies, Brighton, UK, <http://www.uvg.edu.gt/instituto/centros/cea/Scoones72.pdf>

Smith, A. B. with Vitenbergs, A. and Brehaut, L. 2002, *Under a Bilari Tree I Born*, Fremantle Arts Centre Press, Perth.

Solomon, F., Katz, E. and Lovel, R. 2008, 'Social dimensions of mining: research, policy and practice challenges for the minerals industry in Australia', *Resources Policy*, vol. 33, pp. 142–9.

Stafford-Smith, M. 2008, 'The "desert syndrome"—causally linked factors that characterise desert Australia', *The Rangeland Journal*, vol. 30, pp. 3–14.

Stanton-Hicks, E. 2007, Sustainability and the iron ore industry in the Pilbara: a regional perspective, Masters thesis, Institute for Sustainability and Technology, Murdoch University, Perth, <http://www.sustainability.dpc.wa.gov.au/CaseStudies/pilbara/pilbaraprint.htm>

Taylor, J. and Scambary, B. 2005, *Indigenous people and the Pilbara mining boom: a baseline for regional participation*, CAEPR Research Monograph No. 25, ANU E Press, Canberra.

Trigger, D. 2005, 'Mining projects in remote Australia: sites for the articulation and contesting of economic and cultural futures', in D. Austin-Broos and G. MacDonald (eds), *Culture, Economy and Governance in Aboriginal Australia. Proceedings of a Workshop held at the University of Sydney, 30 November – 1 December, 2004*, Sydney University Press, NSW.

Wilson, J. 1961, Authority and leadership in a 'new style' Australian Aboriginal community: Pindan Western Australia, Unpublished MA thesis, University of Western Australia, Perth.

Wilson, J. 1980, 'The Pilbara Aboriginal social movement: an outline of its background and significance', in R. Berndt and C. Berndt (eds), *Aborigines of the West: Their past and their present*, University of Western Australia Press, Perth.

Young, E. 1995, *Third World in the First: development and indigenous peoples.* Routledge, London.

10. Realities, simulacra and the appropriation of Aboriginality in Kakadu's tourism

CHRIS HAYNES

Introduction

Like the previous two chapters, this final chapter is located in the present and recent past. In the sense used by Richard Davis (2005) and other contemporary writers, it imagines colonisation as an extension of the colonial period of the nineteenth and twentieth centuries into the present. It is about some effects of tourism—always a feature of national parks—in Kakadu National Park on Australia's north coast. I argue that tourism generally, especially what is often dubbed 'cultural tourism', has created significant disadvantage for the Aboriginal people of the area. After first introducing this now-famous park, I look at how Kakadu's Aboriginal population is compensated financially, comparing this with the overall value of tourism in the Northern Territory, much of which is generated through marketing representations of Aboriginality. I then look at the complicated mimetic effects arising out of aspects of traditional Aboriginal culture that have been appropriated for touristic advantage in Kakadu. While using quite different data sets and logics, I share anthropologist Lisa Palmer's (2001) earlier conclusion that Aboriginal people have paid a high price in sharing their land with the visitors who enjoy it so much.

Brief history of Kakadu National Park

Arguably the best known of Australia's national parks, Kakadu is situated in the wet–dry tropics of the Northern Territory of Australia, about 250 km east of its capital city, Darwin (Figure 10.1). At just less than 20 000 sq km, comparable in size to small nation-states such as Israel and Belgium, and one-third the size of Australia's smallest state, Tasmania, it is certainly Australia's largest national park. Although its administration has nothing like the complexity of nation-states, or even subdivisions of nation-states, it is much more difficult to administer than most national parks, even those of comparable size.

Figure 10.1 Location of Kakadu National Park within Australia. The internal markings denote road, mining and special-purpose excisions

Maps: Google Imagery 2009 and UNEP/WCMC/IUCN

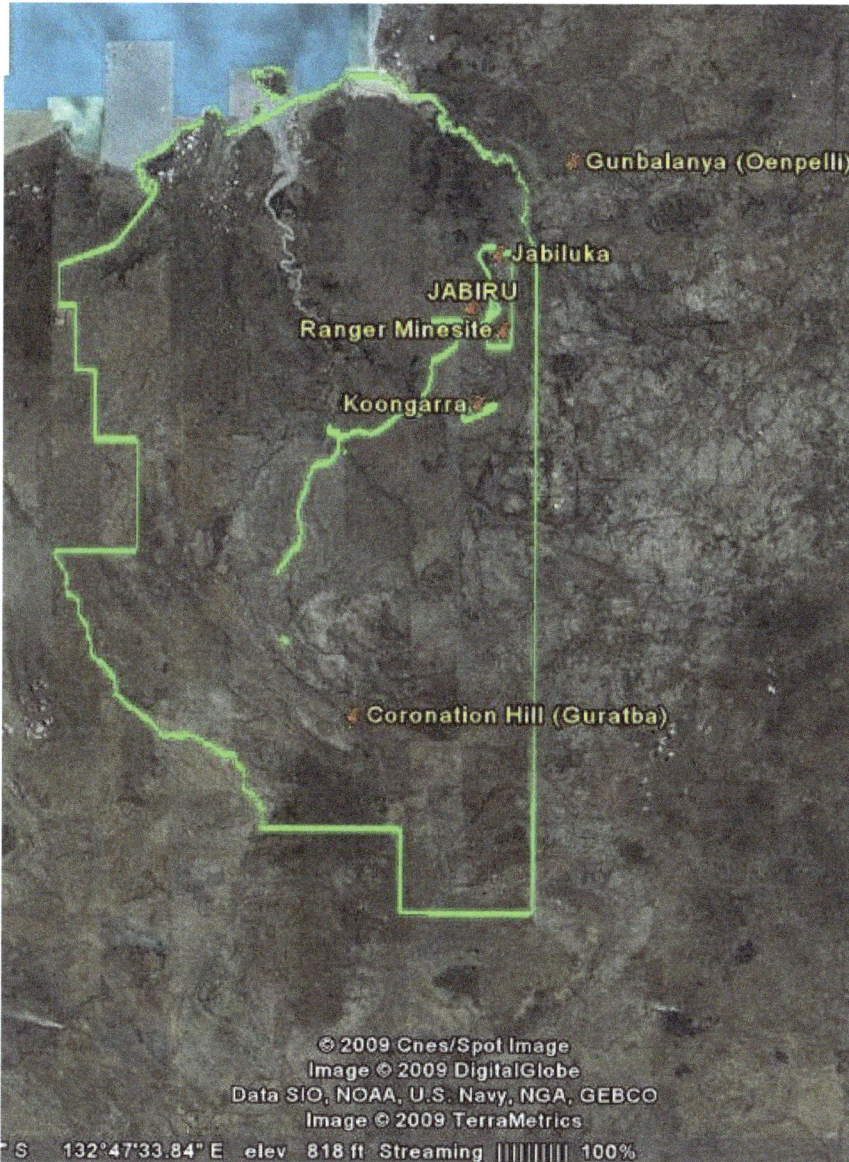

Figure 10.2 Details of boundaries, key features and relevant mining locations within Kakadu. The internal markings denote road, mining and special-purpose excisions. The heavily dissected sandstone sheet that covers western Arnhem Land and extends into Kakadu can be seen extending from the lower right of the image. The park's major river, the South Alligator, lies approximately midway between the eastern and western boundaries. Its catchment is almost completely encompassed within the park boundaries

Map: Google Imagery 2009 and UNEP/WCMC/IUCN

Much of its complexity derives from how it was originally devised. The first moves to create a national park in this area took place in the 1960s, as part of a global movement that saw a doubling in number and size of national parks and other protected areas in that decade (Eagles et al. 2002:8; Worboys et al. 2005:41–2). Kakadu was not formally declared until 1979, and then only as the first stage—about one-third of the present area. The delay in its declaration can be attributed to the discovery of significant ore bodies of uranium near the current town of Jabiru (Figure 10.2) and the contestation those discoveries presented. There was not only a potential national park to consider. There were also broader questions of environmental protection and consequences of uranium mining such as nuclear proliferation and the disposal of nuclear waste to be accounted for. Moreover, the Australian Labor Party Government led by Prime Minister Gough Whitlam had initiated the granting of land rights to those Aboriginal people who could demonstrate traditional affiliation to the land as one means of addressing the social disadvantage of this group (Peterson 1982).

Working out how to allow the mining, while at the same time protecting a beautiful landscape that housed an abundance of natural and archaeological treasures, addressing the wider environmental protection questions and doing justice to the traditional owners of the area, provided unprecedented challenges to policymakers. Policy requirements were eventually resolved through two major moves. The first was the appointment of the Ranger Uranium Environmental Inquiry (RUEI 1977), headed by Justice Russell Fox. Over about 20 months, this commission of inquiry heard complex, and often contradictory, evidence on issues ranging from nuclear threats and the disposal of nuclear waste to the intricacies of how Aboriginal land was owned according to local tradition. The second move followed receipt of the RUEI's final report in April 1977 by the federal government. It set up a subcommittee of relevant ministers to work through the considerable detail of the RUEI recommendations with senior public servants, producing a series of detailed decisions several months later (Commonwealth of Australia 1977). Among the most significant of these were: uranium mining was to be permitted, under strict environmental safeguards (including the establishment of a new agency, with its own legislation, that would police the operations of the mine); the first stage of Kakadu National Park would be created; and almost all of that first stage would be granted to Aboriginal land trusts to hold the land on behalf of traditional Aboriginal owners, subject to its being leased to the state to be run as a national park.

After months of controversial negotiations and considerable duress to both traditional owners and state negotiators (see, for example, O'Brien 2003; Parsons 1978; Peterson 1982), the agreements to allow mining at the first-discovered ore body, Ranger, and the lease of about one-third of the current park to the state were signed in November 1978. Construction of the mine site started soon afterwards, and the first stage of Kakadu was declared in April 1979. A change in the federal government in 1983 saw other uranium-mining prospects curtailed and an eventual increase in park area to its current size in 1991. The final addition was also controversial, with the possibility of non-uranium mines in the South Alligator Valley (Figure 10.2) remaining until the government decided not to permit mining and to include the whole area in Kakadu.

Although only about half the total area has been successfully claimed on behalf of traditional owners so far, with other claims still to be resolved, the park is now administered as if it were all Aboriginal land and decisions are made jointly by traditional Aboriginal landowners and Parks Australia. The fact that Parks Australia is an agency of the federal government is a matter that has been a source of irritation to successive local NT governments, especially those of conservative persuasion in power between the Northern Territory's self-government in 1978 and 2001 (Heatley 1990:130–2). Between those dates, NT Government ministers pushed hard for Kakadu's administration to be handed over to NT partnership. Later administrations have taken a much softer approach, saying that the matter is up to the traditional owners.

Thus, Kakadu, which, like all national parks, is captive to the tension between conservation of the area's natural resources and current use (cf. Eagles et al. 2002:10–12), is subtended by other big issues as well: mining, Aboriginal land rights and local versus national government control. These bigger issues have periodically captured national and international attention, much of it related to the park's inscription on the list of World Heritage properties—a factor that has made Kakadu all the more politically important (Aplin 2004; Trebeck 2007). Such issues have tended to crowd out consideration of the interplay between the interests of the traditional Aboriginal landowners and public use, notwithstanding the importance of such interplay to the Aborigines, as Palmer (2001) tells us.

In the years of my initial close involvement with Kakadu between 1978 and 1985, tourism was relatively weakly developed, but when I returned as park manager, after an absence of 17 years, between 2002 and 2004, visitor numbers had grown considerably. I was frequently confronted by the strains placed on traditional owners—one factor that in turn imposed on the processes of 'joint management', the sharing management between traditional owners and the state, one of the facets of the agreement that set this park up and which was to be the subject of my doctoral thesis (Haynes 2009).

Kakadu's value to NT tourism

Kakadu is variously promoted as a nice, warm place to be in winter; as a spot to catch barramundi and other fish; for its wetlands' other values, such as the abundant birdlife of Yellow Waters; for its scenic open spaces; for the sandstone plateau itself; and the waterfalls and plunge pools, which, notwithstanding difficulties with stray crocodiles in recent years, make ideal swimming holes. Many insiders give much of the credit for Kakadu's popularity to the 1986 film *Crocodile Dundee*, which showed off many of the best features of the landscape. For a sustained period, visitor numbers increased at a compound rate, exceeding 30 per cent (ANPWS 1989:12). Then a limit to numbers of potential visitors appeared to be reached in the mid-1990s, at about 260 000, followed by a gradual decline to less than 200 000 for some years. Numbers have since started to rise again; the park service reported 227 000 visitors for 2007–08 (DNP 2008:102).

Aided by the attractions of World Heritage listing and the controversies that have marked its history, Kakadu's landscape alone is probably enough to draw tourists in significant numbers. Yet, as local commentators regularly point out, there are many other fine landscapes, swimming holes and fishing places in the Northern Territory's 'Top End'. In the eyes of many of the same commentators (see, for example, NT News 2006), what makes Kakadu special is its so-called 'Aboriginal culture'—a term appropriated ambiguously into the tourism literature in more recent years. Here writers might mean the tens of thousands of beautiful images painted on overhanging cliffs and other rock surfaces of the sandstone plateau and other archaeological treasures that have been well documented (for example, Chaloupka 1993). Or they might mean to include other diacritics of the traditional culture: painted bodies dancing; men throwing spears; women gathering spike rush or hunting for file snakes; or just people cooking in the traditional way.

Both notions offer the tourist their own encounter with an exotic Other, and a great deal of Kakadu's promotion, and that of the Top End (the section of the Northern Territory lying north of about 15° S), rests on the potential that such an encounter offers. For example, the web site of Tourism Top End, the tourist industry's peak body in Darwin, advertises:

> The Top End of the Northern Territory is known for its tropical weather, rich indigenous culture, national parks and laid-back lifestyle. It is home to an eclectic mix of cultures whose outdoor lifestyle is complemented by brilliant sunsets, fantastic fishing and a colourful calendar of outdoor events…

Kakadu National Park, the largest in Australia, is situated 250 kilometres from Darwin on the Arnhem Highway. Renowned internationally for its natural and cultural wonders, Kakadu has one of the highest concentrated areas of Aboriginal rock art sites in the world.[1]

The skilled wording of such marketing implies a rewarding experience of the world of Aboriginal people—one that could include not only the artefacts of bygone days, but incorporation of a 'rich Indigenous culture' into the visit.

Whether such potential is in fact realised is contested, often emotionally. For example, Kakadu's own surveys over the years suggest that more than 80 per cent of visitors are either 'satisfied' or 'very satisfied' with their visit, and, while only a minority of visitors to the Top End in fact visit Aboriginal art sites (17 per cent), 94 per cent of these visitors were 'very or fairly satisfied' with the experience. Of the even smaller number (6 per cent) who participate in Aboriginal guided tours, 100 per cent are 'very or fairly satisfied'.[2] Almost all such Aboriginal-related activities take place in Kakadu. On the other hand, many white people in Darwin, notably tour operators, consider Kakadu a frustrating entity that delivers only a fraction of its potential to the visitor—a theme that has recurred over the decades of Kakadu's existence as a national park (for example, NT News 1989, 1996a, 1996b; The Weekend Australian 2009). Many whites express exasperation about how traditional owners, aided and abetted by Parks Australia, the current joint-management partner, keep beautiful and interesting areas closed to park visitors. Not only that, they say, most traditional owners refuse to act out the role of 'traditional' Aborigines, in a game many white people claim would certainly enhance Kakadu's unrealised tourism potential.

Contestation and controversy notwithstanding, visitors continue to come—both to the Top End and to Kakadu. There are several ways of estimating the economic activity they generate. Two of them are considered briefly here—the first based on the aggregate amounts of money spent by tourists in the destination, the method used by Tourism NT, the NT Government's tourism agency. It estimates about 1 million people visit the Top End annually, spending an average of more than $1000 each, thus generating just more than $1 billion in the Top End economy.[3] Extending the logic of this method, Kakadu, with its

1 Tourism Top End web site, viewed 14 February 2009, <http://www.tourismtopend.com.au/pages/welcome-to-tourism-top-end/>
2 Destination visitor survey, Tourism NT web site, viewed 14 February 2009, <http://www.tra.australia.com/content/documents/DVS/First%20Round%20of%20Reports/SRR%20Reports/SRR%20Darwin%20Final.pdf>
3 Tourism NT web site, viewed 14 February 2009, <http://www.tourismnt.com.au/nt/system/galleries/download/NTTC_Research/Quick_Stats_YE_Sep08.pdf> All figures are quoted in Australian dollars.

230 000 or so visitors, could claim to generate tourist expenditure of about $230 million per annum—a share of overall Top End activity that is consistent with economist Pascal Tremblay's (2007:vi) estimate.

Tremblay himself uses a second, more rigorous economic estimation regime, developed by Carlsen and Wood (2004). He argues that its estimates reflect only additional economic activity specifically attributable to the park or region. In other words, the figures discount the fact that tourists would substitute activity in other regions if they did not visit Kakadu or the Top End. By this more conservative methodology, Tremblay estimates the net tourism contribution to the economy by Kakadu is about $15 million—about one-quarter of the total Top End net contribution of $58.1 million.

Aboriginal people's financial share of tourism

The most obvious way by which Aboriginal people in Kakadu benefit financially from tourism is through their work in tourism enterprises, both as guides and as informants—work that so many white people insist Aboriginal people *should* be doing. Some traditional owners and their relatives conduct their own enterprises. Others produce paintings and artefacts that are sold in local retail outlets, but most of those involved in tourism do so as employees in enterprises that are owned by either Aboriginal associations or white people. (Almost all of those actually working in this way are not real traditional owners of Kakadu, but relatives or other people whom traditional owners accept as suitable to be working there.) As well, a few traditional owners have negotiated special deals for tourism to take place in their own areas, and derive a small royalty-style income stream from this source. The annual income from both sources is about $900 000—a small amount in comparison with what Kakadu generates in the tourism economy, but still considerably larger than it was a few years ago.[4]

There are three other ways through which, I argue, Aboriginal people derive income from tourism in Kakadu. These are channelled through the park organisation itself—the first being the traditional owners' share of visitor use fees, negotiated when these fees were first introduced in 1988. This figure was about $1.2 million in 2009.[5] Second, traditional owners receive land rent for the park—currently about $400 000. It could be argued that a proportion of this amount—I suggest half ($200 000)—is compensation for the tourists' use

---

4   This is my estimate. In my calculations, I acknowledge the assistance of several private operators and Aboriginal associations, especially Liam Maher of the Djabulukgu Association.

5   DNP (2008:101) and Senate, 'Budget Estimates', *Hansard*, May 2007—answer to Question No. 34 by Senator Crossin (NT). Since its introduction there have been changes to the way in which this payment is made—notably after the abolition of entry fees by the Howard Government in 2004 and their reintroduction by the Rudd Government in 2009.

of the land.[6] These two sources are shared among about 150 traditional owners. Third, about half of the park's 65 or so employees are Aboriginal, although only a small number of them are in fact traditional owners. These employees earn about $2.5 million per annum, of which I estimate about 40 per cent ($1 million) is attributable to providing visitor services, including guided tours that are available during the peak visitor months at no added cost to park visitors. Thus, if one adds these three payments made through Parks Australia ($2.4 million), Aboriginal income in Kakadu attributable to tourism is about $3.3 million per annum.

Although a total of more than three times the direct tourism income, $3.3 million is still only a fraction of the conservative figures generated by Tremblay—$58.1 million for the Top End and $15 million for Kakadu—especially when one notes the use of Aboriginality to attract visitors to the Top End in general, and Kakadu in particular. Of course, if one makes the comparison with the grand figures of $1 billion for the Top End, or $230 million for Kakadu, the fraction becomes not modest, but tiny. I suggest this could be one factor that has made it harder to persuade traditional owners to embrace tourism in both Kakadu and the Top End generally.[7]

How Aboriginal 'culture' is commodified in Kakadu

Commodification of traditional culture and its recognition are hardly new ideas. As Sahlins (1999:401) notes: 'All of a sudden, everyone got "culture". Australian Aboriginals, Inuit, Easter Islanders…even peoples whose ways of life were left for dead or dying a few decades ago now demand an indigenous space in a modernizing world under the banner of their "culture".' In the sense that Sahlins is describing, it is the subject peoples themselves who are enacting such commodification. Traditional owners and other Aboriginal people in Kakadu do exactly this, showing off so much of 'traditional culture' as suits their purposes, such as to argue identity and the protection of Aboriginal rights, as they do in Kakadu's management plans (for example, KNP and DNP 2007:45), and to earn income through showing tourists an exotic Otherness.

---

6 Tourism is not the only inconvenience attributable to the park that traditional owners have to manage. For example, there are conservation projects such as feral animal control (Bradshaw et al. 2007; Robinson et al. 2005) that create conflict between them and the park service.
7 Some commentators (for example, Tremblay 2008:73–5) point out that an opposite case can be made—that is, that if Aboriginal people had been more enthusiastic in taking up tourism opportunities they would now be much bigger players in tourism, and hence beneficiaries of it. Notwithstanding this argument, while I was park manager, I heard many complaints from Kakadu traditional owners that they were not gaining the benefits from tourism that the many white people in Darwin were receiving.

But what of the gap that appears to open up when one considers another view of culture? By 'culture' here I mean neither Kakadu's archaeological treasures such as the thousands of rock paintings nor the commodified re-enactments such as dancing, hunting and cooking, but rather the Geertzian (1993:5) view: 'The concept of culture I espouse…is essentially a semiotic one. Believing, with Max Weber, that man is an animal suspended in webs of significance he himself has spun, I take culture to be those webs.' If we take such a view then the webs of significance that 'suspend' traditional owners today are, in many respects, quite different from those that suspended the traditional owners of 30 years ago when the park got under way, and radically different from those that suspended their forebears encountered by explorer Ludwig Leichhardt when he descended from Kakadu's sandstone plateau in 1845. We have some clues about how culture changed through the colonial period: about how the whole population almost died out (Keen 1980:34–44), how migration patterns and fire regimes changed (Brockwell et al. 2001), how the remaining traditional owners migrated back and forth to towns and stations, with many eventually settling into casual work for white buffalo shooters, and how they demonstrated an early version of what Altman (2005), for example, calls the hybrid economy, purchasing Western goods while continuing to 'live off the land' much as their ancestors had done, thus engaging in different modes of production.

We know much more about changes that have taken place in the past three decades. In this period, we have seen most of the senior traditional owners die and be replaced as authority figures by people who have received at least some schooling and who do not remember much about the area before the park existed. We have seen rapid, but under-scrutinised changes in technology and infrastructure: the creation of the town of Jabiru, with its shops and other amenities; construction of sealed roads that have cut travel times by two-thirds; the building of modern tourist facilities, district offices and housing for staff throughout the park; and the introduction of phones and internet connections into all park offices—just to name a few.

All these technologies, let alone more complex things such as the intrusion of the state into their daily lives, and the ways by which traditional owners and other Aboriginal people have responded to them, make for transformed webs of significance to contemporary traditional owners. Many of the park's Aboriginal people—those who tend to play the most active roles in the park—now live in the same kind of housing, shop in the same shops and own the same kinds of cars and boats as their white counterparts.[8] Thus, although they continue to have responsibility for, and frequently worry about, their traditional clan estates, these days their firsthand knowledge of 'country' is generated largely through their employment or recreational visits to it in their 'spare time'. Likewise, much of their knowledge of what is told to, or performed for, park visitors is gained with the help of Western technologies such as video and audio recordings. Yet, like Sahlins (1999:409) in his critique of the meaning of Sumo, I argue that the narratives and performances for the tourists are much more than mere diacritics of long-gone cultures; no matter how they are learned and reproduced, they are the work of Aboriginal people themselves and, in this sense, they are 'authentic'.

Other people and agencies commodify Aboriginal culture too. In this sense, I see commodification as appropriation. I have already mentioned the skilled word images of tourism promoters on web sites. Such messages are reproduced, often pictorially as well, in other media, and they continue to be reproduced verbally by the many white tour guides that traverse the park throughout the year as they sell their own versions of the 'authentic' Aboriginal people. In the park's early days, some of the guides enthralled visitors with stories about, for example, 'tribal' murders, 'pay-back' killings and bizarre sexual behaviour. Park service activities such as judicious 'listening in' to tour guides, and its education programs, as well as self-policing by tour operators themselves, have truncated the more outrageous misinformation perpetrated by guides. Misinformation persists, however, and probably always will, as will all kinds of representations of Aboriginal people by whites.

It is relatively easy to identify the strange, even bizarre, appropriations of Aboriginal culture by commercial tour guides. More difficult to classify are the various appropriations by the park service itself. It is on these that I now wish to focus. Done with the complicity of traditional owners themselves, always first created with their explicit permission, these simulacra of past cultures, I argue, expose the tensions that lie between them and the culture of now.

The seasonal calendar and burning off

The brochure that has been handed by park employees to hundreds of thousands of visitors provides considerable information about visitor safety

---

8   Some residents, especially those who are neither traditional owners nor park employees, are not so well off materially. Yet, through the strength of various affiliations with traditional owners, these people are able to continue residence in Kakadu. While they take advantage of access to fishing and hunting, in accordance with the agreement, and therefore live a more 'traditional' life than their more affluent counterparts, their lives have been changed too. For example, most have access to transport, shopping, health services and other forms of social security.

and general information about the park and suggests activities for visitors. This includes information about aspects of Aboriginal culture—here a tripwire to some awkwardness that can arise when representing and appropriating other cultures.

The text (Environment Australia 2003:11) explains how the collapse of original populations disrupted what are thought to have been traditional fire regimes, relying as they did on many small fires that went out during the night in the cooler months (see, for example, Levitus 2005). Backed by Western science (for example, Edwards et al. 2003; Russell-Smith et al. 1998), park managers try to simulate these, mainly by dropping from helicopters permanganate-filled ping-pong balls injected with glycol. These little balls ignite on reaching the ground and theoretically take the place of the former hunter-gatherers and their fire-sticks. Done in the name of good land management, it is called 'planned burning', but it is not the same as what the region's people call *anwurrk*, in which burning off the vegetation is part of being, caring for one's own land and thereby expressing ownership of it (Verran 2002).

The brochure does not explain that 'planned burning' is a metonym of imagined tradition—the practice of which now largely excludes the very people whose ancestors once did it all and in different ways. Unable to argue against the logic, backed by Western science, that white managers are simulating 'Aboriginal burning practices' for the good of the country, traditional owners and the other Aboriginal people have the choice to either comply with these mimetic fire regimes or rebel—lighting fires in the hot periods of the year during which fires spread rapidly and can burn for weeks on end. So, while Sherry Ortner (1984:154) famously notes that 'hegemony is always more fragile than it appears', in Kakadu we see the fire program dominated by whites in the name of 'authentic Aboriginal culture' (and Western science too) and only sporadic frustrated resistance by traditional owners and their countrymen and women.

The Gundjeihmi seasonal calendar (Figure 10.3) is also reproduced in the brochure (Environment Australia 2003:10). This was in fact the product of an afternoon's work in December 1978 (and a few hours of later checking) by then traditional owners Toby Gangali and Mick Alderson, with me asking questions and acting as scribe. (Note that the original spellings have been retained in Figure 10.3.) At the time, Mick was quizzical: 'Why would whitefellas want to know about all this?' My response—'So that they know how blackfellas are smart'—bemused but still satisfied him, as it seems to have satisfied many traditional owners since then. Yet this form of appropriation, this mimetic transformation of an abstracted traditional knowledge on to paper, constitutes a double imposition on Aboriginal people.

SEASONAL CALENDAR FOR THE
KAKADU REGION IN GUNDJEIDMI (MAIILI) LANGUAGE

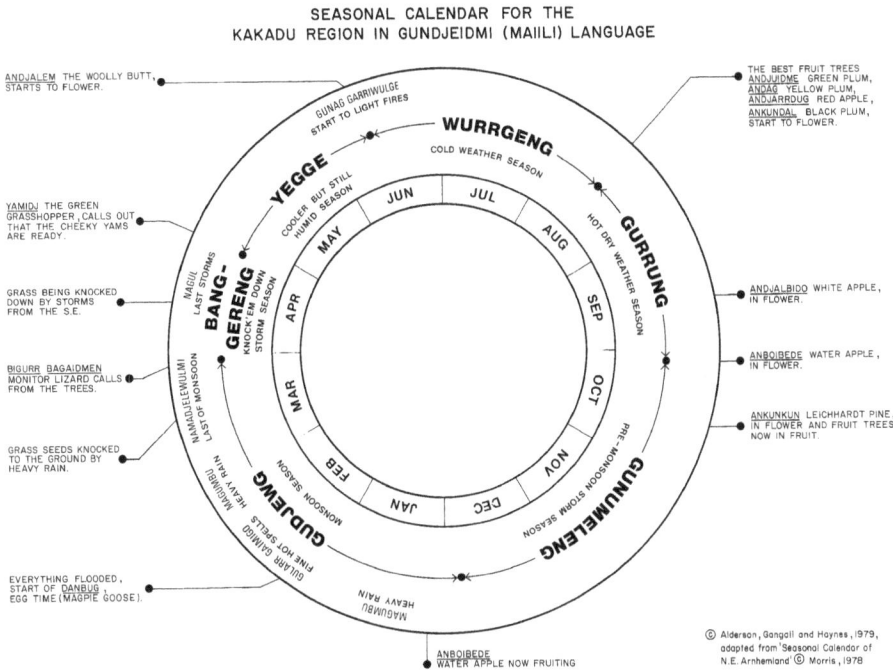

Figure 10.3 Seasonal calendar for the Kakadu region in the Gundjeihmi (Maiali) language

First, its very documentation (and subsequent re-presentation in almost uncountable numbers of books, in the park brochures that have been handed out to literally millions of people, on stone tablets at the park's visitor centres, and even on T-shirts) means that for white people it is privileged as a way of knowing, in recognisable iconography. It can be used, and is used, as a means of telling Aboriginal people what their 'authentic' culture is—implying that they themselves are *in*-authentic. For while the park service and its individual white actors do recognise that Aboriginal lives are not the same after three decades of mining, the park and all those visitors, they tend to frame that recognition in the manner of the structural-functionalist anthropologists who periodically talked about the collapse of former cultures (for example, Berndt and Berndt 1988:492).

This leads into the second imposition on Aboriginal people—part of mimesis itself. The images here are the representations of the seasonal calendar and how the state both practises and represents planned burning that is based on *anwurrk*—but is not *anwurrk*. As the person who enthusiastically documented the seasonal calendar in the first place, and one of those who (also enthusiastically) persuaded the park service to imitate Aboriginal fire regimes (Haynes 1985),

I work through the following argument as a cautionary tale as much, if not more so, against myself as against the park service or other white people who have worked there.

Considering Sir James Frazer's (1890) musings about imitation, Michael Taussig (1993:65) notes: 'How much more complex than Frazer's "like affecting like" this magical power of the image becomes! This power intrinsic to mimesis and alterity on the frontier is as much a destructive as a healing force.' As I thought at the time (like Frazer), what could have been more assuring and flattering to traditional owners than imitation? When I responded to Mick Alderson's question about why whitefellas would want to know all this with 'so that they know how blackfellas are smart', I meant it as one means of healing: as a means of rapprochement with traditional owners; as a means of driving into the background the overt and vicious racism that was abroad three decades ago when the park was declared; and as a means of convincing park visitors that Aboriginality meant not just the antiquity of the rock paintings but the culture of a clever people. I had no idea then that simple things such as the introduction of roads, park radio and phones, and the more complex phenomena such as the intrusion of the state into their daily lives, as well as their responses to all this and more, would transform culture and open the way for the destructive forces that lie within mimesis to appear.

In another theoretical view of mimesis—one that lays bare the double-sided and corrupting nature of imitation—Homi Bhabha (1994:91) notes:

> Under cover of camouflage, mimicry, like a fetish, is a part object that radically revalues the normative knowledges of the priority of race, writing, history. For the fetish mimes the forms of authority at the point at which it deauthorises them. Similarly, mimicry rearticulates presence in terms of its 'otherness' that which it disavows.

The park service's imitation of the seasonal calendar (while transforming it into an alien, written object) and its imitation of as much of traditional fire regimes as suits 'good conservation', rearticulates traditional forms of authority and simultaneously de-authorises their value to traditional owners. Bhabha (1994:88) points out elsewhere that mimesis involves metonymy—taking part of the whole to represent the whole. In so doing, here it not only de-authorises the value of these traditional forms of authority, it de-authorises the traditional owners themselves as well.

The argument here is that while traditional owners are generally pleased to have had their traditions and customs recognised, that same recognition can, and does, cause them grief too. The challenge to their authenticity is always there, whether it is being actively discussed or not. As Francesca Merlan (1998:150) notes: 'Representations of Aboriginality as made most powerfully by others come to affect who and what Aborigines consider themselves to be.'

Exploring the future

The appropriation of Kakadu's Aboriginality has been manifestly beneficial to the tourism industry of the Top End. I have argued that such appropriation has not yielded particularly good results for the Aboriginal people themselves. First, although one can endlessly dispute which sets of figures should be used for comparison, the Aboriginal share of the tourism economy is small. Second, they have partially given up, or had taken from them, in various forms, their capacity to represent their own culture.

While discussing the agency of web sites, government organisations and tour guides, I admitted that representations of Aboriginality, even powerful representations, are one part of the future. One consequence, then, is that, as Merlan says, Kakadu's traditional owners will continue to think of themselves as, in part, within the referential framings of white Others. The question here is how Aboriginal agency might be demonstrated within the fields of power that have been so clearly established. And there are two sub-questions: how might Aboriginal people take a larger share of the tourism cake; and how might they take back some of the ways by which they might represent themselves?

I suggest that possible answers to both sub-questions could already be demonstrated in response to an initiative of a previous federal government of Prime Minister John Howard. Early in 2006, Parliamentary Secretary for the Environment, Greg Hunt, launched a new program that had followed about a year of consultation between the government and the Kakadu Board of Management. My fieldwork was at the periphery of it, and nothing I heard from my participants made me inclined to take much notice of this initiative, which was supposed to encourage Aboriginal people to build on their small existing involvement by establishing their own enterprises and, in particular, building links with the tourism industry. Inured by three decades of watching Aboriginal reticence about becoming seriously involved in tour guiding, it was hard for me to view the program as anything other than yet more bullying of traditional owners by the state, in order to expand tourism and create more jobs for Darwin-based whites.

The number, robustness and value of Aboriginal tourism enterprises have increased, however—albeit from a tiny base. I estimate that the current income gained by Aboriginal people—$900 000—represents an increase of about 50 per cent over the amount generated in 2006.[9] Although the potential to grow this income is limited, both by the numbers of Aboriginal people available to do the work and by what the tourist market is prepared to pay for cultural tours, Aboriginal participation is increasing. On interviewing several newcomers recently, journalist Fiona Carruthers (2009) noted: 'The signs of change are everywhere.' The new Aboriginal participants also appear to be realistically enthusiastic about their prospects, as former park ranger and now partner in a small tour operation Fred Hunter noted on television in August 2008:

> You know, working with parks for quite a number of years I never saw hardly any Indigenous guides, hardly at all…and in just the last couple of years, just seeing the different companies starting up, it's been really good and there needs to be more of it, especially people from this country talking about their country and about their culture. (*7.30 Report*, ABC Television, 28 August 2008)

There is, as well, potential to increase the passive incomes through royalty-style payments such as shares of park fees and access into special places that require supervision. After all, as I have shown, the real Aboriginal share of tourism is paltry.

Perhaps the real dollar increases are less important than traditional owners and other Aboriginal people reappropriating ways in which their culture is represented, as a means of decoupling themselves from the mimesis in which they have become unwittingly involved. Tour guiding is not the work that most Aboriginal people prefer. Yet if tourism is more firmly controlled by Aboriginal people themselves, it will be they who have much greater control over what visitors should know, recovering past injustice and allowing the un-complication of the complicated. In saying this, I am agreeing with Lisa Palmer's (2001:267) conclusion:

> The key to imagining Kakadu as an Aboriginal place lies in the relationship people construct with each other through their relations with the landscape. If the landscape is viewed as a living subject where relationships to the land and to each other continue to change with time, a new construction of Kakadu can emerge.

Palmer's emphasis here is on reconstruction of how people interact with land, but important keys also are the possibilities that are allowed through each changing with time, in particular in ways that allow Aboriginal people to retake ground that has been lost in the rush to represent their culture.

---

9 I estimate that between 2006 and 2008, the number of Aboriginal individuals involved in tourism (including artists) has increased from about 60 to 90, and income has increased from $590 000 to more than $900 000.

The emphasis of this chapter has been directed towards some ways in which Aboriginal people have participated in the economies of the market and the state. This is not to deny that other economies (those based on traditional exchange, mutual obligation and demand sharing, for example) are at work, as they still are in Kakadu. For in many ways Kakadu's Aboriginal people still transact business in ways similar to those described by Lorraine Gibson in Chapter 8: maintenance of family relations is often privileged over work as it is defined by the market economy. My purpose has been not to deny the richness and complexity of the hybridity of the economies here, but rather to demonstrate how Aboriginal participation in what Noel Pearson (2000, 2001) calls the 'real world' has in fact resisted the welfare colonialism articulated by Robert Paine (1977). Indeed, rather than a situation in which value as defined by Western thinking is flowing from the centre to the periphery, I suggest that Aboriginal people are being short-changed in their contributions to the tourism of Australia's north.

Acknowledgments

I gratefully acknowledge Liam Maher's considerable assistance in the compilation of the tourism value estimates. Jon Altman, Tess Lea, Lisa Palmer and Pascal Tremblay provided valuable comments on earlier drafts of this chapter.

References

Altman, J. 2005, 'Economic futures on Aboriginal land in remote and very remote Australia: hybrid economies and joint ventures', in D. Austin-Broos and G. Macdonald (eds), *Culture, Economy and Governance in Aboriginal Australia*, Sydney University Press, NSW, pp. 121–33.

Aplin, G. 2004, 'Kakadu National Park World Heritage site: deconstructing the debate, 1997–2003', *Australian Geographical Studies*, vol. 42, pp. 152–74.

Australian National Parks and Wildlife Service (ANPWS) 1989, *Australian National Parks and Wildlife Service. Annual Report 1988–89*, Australian Government Publishing Service, Canberra.

Berndt, R. M. and Berndt, C. H. 1988, *The World of the First Australians*, (Fifth edition), Aboriginal Studies Press, Canberra.

Bhabha, H. K. 1994, *The Location of Culture*, Routledge, London and New York.

Bradshaw, C. J. A., Field, I. C., Bowman, D. M. J. S., Haynes, C. and Brook, B. 2007, 'Current and future threats from non-indigenous animal species in northern Australia: a spotlight on World Heritage Area Kakadu National Park', *Wildlife Research*, vol. 34, pp. 419–36.

Brockwell, S., Clarke, A. and Levitus, R. 2001, 'Seasonal movement in the prehistoric human ecology of the Alligator Rivers region, North Australia', in A. Anderson, I. Lilley and S. O'Connor (eds), *Histories of Old Ages: Essays in honour of Rhys Jones*, Pandanus Books, Canberra, pp. 361–80.

Carlsen, J. and Wood, D. 2004, *Assessment of the Economic Value of Recreation and Tourism in Western Australia's National Parks, Marine Parks, and Forests*, Cooperative Research Centre for Sustainable Tourism, Gold Coast, Qld.

Carruthers, F. 2009, 'Walkabout on the wild side', *Australian Financial Review [weekend edition]*, 29–31 May 2009, pp. L10–11.

Chaloupka, G. 1993, *Journey in Time*, Reed, Chatswood, NSW.

Commonwealth of Australia 1977, *Uranium: Australia's decision*, Australian Government Publishing Service, Canberra.

Davis, R. 2005, 'Introduction: transforming the frontier in contemporary Australia', in D. B. Rose and R. Davis (eds), *Dislocating the Frontier: Essaying the mystique of the outback*, ANU E Press, Canberra, pp. 7–19.

Director of National Parks (DNP) 2008, *Director of National Parks. Annual report 2007–08*, Australian Government, Canberra.

Eagles, P. F., McCool, S. F. and Haynes, C. D. 2002, *Sustainable Tourism in Protected Areas: Guidelines for planning and management (best practice protected areas guidelines)*, IUCN, UNEP and WTO, Gland, Switzerland, and Cambridge.

Edwards, A., Kennett, R., Price, O., Russell-Smith, J., Spiers, G. and Woinarski, J. 2003, 'Monitoring the impacts of fire regimes on vegetation in northern Australia: an example from Kakadu National Park', *International Journal of Wildland Fire*, vol. 12, pp. 427–40.

Environment Australia 2003, *Kakadu National Park: Visitor guide and maps*, Commonwealth of Australia, Darwin.

Frazer, J. G. 1890, *The Golden Bough: A study in magic and religion*, Macmillan, London.

Geertz, C. 1993, *The Interpretation of Cultures*, Fontana Press, London.

Haynes, C. 1985, 'The pattern and ecology of *munwag*: traditional Aboriginal fire regimes in north central Arnhemland', *Proceedings of the Ecological Society of Australia*, vol. 13, pp. 203–14.

Haynes, C. 2009, Defined by contradiction: the social construction of joint management in Kakadu National Park, Unpublished PhD thesis, Charles Darwin University, Darwin.

Heatley, A. 1990, *Almost Australians: The politics of Northern Territory self-government*, North Australian Research Unit, The Australian National University, Darwin.

Kakadu National Park and Director of National Parks (KNP and DNP) 2007, *Kakadu Board of Management and Director of National Parks. Kakadu National Park. Management plan 2007–2014*, Australian Government, Darwin.

Keen, I. 1980, 'The Alligator Rivers Aborigines: retrospect and prospect', in R. Jones (ed.), *Northern Australia: Options and implications*, Research School of Pacific Studies, The Australian National University, Canberra, pp. 171–86.

Levitus, R. 2005, 'Management and the model: burning Kakadu', in M. Minnegal (ed.), *Sustainable environments, sustainable communities: potential dialogues between anthropologists, scientists and managers*, SAGES Research Paper No. 21, University of Melbourne, Vic., pp. 29–35.

Merlan, F. 1998, *Caging the Rainbow: Places, politics and Aborigines in a north Australian town*, University of Hawai'i Press, Honolulu.

NT News 1989, 'Buffalo slaughter "hurting tourism"', *Northern Territory News*, 4 November 1989, p. 3.

NT News 1996a, 'Kakadu war: tour guides blast feds', *Northern Territory News*, 13 March 1996, p. 6.

NT News 1996b, 'Park poser 21 years on', Editorial, *Northern Territory News*, 13 March 1996, p. 10.

NT News 2006, '(Kakadu) (Kakadon't) Kakatrue', *Northern Territory News*, 18 March 2006, pp. 16–17.

O'Brien, J. 2003, 'Canberra yellowcake: the politics of uranium and how Aboriginal land rights failed the Mirarr people', *Journal of Northern Territory History*, vol. 14, pp. 79–91.

Ortner, S. B. 1984, 'Theory in anthropology since the Sixties', *Comparative Studies in Society and History*, vol. 26, pp. 126–66.

Paine, R. 1977, 'The path to welfare colonialism', in R. Paine (ed.), *The White Arctic: Anthropological essays on tutelage and ethnicity*, Memorial University of Newfoundland, St John, pp. 3–28.

Palmer, L. 2001, Kakadu as an Aboriginal place: tourism and the construction of Kakadu National Park, Unpublished PhD thesis, Northern Territory University, Darwin.

Parsons, D. 1978, 'Inside the Ranger negotiations', *Arena*, vol. 51, pp. 134–43.

Pearson, N. 2000, *Our Right to Take Responsibility*, Noel Pearson & Associates, Cairns, Qld.

Pearson, N. 2001, On the human right to misery, mass incarceration and early death, The Dr Charles Perkins Memorial Oration at the University of Sydney, Cairns, Qld, 25 October 2001.

Peterson, N. 1982, 'Aboriginal land rights in the Northern Territory of Australia', in E. B. Leacock and R. B. Lee (eds), *Politics and History in Band Societies*, Cambridge University Press, UK and Paris, pp. 441–62.

Robinson, C. J., Smyth, D. and Whitehead, P. J. 2005, 'Bush tucker, bush pets, and bush threats: cooperative management of feral animals in Australia's Kakadu National Park', *Conservation Biology*, vol. 19, pp. 1385–91.

Ranger Uranium Environmental Inquiry (RUEI) 1977, *Ranger Uranium Environmental Inquiry: Second report*, Australian Government Publishing Service, Canberra.

Russell-Smith, J., Ryan, P. G., Klessa, D., Waight, G. and Harwood, R. 1998, 'Fire regimes, fire-sensitive vegetation and fire management of the sandstone Arnhem Plateau', *Journal of Applied Ecology*, vol. 35, pp. 829–46.

Sahlins, M. 1999, 'Two or three things that I know about culture', *Journal of the Royal Anthropological Institute*, (NS) vol. 5, pp. 399–421.

Taussig, M. 1993, *Mimesis and Alterity: A particular history of the senses*, Routledge, New York.

The Weekend Australian 2009, 'Tarnished treasure: Kakadu becomes Kakadon't', *The Weekend Australian*, 17 January 2009, p. 1.

Trebeck, K. A. 2007, 'Tools for the disempowered? Indigenous leverage over mining companies', *Australian Journal of Political Science*, vol. 42, pp. 541–62.

Tremblay, P. 2007, *Economic Contribution of Kakadu National Park to Tourism in the Northern Territory*, Cooperative Research Centre for Sustainable Tourism, Darwin.

Tremblay, P. 2008, 'Protected areas and development in arid Australia—challenges to regional tourism', *The Rangeland Journal*, vol. 30, pp. 67–75.

Verran, H. 2002, 'A postcolonial moment in science studies: alternative firing regimes of environmental scientists and Aboriginal landowners', *Social Studies of Science*, vol. 32, pp. 1–34.

Worboys, G. L., Lockwood, M. and de Lacy, T. 2005, *Protected Area Management: Principles and practice*, (Second edition), Oxford University Press, South Melbourne.

Index

www.ingramcontent.com/pod-product-compliance
Lightning Source LLC
Chambersburg PA
CBHW061245270326
41928CB00041B/3431